Beth Chatto ran her own Gar‹
Plants at Elmstead Market near Colchester. Winner of ten
Gold Medals at Chelsea, she also held the Royal Horticultural
Society's Victoria Medal of Honour and an honorary doctor-
ate from Essex University for her services to horticulture.
She is the author of a host of gardening classics and is also
co-author of *Dear Friend and Gardener*, written with her
long-standing friend and fellow gardener, Christopher Lloyd.
She died in 2018.

By Beth Chatto

The Dry Garden
The Damp Garden
Beth Chatto's Garden Notebook

BETH CHATTO
The Dry Garden

Drawings by
MARGARET DAVIES

W&N
WEIDENFELD & NICOLSON

First published in Great Britain in 1978 by J. M. Dent Ltd
First published in paperback in 1981
Reissued in 1998 and 2011
This paperback edition published in 2018
By Weidenfeld & Nicolson
an imprint of The Orion Publishing Group Ltd
Carmelite House, 50 Victoria Embankment
London EC4Y 0DZ

An Hachette UK Company

3 5 7 9 10 8 6 4 2

A CIP catalogue record for this book is available from the British Library.

ISBN (paperback) 978 1 4746 1096 4

Printed and bound in Great Britain by Clays Ltd, Elcograf S.p.A,

MIX
Paper from
responsible sources
FSC® C104740

www.orionbooks.co.uk

CONTENTS

· · · · · · · · · · · · · · · · · · ·

LIST OF PLATES

....

The Dry Sunny Garden

between pages 78 and 79
1. *Euphorbia characias* subsp. *wulfenii*
2. The west-facing entrance border to White Barn House
3. *Iris pallida* 'Variegata'
4. *Acanthus spinosus*
5. *Eriophyllum lanatum*
6. *Leuzea centauroides*
7. *Bergenia cordifolia*
8. West-facing steps at White Barn House: *Parahebe catarractae* and *Agave*
9. *Genista hispanica,* helianthemums, *Artemisia* and *Ballota* in an island bed
10. *Allium karataviense*
11. *Agapanthus campanulatus*
12. *Senecio cinerea* 'White Diamond'
13. *Yucca filamentosa* 'Concava Variegata'
14. *Cistus* × *purpureus*

The Dry Shady Garden

LIST OF LINE DRAWINGS

....

ACKNOWLEDGMENTS

....

I am indebted to more people than I can mention for their help and encouragement in making my garden and writing this book.

Without doubt my first and greatest blessing has been to be married to a man whose life-long hobby has been to study the natural homes of our garden plants. Without Andrew neither my garden nor a book would have been possible. How many times I go to him to ask the origin of a plant, the kind of conditions in which it will be growing, and what other plants may be found with it. Often he can answer with such a wealth of information that at times, it seems as if he had stood on the spot where the plant was found. To his despair I do not always follow his advice to the letter, but ignoring a plant's natural environment leads to failure in performance as well as design.

To our dear friend Sir Cedric Morris I shall forever be grateful. No one could have had a more generous teacher. His wonderful collection has been an education to me in the sheer wealth of good plants and bulbs we can grow. My garden is full of 'Cedric' plants, given to me by him, clumps in spadesful, pocketsful of sticky fruits and brittle seeds – handsful of unfamiliar cuttings. Many of these have been spread again to other gardens, continuing the living thread which links dedicated plantsmen and women, past, present and future.

Another great plantsman, Graham S. Thomas has influenced me both by his writings and, in the past, by his very individual and beautiful exhibits for the Sunningdale Nursery at the Chelsea Shows. His books are a rich feast of knowledge, combining meticulously verified detail with wide personal experience, spiced now and again with a neat dry wit. His love and knowledge of plants is no less evident in the delicate drawings with which he illustrates his invaluable book *Perennial Garden Plants*. I am very grateful to him also for his kindness and patience in reading my typescript, and for chastising me properly for my carelessness concerning the intricacies of typeface in printing plant names. The page *does* look and read much better when it is right even though it seems vastly complicated to a beginner.

At this point I would like to thank Graham Rose, gardening correspondent of the *Sunday Times*, and his editor, Philip Clarke. They visited my garden in June 1976, and the result was an article on how to deal with drought. The interest aroused by this article finally persuaded me to put down my spade for a while and try to put some of my ideas about gardening into a book.

Only at a very late stage in the production of the book did I have the good fortune to find Margaret Davies, who has taken my plans and scribbles of sketches, and interpreted them with such style and beauty. For her understanding, patience and great skill my very sincere thanks.

Not having learnt myself the complicated art of plant photography I am much indebted to Neville and Pat Brindley (Pls. 3, 5, 9, 12, 13, 14, 18, 19, 24, 26, 29) and Michael Warren (Pls. 2, 6, 7, 8, 15, 17, 21, 22, 23) for visiting my garden and providing their expert skills for my illustrations. My thanks also to the Harry Smith Horticultural Photographic Collection for more photographs (Pls. 1, 4, 10, 11, 16, 20, 25, 27, 28).

I would like to express my gratitude to the staff of Messrs Dent for their help in steering me through this novel experience.

Finally, I would like to say a very warm thank you to my staff whose hard work and dedication have given me the time to write this book.

December, 1977.   Beth Chatto,
                                                    Elmstead Market,
                                                         Colchester.

INTRODUCTION

....

Sometimes, in summer, I imagine I could fill up pages without drawing breath, I have so much to say about the way a newly planted area is filling up, or what a fool I have been to have planted something in past years which now I have to battle to eradicate. My worry at the moment is where to begin. Perhaps I should introduce myself, if you have decided to start with the introduction. I usually read introductions years after I have become familiar with the contents of a book and sometimes realize that I would have understood more if I had known the writer a little better before I began.

I am an East Anglian, born and bred, so coping with a dry garden is no new phenomenon but a way of life. I have had two gardens in the last thirty or so years. My first was just west of Colchester, on the chalky boulder clay. In practice this was not an easy soil to handle. In winter, when thoroughly wet, you could slice it neatly with a spade, like lumps of liver. It was speckled white with the little nodules of chalk showing clearly. Short of humus, that is decayed vegetable matter, it set like concrete in periods of drought. To catch the soil just right was the problem, that brief spell when it is possible to pull up weeds without removing the precious layer of top soil. A few days of drying winds and the weeds would set firm, only to be eradicated with wrist-aching jabs of a sharp fork.

East Anglia has been called the Granary of England, for it can generally rely on good harvesting helped by long periods of bright sunshine, low rainfall and drying winds. We have well-known firms of seed growers, and their fields make a pretty sight with the vividly coloured blocks of marigolds, wallflowers, sweet peas and other garden favourites which set good seed, shelling out hard and clean. Cricketers and holidaymakers revel in the good weather. But for us gardeners in East Anglia, every year brings weeks and often months of concern for our plants, the 'good' weather for the sportsman and camper becoming the despair of the grower.

By the middle of June my Colchester garden was fading, the grass was indistinguishable from the gravel paths and would remain so until the hoped-for September rains. Many years little measurable rain fell from May to September. Of course, the roses had black spot, the leaves of the Michaelmas daisies turned brown and hung like limp rags, the flowers of the lovely border phlox withered as they tried to bloom. Misguided attempts to grow even such easy primulas as *Primula denticulata*, the Drum-stick Primula, were properly punished, while as for astilbes, I should have known better.

But some plants hung on – in fact they looked better as the sun burnt brighter and the air became drier. Quite early in my gardening career I began to realize that it was the plants which *had* and *kept* good foliage that made the most satisfying picture in the garden. Outstanding in the droughts were the grey and silver foliaged plants – these became whiter as the grass baked biscuit colour. Cistus bushes made handsome contrast with their dark evergreen leaves, filling the air with a strange aromatic scent when there was enough dew on a warm summer night.

Then came my first trip abroad, to the Alps, followed by others to the mountains of southern France and Corsica. My first impression on that long ago visit to the Valais in Switzerland was of incredulity. Here were so many of my garden plants beautifully grouped and arranged, the rocks smothered with Cobweb House Leeks and *Sedum*, while the hot stony slopes were gay with *Dianthus*, *Helianthemum* and *Euphorbia*. What marvellous landscaping and not made by man!

Like most amateur gardeners, I was not very well read, and had not fully realized that all of our garden plants, except of course the cultivars, grow wild somewhere; and here I was seeing for the first time how right plants look when they grow together, in association, in the conditions to which they have become adapted. I noticed too that the associations varied whether we went a thousand feet or so higher, or whether we were on the north side of the mountain where the conditions were cooler and shadier. I learnt that some plants, although they appeared to be growing in poor gritty soil in blistering bright sunlight, were in fact revelling in the cool trickle of melting snow water that ran not far beneath the surface. These are among the most difficult for us to grow.

The Mediterranean plants that grow well with me come from a very variable climatic zone, but basically the winters are mild with scattered rain storms, while the summers are long, hot and practically without rain. Because the range is so wide a few of my plants are susceptible to hard frost, a few dislike too much wet cold which causes rotting. But by far the majority can stand anything our winters can offer, coming as they do from mountain sides which experience moderately cold weather with some frost. (I am not referring to the high alpine plants which spend their winter under the protection of a heavy snow blanket.)

The feature they can all face up to is the famous Mediterranean sunshine. Long days of continuous scorching sun are hard to bear. Those plants that can survive are precious. It sounds so obvious, but is worth stating I think, that I find it best to plant plenty of something that looks good most of the time rather than struggle to keep alive plants which at best only accentuate the fact that what you have to offer them is not what they need.

With time, study and observation, I began to learn about the many groupings, or associations of plants that are still to be found growing in their natural habitat. I have already mentioned briefly how these change according to altitude, sun or shade, wet or dry conditions. Another factor that has altered plant communities is the scavenging hand of man, aided by the ever-hungry goat. Great tracts of land bordering the Mediterranean were once covered by evergreen forests consisting of evergreen oaks like the Holm oak, and pines, with a lower storey of small evergreen shrubs. Where there was enough light and air, usually because the terrain was steeper and poorer, there was room for plants and bulbs. Today the shrunken forests are limited to those few areas not yet considered worth exploiting by man.

When the trees were felled to make charcoal – needed for cooking the delicious dishes that can result from stewing kid with wine, garlic and the aromatic herbs from the stony hillsides – another type of plant community evolved, the *maquis*. It consists of many of the evergreen shrubs that had been part of the under-storey of the evergreen forest, including *Cistus*, rosemary, juniper, *Genista*, lavender, Spanish broom, tree heathers – all of these and many more, often making impenetrable thickets more than 10 ft/3 m high, were fine places for rogues and robbers to hide in olden days, and places of refuge to this day for those families in places like Corsica that still carry on inherited vendettas.

Garigue is the name given to the next and last stage of deterioration in the plant life of the Mediterranean area. Here, man's activities – tree felling, grazing, and cultivation followed by neglect – have all contributed to the impoverishment of the land. Removal of trees causes loss of protection from drying winds, humus cannot form, and the soil is eroded, washed or blown away. Only the coarse rock fragments are left, and bare rock. Such an area can be seen in the limestone *causses* of southern France, high table-lands with soil now so thin it can scarcely be used. A few inches beneath the surface are calcareous rocks. In many places there is no soil at all, the fractured limestone looking like pavements. Driving across one sees little except here and there in a fold or hollow the dark forests of recently planted pine whose interiors are so dark and forbidding no other plant will keep them company.

But one very early morning, when the dew had not yet been lifted away by the hot glare of the sun just appearing over the horizon, I was drawn to go out and explore the apparently endless emptiness. I found that what had looked from a distance like a frozen mist carpeting the ground were the waving feathery fronds of *Stipa pennata*, each spangled with dew, wave after wave blowing across the stony desert. As I wandered I found brilliant lime-yellow patches of a *Euphorbia*, very like *Euphorbia seguierana* subsp. *niciciana*, thyme mats, lotus, silene and other little plants I could not identify. Then I noticed that the slope was faintly terraced, and felt sure that many, many years ago that area had been cultivated with vines, and probably olives too. I found scattered scrubby little gooseberry bushes, with tiny fruits the size of currants. Had they survived from the cultivations, or did they grow wild there originally?

Helleborus foetidus, which I have found wild all over France from north to south, in woods and in the open, was there too. Some splendid specimens were tucked for shelter against an outcrop of stone, with their roots well down a crack in the rock where the humus from plant remains is blown by the wind, making rich feeding deep down, and where some moisture will remain. Back home on my starved Essex gravel I must prepare the soil well for *Helleborus foetidus* or else find a place in the shade, for I have had them shrivel under the combination of drought and drying wind.

Garigue is always to be found on the hottest and driest slopes. There are few scattered shrubs, small, often spiny or prickly. Foliage is thick and leathery, or felted with hairs or white wool. Plants we all know such as sage, lavender, garlic and rue all come from the garigue, together with our favourite garden bulbs – tulips, iris, crocus and fritillaries. Brought to life by the warm wet winters, the sheets of flowering bulbs stand exposed among the mat plants and sparse grasses. Spreading out their leaves to the warm spring sunlight they quickly store up reserves to remake their deep-down bulbs. Many, such as the alliums, flower without leaves; only curling shrivelled ribbons are left at the base of their stems.

When I realized that many of these plants were the very ones that were among my favourites for endurance in my Colchester garden it was inevitable that when I came to make my present garden I should make a Mediterranean garden. Now, after thirty-eight years my dry gardens have grown, and I have added to those plants that come from the plant communities of the Mediterranean, plants from the Californian chaparral (which corresponds to the maquis) such as *Zauchneria* and *Romneya*, with *Artemisia purshiana*, and *Seriphidium tridentatum* (syn. *Artemisia tridentata*) from the semi-deserts of the Great Basin. In addition some of the alliums, eremurus and many vivid scarlet tulips come from the great mountains of Soviet Central Asia and Afghanistan, from places with romantic-sounding names like Bukhara and Samarkand.

FOREWORD

....

by Monty Don

I first saw Beth Chatto in the mid-eighties from a distance at Chelsea Flower Show. I was still in my twenties and feeling remote from a well-fortified gardening establishment of which Beth seemed to be an established member. By then she had won a long succession of gold medals for her Chelsea exhibits and published *The Dry Garden* and *The Damp Garden* which I referred to constantly. I still do. But her exhibit that Chelsea stood out from all others in its naturalistic display of her exquisite plants. In those days that challenged all the preconceptions of how plants might best be displayed and yet, once you saw Beth's stand, it seemed blindingly obvious to show them in a garden rather than a formal nursery setting. She might have been a member of the gardening Great and Good, but I could immediately relate to her as a lover of gardeners rather than just a potentially intimidating expert.

This was the key to Beth's love of plants. She was a superb plantswoman but she was first and foremost a gardener. If she admired a plant, then wherever possible she would use it to best effect in her garden at Elmstead Market near Colchester. It was the making of this garden, with its various developments and extensions in unpromising heavy East Anglian clay, that provided the impetus for her nursery and her books.

My first sight of her at Chelsea showed me a slim, neat, sprightly person with a kind face but some steel in the eyes. She had a reputation for not suffering fools and did not take any prisoners. When I met her properly for the first time some years later, in her garden, that steel was evident. I was very aware that despite being the *Observer*'s gardening editor, with lots of television programmes under my belt and three gardening books published, I was a horticultural upstart with, compared her at least, a derisory amount of knowledge. So I was slightly anxious. She greeted me by looking into my eyes and saying 'How can I say this . . . [long pause] . . . I think that you write so much better now.'

Ouch. But there is an openness in that kind of directness and we got on well. There was none of the patrician confidence about her garden that almost invariably comes with inheritance. The site, fourteen acres of it, had all been made by her over thirty-six years with an industry, patience and canniness that comes from leading a living from the soil. She and her husband Andrew farmed the land around the site for eighteen years before they built a house and started to make the garden. In *The Damp Garden* she writes about the muddy ditch in the middle of a tangle of scrub lying in a dip between two farms, the top slopes being thin gravel and the bottom muddy silt, good for nothing agricultural. From this she created a garden that made a virtue from what others would deem adversity, allying her husband's work on the natural ecology of plants with her own superlative plantsmanship that amounted to more than just knowing the facts about a vast range of plants. Whereas quite a few people acquire plant knowledge, Beth had the much rarer attribute of plant wisdom. She did not just know about plants, she understood them.

Because of the wide range of conditions and the extraordinary breadth of her plant knowledge, Beth made a garden composed of a huge diversity of plants despite the unpromising site and the harshness of East Anglian weather which can see as little as fourteen inches of rain a year and bitterly cold winters with the east wind sweeping in unchecked across the North Sea from the Urals.

But, with her determination, thoughtfulness and depth of plant understanding she put these conditions to her advantage and in doing so created one of the most original and influential garden areas of her age. Where there had once been the visitor's car park was dug up and made into a gravel garden with great sweeps of planting with gravel spaces – too loose and wide to be called paths – between them. From the start it was a self-conscious exercise in displaying what can thrive in the most arid part of the country and was never to be watered.

Her first book *The Dry Garden* had preceded this by over a decade but that was essentially a guide to coping with dry conditions. *The Gravel Garden* took this experience – and re-editions of the book – to another level by celebrating them. It shows that dry gardens which are never watered, even in the worst drought, can look staggeringly beautiful for much of the year. It was a kind of gardening revolution and typical of the intelligence, careful research and practical energy that Beth bought to both her garden and her books.

The first edition of *The Dry Garden* was published in 1978 and it was followed four years later by *The Damp Garden*. Beth always made a virtue of the fact that her chosen site contained the worst combination of conditions – both arid, thin soil with minimal rainfall and boggy areas of impossibly heavy clay. Immediately the rest of us, struggling with what we thought were heroic odds, realised that this slight, spare middle-aged woman had overcome far worse and made of them one of the country's great gardens. The tone was both instructive and instructional. If she had managed to turn harsh wasteland into a beautiful garden so could you – stop complaining and get stuck in!

I loved her for this. It was the perfect combination of working with nature, making the most of conditions and a refusal to be beaten. At a time when gardening could sometimes seem to be a cross between an exercise in good taste and Latin O level, Beth made it a creative adventure – which of course it should always be.

Her creativity was expressed with a painterly eye. She was greatly influenced by her friendship with the painter and gardener Sir Cedric Morris, who not only shared his love of plants and collecting but also encouraged her to compose plants together in a border rather than just pander to their horticultural needs. Beth's own instincts for this were also expressed in the years of giving talks and lectures on flower arranging from the early 1950s and she says in the introduction to her *Garden Notebook* that

> Like many other women in those dreary years of shortages and ration books, I was hungry for new contacts and ideas, and found my eyes opened to see plants in a new way. Perhaps as a painter must do – so I began to look at plants carefully and critically.

She began travelling the country lecturing and demonstrating, using plants from her garden – many of which had been given to her by Cedric Morris. Gradually she needed more plants than her garden could provide and thus the nursery was begun. Those early years speaking to small groups about flower arranging gave her the confidence and the common touch as well as the expertise that is so evident in all her writing.

When Beth Chatto wrote about plants, be they for dry or damp conditions, woodland or prairie, you knew that it was always from personal experience. This deeply practical, resourceful person was sharing her knowledge and advice rather than dispensing it from on high. There was always a modesty in this despite the rigour and remorseless attention to detail.

In her *Garden Notebook*, published in 1988, that detail has the room to become elegiac. Her connection to land and place, focused on her garden, is as intimate and detailed as Gilbert White's Selbourne or Richard Jefferies' Wiltshire. She is a very English writer who loved the land as well as the more narrow focus of horticulture, and delighted in all the precious moments that nature offers in a thousand ways across the year. She was, in Thomas Hardy's own poetic epitaph, a person who 'used to notice such things.'

I return to her books constantly, always finding new advice and fresh ways to look at plants and gardens. For those who are new to her work, then you are entering into a life-long relationship with a wise friend and gardener.

Soil and Climate

The Soil

It is not always obvious, especially to new gardeners, that some plants do not take kindly to being pushed into the nearest empty space. In the wild the type of plants found growing will vary sometimes within a mile or two. I always find it interesting travelling across the clays and gravels of Essex to drive onto the hills of Cambridge, and suddenly see clouds of Old Man's Beard, Small Scabious, or Ladies' Fingers, *Anthyllis vulneraria* which tell me I'm on the chalk. Similarly, on a tract of poor sandy soil, there will be few oaks, but plenty of pines and silver birch, with heather beneath.

Many enthusiastic gardeners, anxious to be advised on what they shall plant, are floored by the simple question 'What kind of soil do you have?'. There is not really a simple answer to this. Soil has been formed over thousands of years by the interaction of climate, vegetation and the parent bed rock, and there is nothing we can do about this. But it is helpful to know whether your soil contains chalk or limestone, because some plants cannot abide it. (Fortunately for the purpose of this book we shall not be interested in lime-hating plants as most of them insist on plenty of moisture also.)

The most important thing about soil is its texture, because that affects two of the vital requirements for plant growth, water and air. Basically soil is broken-up pieces of rock which have been split, crushed or tumbled about. It is classified according to the size of the particles or stones. If your soil seems to be composed mostly of stones the size of peas and beans or over, and most of your forkful falls through the prongs because the finer soil between is coarse, then you can say you have a gravel soil. Water drains through this like a colander, and nutrition for plant life is lacking because it is easily washed down through the loose stone. Drought is a big problem on such a soil.

A sandy soil consists of much smaller particles without the large stones. Still very free draining and short of humus, it is a dry soil unless it has a high water table, or frequent rainfall. But it is light and easy to work, and warm and well aerated, especially in winter. This factor enables you to grow many plants that would perish when dormant in a cold soggy soil.

Clay is the opposite of sand. The soil particles are very fine indeed, producing when wet a dense plastic texture. It is difficult to work and late to warm up because of the high water content.

Loam is the ideal mixture of these component parts. In a good loam there is enough clay to retain moisture and minerals, with sufficient sand to allow aeration, thus keeping the soil warm and sweet. Few gardeners are faced with a soil composed of only one of the component parts. They will probably have something ranging between a sandy loam and a clay loam, with or without stones. It may be alkaline, that is, it has some chalk or lime already in it, or it may be neutral or acid.

A simple way to judge your type of soil is to pick up a handful when it is moderately wet, squeeze it tightly and open your hand. If it sticks into a tight ball like plasticine you have a heavy clay soil. If it holds together as a soft mass you have a medium soil. If it falls apart easily you have a light sandy soil.

Now the substance that makes all these different types of broken-up rock into fertile soil is humus. Humus is thoroughly decayed vegetable remains in such a state that it can be utilized by plants for healthy growth. As well as providing nutrition for plants, humus also greatly improves the texture of the soil, helping to open up a close soil, thus warming it by allowing freer drainage, while in a light sandy soil it acts like a sponge holding moisture.

During the last great Ice Age, an ice cap practically covered the country in our area, just to the west of Colchester. As the ice sheets ground down over the chalk and limestone areas to the north of us they deposited a thick layer of clay mixed with ground-up chalk. This was the boulder clay of my first garden, which – if unlike me, you make a habit of reading introductions – you will know, sliced like liver with white spots (being full of chalk nodules) when it was wet. To try and improve the texture I added as much garden compost and leaf mould as I could make and lay hands on, but every summer's drought brought a hard capped surface that eventually split into deep cracks. Most years, from mid June through the long dusty days of July and August into September, when there would at least be some relief with cooler weather and dewy nights, my enthusiasm for the garden hit rock bottom. The burnt grass and bedraggled beds of brittle stems and papery leaves were all an eyesore. Heart-breaking, too, for earlier there had been dreams, plans, planting and watching daily, if not hourly, while strange new shoots unfolded, and young fresh foliage covered the bare earth with a living carpet. Already I was captivated by leaves, their shapes, colours, textures. I liked best those parts of the garden which never seemed bare. However miserable other parts were looking it was always a delight to see the velvety mats of *Stachys byzantina* (*S. olympica*) creeping out onto the paving, backed by a robust shrub of *Brachyglottis* Dunedin Group (*Senecio* Dunedin hybrid) 'Sunshine', long known incorrectly as *S. laxifolius* or *S. greyi*. Neither of these plants are considered choice or uncommon but, showing no distress, they created an atmosphere of peace and plenty.

3

I began to think about collecting more plants that were adapted to drought, to group together in the sunniest, driest parts of the garden.

Then we decided to start again, to make a new garden on some land to the east of Colchester, about twelve miles from the coast.

When the ice cap started retreating, great rivers of melting ice must have gushed out over our east coastal strip, piling up gravel banks where the current was strongest, depositing sand and fine soil or silt where the water was shallow and still. The greater part of my present 10 acres of land is red gravel mixed with sand, spewed out of a melting glacier about 10,000 years ago. I am also fortunate to have the shallow valley formed by that ancient water course with still a small flow of water trickling down the centre. Although it was the possibility of one day using that small trickle to make a bog garden that drew us to this site, I must confess that on closer inspection I was appalled at the state of the rest of the land. None of it had been cultivated in our time, being too wet in the hollow, and too dry everywhere else. Several acres of dry sand and gravel were covered with coarse grasses, bramble bushes, wild rose, stunted oaks, and plenty of sorrel, indicating acidity.

On a sloping sandy bank were tall bracken beds which screened a badger's set. All around was a vast mound of fine white sand thrown out by this elusive burrower. It was June 1959, and we were busy ferrying boxes of stock plants, bulbs and cuttings from our old garden seven miles away to the site of this new venture. I sat one drowsy afternoon on the side of the badger's bank and let the hot sand trickle through my fingers like an egg timer. Well, I thought, we are certainly going to have to learn a lot about plants that will put up with this! Shall we really be able to create a garden under these conditions? That year, from November '58 to November '59, our rainfall was 14.65 in./370 mm.

The Climate

This brings me to my next point which must be considered when planning a garden – the climate. Although areas of heavy rainfall have their problems, the condition which causes more concern I would think is that of drought. Drought is, of course, relative. Another district may have the same rainfall, but with a good retentive soil, plus freedom from wind, plants will suffer less from drought. Again, people who live in areas that are used to higher rainfall and suddenly have to put up with less will be finding their plants distressed. They are suffering from drought but it is not to the same degree. It will have worse effects because the plants chosen have not been selected for their capacity to adapt to drought.

Here in East Anglia fruit orchards that have had perhaps fair supplies of rain in early summer develop soft large leaves which collapse easily in a period of sudden heat, or several days of tearing wind. Whereas another year, when a dry spring merges into a dry summer, the trees grow smaller tougher leaves and produce a stronger sap to suck up what water is available. In other words, they adjust themselves, and have time to do so. This is why flooding a plant with water in a drought and then forgetting it, or not being able to carry on watering, is so damaging.

Our average 20 in./510 mm of rain falls more or less evenly throughout the year. Because the clouds from the west have shed most of their load over the western and central part of the country, the rainfall is always light. We rarely record more than 3 in./75 mm in a month. For six months of the year the average monthly total will be less than 2 in./50 mm, and three months will register less than 1 in./25 mm. The light summer rainfall, although bringing some relief, often does not penetrate far into the soil before it is followed by two days of devilish wind which does far more harm than the sun. Still days are a balm to the spirit as well as the poor plants, a state of peace which probably only gardeners and growers really appreciate to the full. July and August are often overcast; irritatingly no rain falls except for the occasional thunderstorm, but plants will respond to cooler temperatures even when they are short of water. April and early May can be relied on for a drought or period of very low rainfall, combined with chilling winds out of the north-east – our 'blackthorn winter', when tender young shoots and new leaves unfolding can be blackened.

2

Moisture Conservation
and Soil Improvement

I really don't hold with watering. Of course I water new plants in, to settle the soil around the roots and prevent air pockets, and I do give extra water to keep them going until they are established. But I do not make a practice of watering the garden in periods of drought, although I must confess the Big Drought of 1976 almost overcame my resolve not to water some of the borders. There were signs of distress in many plants, but although a few died, being newly planted, the established ones hung on, and some looked astonishingly well.

This would not have been the case if we had not added plenty of moisture-retaining material. Many of the Mediterranean-type plants which stand drought, such as the grey artemisias and succulent sedums, will grow in many peoples' gardens without any additional organic matter – indeed they would be overfed and grow out of character on too rich a diet – but I am dealing with a soil and climate where the native weeds sometimes curl up and die. Some of my borders, I can confidently say, are on the poorest, driest soil in the country! I know that I must first cosset the soil if I am to achieve anything worthwhile, and secondly, consider only those plants that will put up with low rainfall and complete exposure to sun and wind.

Whether your soil is sand, gravel, chalk or clay based, well-rotted vegetable matter will greatly improve the texture, retaining moisture, providing aeration in dry soils and improving fertility in all types. The difficulty is how to obtain enough of this invaluable material. Wherever you live, and whatever you use, money or effort – or both – will be needed.

Garden Compost

The most economical material so far as cost is concerned is garden compost. But it does mean effort, and an attitude of continual conservation. Barrowloads of weeds, cut-down plant remains and fallen leaves are yearly removed from the beds, and if nothing is put back, however initially good the soil, you will, over the years, have removed most of your top soil and exhausted the nutrients from the layer you have left. A compost heap is a pile of such materials, neatly stacked to rot, which you can then return to the garden to replace what you have taken out.

I value my compost heaps more than any other organic material I use, and prefer it to manure for putting into the holes when planting as it is immediately available to the plants, being black, crumbly and sweet smelling. If you have room it is a good idea to make at least two heaps, one ready to use, one half rotted, which will be turned onto the empty space when the first has gone out. Turning the heap can reactivate the rotting process, but is not vital.

I must confess I make my heaps pretty haphazardly. We have set aside an area surrounded by three walls for our composting. During the growing season barrowloads of waste are dumped; everything from the garden is utilized except really woody things that will not rot down. I am not too fussed about weeds like twitch grass and sorrel – sorting out weeds to save and weeds to burn usually means the whole lot goes on the bonfire. I have found that most weeds are rotted down, and those that may have escaped near the edges of the heaps are perfectly obvious, like the strong white strings of twitch, or orange threads of sorrel, and can be collected up and burnt as you dig out the heap. I have learnt, though, that pernicious nuisances like celandines, and certain alliums which have become one of my pet hates, must be kept separate, and these do go into a different barrow and

8

end up on the burning heap. Worn-out soil compost from potting contains a little peat which cannot be wasted so that is also tipped onto the heap.

All refuse from the house is put into a shallow area, surrounded by brick, and covered with a wire netting lid to keep out rats. We also see that rat bait is frequently laid round the whole composting area, as they love to over-winter in the warm heaps, coming in from the surrounding farms. But you need to guard against rats just as much in town gardens as in the country. Going back to this refuse pit, I have a friend who adds to the vegetable peelings and emptied tea pots all her old letters, newspapers and cotton rags, in fact everything rottable, except for man-made fabrics like nylon. When we put a fork into her pit to see how it was getting on we turned over a mass of wriggling red worms all having a fine feast. I find myself that too much paper can accumulate, unless it is regularly watered to keep decomposition active.

Every few months this pit of wet waste is scooped out and added to the piles of weeds. I don't add soil as enough of that seems to come from weeding, but occasionally I add a sprinkling of some activator like Garotta, or you can use a little sulphate of ammonia with a sprinkling of chalk to prevent acidity which slows down the fermentation process. When the heaps are really active in the growing season it is possible to push your hand deep into the pile and be compelled to draw it out again smartly, the heat that is generated being too hot to bear. We turn our heaps by using the fork lift on the front of the tractor, every now and then having a tidy-up, making a long neat heap against the wall, and leaving room for a new heap to begin alongside.

In a small garden, and with no such mechanical aid, it is important not to make your heap too big, although it needs to be big enough to generate heat. Two smaller heaps about 4 ft/1.2 m across are easier to manage. The books tell you to cover the finished heap with soil, obviously to keep in the heat. I'm sure this is a good thing, especially with smaller heaps, but I'm afraid we never make time for that. The outside layer of unrotted material we throw down to form the basis of another heap. Some books tell you to build your heap around poles, which are subsequently taken out to allow aeration, but this would only be necessary I think if you were using purely soft vegetable waste like lawn mowings which pack down too tightly and do not rot well on their own. Similarly you need to take trouble with autumn leaves, especially if you have large quantities of them. They should be stacked in layers, a layer of leaves, then a layer of soil, plus activator; ideally the whole thing should be watered as you go along, especially if the leaves are very dry. A top layer of soil will keep the last layer of leaves from blowing away. These heaps will take two years at least to become well rotted down, but when they are they are worth gold, because they are almost weed free.

I won't pretend that my compost is free of weed seed. It is not. I don't usually spread it around on top of the soil, but use it well dug in. You can see where it has been put by the healthy-looking weeds that do emerge, especially chickweed. But they are easily dealt with in ways that I will describe later. What matters is that my plants grow away well in that important first season. If I planted in the existing 'soil' they would stand still making up their minds whether to live or die; if they survived they would always look stunted. But with a generous diet of my compost I can look back at the end of the year, and feel delighted how well they have done!

Farmyard Manure

I suppose the next source of humus that we look around for is farmyard manure. This can be bought at a price. If you live in a suitable area, and have room to receive it and stack it, it is worthwhile ringing your local manure company and getting them to quote you for a load. Any kind of animal refuse, well mixed with peat or straw, is worth every effort to obtain. If you can lay your hands on chicken house litter, pig manure or horse manure you will be laying up treasure for your garden. But be sure to 'dilute' these manures; ideally they should be layered with either compost, straw or peat and stacked for a few months. They can be too strong if used fresh and neat.

I prefer to use farmyard manure on top of the ground, utilizing it as a mulch around trees and shrubs, and greedy feeders like hostas and hellebores, where the rain will wash in the soluble nitrogen, the birds and frost will break it up, and the worms drag it down into the soil.

Worms and Soil Bacteria

If you rarely see worms when you dig your soil that is a sure sign you are short of humus, unless the soil is very dry when they sensibly go down deeper, coming to the surface as soon as rains fall. Worms do much good. They make burrows in the ground which let in air and water, especially valuable in heavy soils. They drag leaves into the soil and digest them, so helping to make a mixture of soil and leaf mould. By continually bringing up fresh enriched soil to the surface they disturb it so much that slimy moulds cannot grow.

Darwin studied the lowly earthworm, discovering how indebted we are to its labours. In his book *Earthworms and Vegetable Mould* he shows that each year worms bring up about 1/50th of an inch of soil, so that if you put a tenpenny piece on the soil now, and it was left undisturbed, in fifty years it might be covered with one inch of soil. Pavements that were on the surface when the Romans occupied Britain are now covered with a thick layer of soil.*

Helping out the earthworms is a vast population of unseen workers. Termed soil bacteria, these micro-organisms all play a part in the strange underworld of the soil. The Goodies change dead remains of plants and animals into valuable plant food. The Baddies can cause infections in wounds of both plants and animals. Eel worms, minute creatures which infect roots of plants such as phlox, are among the troublesome Baddies.

* From *Lessons on Soil* by J. M. Russell.

Peat

Most gardeners feel they ought to use peat. Certainly if you haven't space, time or energy to make compost, and your next-door neighbour would understandably be upset if you had a steaming load of muck left at your entrance (even though it smells so deliciously nitrogenous in the country!) then peat it must be, for those plants that justify the expense! I do not think it matters whether it is moss peat, or sedge peat – whatever is handiest and least costly. The demand for it is so great that it can never be cheap unless you live on top of it – and then you won't want it, but will be pining for some well-drained gravel.

Do wet your peat well before using it. Do not use it straight out of the bag. If you can easily lift a bag of peat then it is not wet enough. It will absorb ten times its weight in water, I am told. I have an old-fashioned long zinc bath; I put half a bale of peat into it, flood it with water, stir it round like pig meal, then add more until the bath is full. Then I leave it to soak until it is black and heavy. For small amounts you could use a bucket or the wheelbarrow. A good handful of this, well mixed into the hole for a plant, a bucketful for a tree or a half-bucket for a shrub gives them a good start. But it does not *feed*. Its effect is mechanical, preserving moisture, and helping to aerate and warm a clay soil.

Other Organic Material

Other aids in water conservation to be dug into the soil are spent hops if you can find them, and although I have no experience of sewage sludge, I understand it has been produced in an acceptable form by some enlightened councils so it would be worthwhile investigating in your area.

I used to use a bagged dried organic manure produced by an enterprising farmer in Norfolk. It is no longer available to me but could be produced by enterprising companies elsewhere. A magic mixture involving, I imagine, dehydrated FYM, fishmeal, perhaps meat and bone, it was light and pleasant to handle, and very useful as a top dressing in spring among small plants. I had to restrain myself from being too generous when using these kinds of concentrate – too much can kill plants more efficiently than neglect.

This is how I Plant

If a piece of ground is smothered with really difficult weeds like creeping thistle, twitch, docks or bracken I use appropriate weed killers the season before. These stubborn perennials need a systemic poison to work through their systems. If there are not too many we dig them out, as I do not care to use poisonous materials more often than is really necessary. Black plastic sheeting (or old carpets if available) fastened down for at least six months to exclude light, will destroy most deep-rooted weeds, as well as weed seedlings.

Then compost, or well-rotted muck, or both, are spread over the entire area if we have enough, and either dug well in or rotavated. If we are short of humus we cultivate first to clean the ground, then put as much as we can spare of whatever we have got into every hole as we plant. We make sure that the addition is well mixed into the soil, and not left as a separate layer.

Where you have a heavy clay soil a good thick dressing, well forked in, of pea-sized grit will help to lighten the soil. I have also seen clay soil burnt. It was a slow and laborious business, but the results were rewarding. Clay was heaped onto a bonfire, more fuel and more clay being added – it seemed to go on for weeks. The result was a brick-coloured crumbly substance which was spread with the ashes, and lightly forked in to improve the top spit. I have learnt not to dig my precious compost into raw clay. Whenever possible I pile up material on top of the clay and have sometimes waited two years before I have accumulated a sufficient depth of improved soil. I have used worn-out potting soil, peat, sand, garden refuse, rotted straw – anything that will make an easily workable top layer, and also enable the plants to establish roots quickly on their way down to the moisture-holding clay. Such extreme measures need only be used when there is no top soil at all on the clay.

When the holes I dug in the summer to take trees in the following winter filled with water like wells, I realized that this was the wrong thing to do too! It is better to dig, incorporate some kind of humus, then plant and fill in immediately. If you are tree planting on a slope, you can dig a little drain-away if the soil is very wet. If not, try to plant as shallow as is practicable, then pile in compost, garden refuse, better soil from elsewhere on top, if possible, and gradually make a mound above the clay.

The Effect of Mulching

In the last three or four years, my garden has been vastly improved in looks, performance and maintenance by mulches. I cannot now abide to see bare soil, it looks so raw. Mulches look good, making it possible to walk over the beds without leaving footprints or panning the soil. But they don't just look nice. They are there for two very good reasons.

(1) *To prevent evaporation of water from the soil.* Having done all you can to provide a sponge to hold water in the soil you don't want it to be dried out too quickly by wind and sun. It is no use putting a mulch on dry soil.

During the spring of 1976 we could not put any mulch down as the soil was bone dry until July, when we had a sudden freak thunderstorm. It takes a tremendous wetting to penetrate a good mulch, usually the whole of the winter rain here. In summer the light rainfall is usually evaporated before it has penetrated the mulch layer.

(2) Equally valuable, if not more so, is the effect of *preventing the emergence of seedling weeds.* My light soil, newly dug, can produce a crop of weed seedlings thick as hairs on a cat's back within a couple of days, and by the end of a fortnight there is the tedious job of hoeing them out. Left much longer newly planted treasures are over-run.

The two materials I now use are straw and pulverized bark.

14

Straw mulching. On my trees and shrubs, at the back of borders, I use straw which so far I have obtained easily. (Bracken cut in autumn could be used as effectively.) We put it down in autumn, after it has rained, making a nice thick eiderdown on my poor gravelly soil. The winter rain soon helps to darken it, while a light scattering of some nitrogenous fertilizer in spring, like sulphate of ammonia, helps the soil bacteria to turn it into humus. The nitrogen created by the breakdown of the straw is then available to the plants. A flourishing worm population drags all vegetable waste down into the soil where exploring roots can find it.

We only ever dig among our shrubs, once they have been planted, if we are adding something new. For weeks in the growing season, after there has been no measurable amount of rain, it is possible to move aside the latest layer of straw and still see last year's dressing, now a thin layer of black humus, while the soil beneath is still moist. Elsewhere the top spit, uncovered, will be bone dry. Admittedly, in many areas during the 1976 drought the soil did dry out beneath the straw, with trees and shrubs transpiring gallons of water, and no rainfall for months. But although they were showing some distress none died, and all picked up quickly when enough rain fell to penetrate the straw. I feel certain that in late summer these straw mulches attract dew, and this, along with cooler days, causes the shrubs to perk up considerably, even though it hasn't rained.

Pulverized bark. I prefer to use a much finer mulch among herbaceous plants. I started using peat, which was very effective, but nearer to hand I found crushed or pulverized bark. This is produced by the Forestry Commission, and sold through garden centres, or in bulk by wholesale firms.

It was much coarser when I first bought it – little chips of bark that looked attractive, but slid off one another like 'Tiddly Winks', making it easy for a really determined weed seed to elbow its way up to the light and so survive. But now, if the ground is clean to start with, I find that a 2 in./50 mm (at least) layer of finely crushed bark stifles the young weed seedlings before they can struggle to the surface. Provided the soil is wet I like to put it down as soon as I have finished planting. Sometimes this is not possible, the planting having taken several weeks in spring to complete. Then the whole bed is carefully weeded and hoed with a small onion hoe, after which the bark is put down immediately. We use our weeding buckets, pouring the bark onto the ground, only levelling the heaps out slightly, and seeing that it is well tucked round the plants. Sometimes, when plants are very small, we have to put on a lighter dressing, adding to it when we go round about six weeks later and everything has grown. It is important, too, to watch over new plantings, and see that precious young things do not get smothered by bark having been blown over them by our north-east winds – which are the curse of the spring months – or scratched over them by blackbirds and thrushes.

I won't say that we get no weeds at all in the beds after this. But I can say that in comparison with what we have done in the past, weeding becomes a luxury, not a dread. Of course the odd tussock of grass makes headway, and chickweed makes luscious mats if not dealt with quickly. But it takes so little time to pull out the few odd weeds, leaving more leisure to admire the plants, which make up twice as well. Again they look so much better against the warm brown carpet, which invites us (not the visitors!) to walk among them to inspect them more closely.

The bark mulch must not be disturbed. Any little nodules of soil brought to the surface will sprout weeds, so be careful not to bring up fresh soil when taking out the odd weed. If you do poke about here and there, as inevitably I do, adding a few newcomers, then you will probably need to add a bucketful or two of bark mulch just where it is thin.

I find that the rate of growth of plants under a mulch is quite astonishing. Generally I do not need to add more, for by the end of the first year the soil is often two-thirds covered by the plants themselves. The edges sometimes need a top-up the second spring, where perhaps the wind has blown the earth bare. I aim to get my plants growing vigorously, so that they will eventually cover the surface, providing natural weed control, and protecting the soil crust from sun and wind.

Peat mulching. It would be unfair not to say a few words about peat as a mulch, my main reason for not using it being that crushed bark is available from a reasonable distance. For many people peat is probably the only sterile material they can lay their hands on. I did use it here in my first experiments with mulches, and was very satisfied with it, both for repressing annual weeds and conserving moisture. I used Shamrock peat, and preferred the coarse variety. It did not blow away when dry, and is very long lasting, still covering some beds efficiently after three years.

Spent hops. I have seen spent hops looking splendid on beds of shrubs at Kew, but all efforts to obtain them here have been unsuccessful. I was once staying with a friend in a hop-growing part of the country, when almost at dusk one evening a large load, wet and very beery smelling, was deposited just inside her entrance, effectively stopping, in more ways than one, anyone entering or leaving. We had to fetch spades quickly to provide room and fresh air for the postman next morning.

It dampened my enthusiasm rather, but would I imagine be quite easy and pleasant to use if it were stacked a while, to dry out.

Other mulches. Some plants really object to having damp necks and sodden foliage, especially in our cold wet winters. This is especially so with the high alpines, used to sun and drying winds in summer, but often buried under dry snow in winter. I do not surround these plants with peat or bark, which would encourage rotting in winter, but dress the ground with gravel. About a two-inch layer seems to be effective in protecting the made-up soil beneath from rapid water loss.

Weed Control

With all mulches, except thick straw, it is worth remembering that seeds falling *onto* them will germinate. So try not to let plants like foxgloves or poppies shed their seed like pepper shakers. I do find that here and there, especially on the damper soil, the extreme edges of the beds carry a bit of Annual Meadow Grass by the end of the season. This shows where we have mowed without the box and the grass seed has shot over the bark, usually on the corners!

What about bindweed, docks and such perennial problems? Any perennial weed if already established in the soil will push up strongly through any mulch, usually looking quite handsome in isolation! Sometimes they can be dug out easily. But for large woody docks, or dandelions deepseated in a thyme mat or crevice, I use a weak solution of systemic weed killer, containing 2, 4-D (one of the proprietary brands suitable for dealing with broad-leafed weeds in the lawn, like Tumbleweed). I keep a special watering can, old saucepan and inch-wide paintbrush for the purpose. Another aid can be an empty liquid soap container, refilled with diluted herbicide, very handy to squirt into the centre of a plantain. A few dabs with the paintbrush on the young growing points and the poison is taken down into the cell sap. Slowly, in about three weeks, the plant becomes distorted and dies. Nettles growing through a shrub can be next to impossible to dig out, but just a touch against every tip is enough to banish them.

Bindweed and sorrel, both very common on light and acid soils, do not give in at all easily. They have intricate rambling root systems, bindweed going down many feet, with tremendous power to produce viable buds. It is tempting to pull off the long runners, and if you garden a sufficiently small area, and are prepared *to do so conscientiously* every week, you will starve the roots. With rather more to cope with I paint mine, some time in May or June, when there is enough growth to give a good cover. I have found that it does not work if the mixture is too strong. If the bindweed turns brown and quickly dies off it will soon be up again. When the solution is right the foliage and stems become twisted and yellow. Much smaller, weaker growth will return after a considerable time, and a second dose on those will usually finish them off. I have eradicated carpets of bindweed by this method. But, of course, with seed having fallen in the soil over many years, it is advisable to watch out for new plants every year and cope with them as they appear.

Concentrated Fertilizers

A brief word on concentrated fertilizers. If you can only use peat as the organic material to improve your soil you must add something else as a feed for your plants. General fertilizers are available, containing a balanced mixture to provide the necessary elements for plant growth, primarily nitrogen, phosphorus and potash. Read the small print and do not exceed the proper dosage, too much can kill plants.

Organic fertilizers like bonemeal, meat and bone, or dried blood are all excellent, but expensive. So are concentrated fishmeals if you can endure the smell. Personally, I rarely use concentrated fertilizer. Too much nitrogen can cause weak sappy growth and spoil the character of some plants, such as the greys. It would be unwise, knowing we shall probably have several droughty spells during the growing season, to encourage too much top growth, which flags immediately conditions get tough. Drought-loving plants look better, and survive better, on a thin diet. I believe strongly in a good start, then once they are established they must make it themselves.

3

Some Principles on Basic Design in Dry Gardens

Even before digging and delving to prepare your soil for drought-resisting plants it is necessary to consider the garden overall. As far as possible, I think, the aim should be to have no square foot that does not provide interest some time during the year, preferably for much of the year. Obviously the smaller the garden the more this applies. No garden is too small to provide continual delights; even a small sink or trough, properly planted, can give pleasure *ad infinitum*.

In Place of Parched Grass

If you have a really small plot, under 30 × 30 ft/10 × 10 m and drought is a yearly problem, then I would forget about grass, either as paths or for a sitting area. Next, I would reduce these functional areas so they use as little space as possible, without skimping the design.

Owners of much larger gardens may find something helpful in this note, because the areas around the house are so important in providing a relaxed atmosphere – which several yards of parched grass does nothing to create.

Gravel. The next thing is to decide what shall be used in place of grass. Gravel, I suppose, is cheapest. Well-made gravel paths, hoggin based, well rolled, and occasionally raked to freshen them, look good and are easily maintained with a watering can and a soil poison like Simazine. If they have become infected with annual weeds, a watering of Simazine and Gramoxone combined will clean them up. Gramoxone burns off the top growth like a flame gun; Simazine, being slow acting, will destroy the roots and prevent further germination. An annual treatment is enough.

There is a happy medium concerning the size of gravel. Stones that are too small, even pea grit, are inclined to pick up on your shoes and are too easily scattered by car wheels. I have a place where paving meets gravel drive and it constantly needs sweeping. There is not always time available to do such repetitive and boring jobs. On the other hand, stones the size of a pigeon's egg are a nightmare to walk on, and it is impossible to push a loaded barrow on them. Something between the two is about right. Again, if you put too thick a layer of gravel down, it takes years to work down into the hoggin, and you struggle over it, as on a pebbly beach!

Edging the gravel paths was another problem, to keep the stones from falling onto the borders. I could not find anything suitable (that I could afford anyway!) when we started the garden, so I decided we would make something that would serve the purpose. I found five long straight planks, laid them on a bed of flattened sand, separating them by house bricks to give me the width. Then I broke up some old seed trays to make divisions, roughly the length of a brick. We made a dry cement sand mix, added a little powdered colouring to tone with the gravel, and making a porridgy mixture plopped it in between the boards and smoothed the top. After a couple of days my 'bricks' were hard enough to move, stack carefully, and fill up the boards for another batch! It did not take long to make enough. When thoroughly hardened we laid them by making a shallow trench, putting in a little wet cement, setting our 'brick' edging level on top, and grouting between with plain cement. They went beautifully round curves. I was delighted with them, and they do not perish in frost, like clay bricks. I have to confess that in recent years I have 'sunk' to using 4 in./100 mm concrete blocks, sinking about half the block. They are heavy to handle, but only need a little cement between them, and make a very strong edging for large areas. They look (almost) as good as my tinted 'bricks', and are easily obtainable. These edgings not only keep soil from spilling onto gravel but make a definite edge to spray against when weed killing. Plants grow out over them making the lines less formal.

Paving. Gravel is not very comfortable to sit on. Chairs wobble, and it is more than likely there will be an ant's nest in the vicinity. Paving is really the answer for the sitting area, or patio. And it is preferable for the path, which allows you to walk comfortably all round the house in wet weather. Remember, though, that it can be slippery in frosty weather.

Paving, or a paved path, laid right up to the walls of the house looks harsh. I love my house wall beds. They provide shelter for all kinds of plants, which in turn soften the outlines of the house. What kind of paving? There is a wide choice, only limited by one's taste and ability to pay the bill.

Seventeen years ago, in total ignorance, we made our own. Living in an area where there is no natural paving material, and not caring too much for the pastel shades of concrete slabs available I declared again that we would make our own, leaving the bothersome business of deciding just how we could do it to my husband. Although quite unused to the building profession he gallantly set to, hired a cement mixer, and thus we began.

Two different levels had been made by the bulldozer on the hot gravelly slope for the site of our single storey, split-level house – which now crouches down over the slope rather like a mushroom, its weatherboarding painted white, as are many traditional Essex farmhouses. We intended to pave all round the house, but the main area meant for sitting out was on the south-west side, about 30 × 20 ft/10 × 6 m. We bought a number of straight planks, so armed with these and a spirit level we knocked in little stakes which soon showed a considerable slope away from the house. We made up this ground with hardcore and spare soil from elsewhere. Then we rolled it. We discovered later that it would have been wiser to have had more reinforcing material, as some of our slabs have moved a little – but for novices it could have been worse.

Next came the fun of designing the blocks. I wanted to make random paving in squares and oblongs. To Andrew goes the credit of carefully laying wooden surrounds, properly blocked up to make the levels right, ensuring that rain would run off in the right direction.

We made a coarse sand/stone cement mix, put down about a 4 in./100 mm layer, leaving it to set, then went on constructing our pattern of large and small blocks. When the base was completed we made a sand/cement mix to which we added three different powdered colours we had chosen to match the pebbles in our gravel. To vary it further we intermixed the colours. As this top layer set we carefully lifted out the wooden slats, and filled in the cracks with cement. I decided not to leave spaces for crevice plants. I knew there would be plenty of plants all round the terrace, to soften the edges, and enough room to sit, and have a few tubs or pots of plants. Too much planting in this case would look overdone.

When it was complete it looked so large and empty Andrew thought it looked like a railway yard – but now, with a *Magnolia* × *soulangiana* making a sunshade near the house, and plants, shrubs and climbers spilling all round, it is almost smothered at times.

The little paved area that leads to the front door we made in a different fashion. We made blocks individually, on sand, not so large that we could not lift them, and then laid them on a bed of sand. We left oblong and square spaces carefully chosen so that they need not be walked on; then I laid, in cement, smooth round cobbles, about the size of a hen's egg, flat to come level with the paving. When the cement was dry I cleaned off the pebbles by washing them with a weak solution of spirits of salts.

Elsewhere I have laid strips of bricks and cobbles but this was not too successful. Some of the bricks have crumbled with frost. The failings caused by our inexperience help perhaps to give the paved areas the appearance of having been laid centuries ago, but although there is charm, with the moss and lichen growing in the broken cracks, we would know better next time.

Boundaries

Hedges are a waste in the small dry garden, to be avoided wherever possible. If you must have one as a boundary between you and your neighbour, put your service path alongside it so that you are not faced with the problem of what to plant on the roots of a privet hedge. (Why always privet?!)

If you have a like-minded neighbour on the other side you could each build up a shrubbery border, back to back, which complemented each other's planting. His *Cupressus arizonica* could make a fine feature to back your *Genista aetnensis* and *Cistus ladanifer*. An unseen wire netting fence would keep the children in bounds, but also would not rob the soil of anything. While the trees and shrubs were growing you could train up all kinds of temporary fancies like ornamental gourds or Canary Creepers to hide it.

Unsuitable Trees for Dry Gardens

Large soft-leafed trees are not adapted to stand drought conditions. They won't do well, and look unsuitable with thymes and heathers. Trees and shrubs with small, tough leaves will do much better, such as rosemary, lavender and cistus, with junipers and some forms of cypress to add height and drama.

4

Plant Grouping in Dry Gardens

If this book is to be of any practical help to you who read it I can only write with confidence of the plants and their groupings which have pleased (or displeased) me. So I am going to describe some of the borders that I have made in my present garden during the last thirty-eight years. Some will be larger than average borders; I am fortunate to have room to experiment. But within these borders there may be ideas which could easily be translated into a much smaller area. I hope so.

Of all the activities that possessing a piece of land forces upon us, planning can result in euphoria or despair. The image in your mind of what to plant, where to plant it, and what it shall be put beside, can be either a total blank or a picture of mature perfection, impossible to achieve.

You may be one of those people who, in the tantalizing jumble of a junk shop, can pick out a piece of furniture or a picture and take it home knowing exactly where to put it so that it will look like an heirloom. I try to do this with plants. They need a background, a middle ground and a foreground. There will be star performers, but there must be a supporting cast. All will contribute to the scene, making highlights and shadows.

The great thing about gardening is that you don't have to stick to something if it doesn't work out. You can dig out your failures and start again. The important thing is to *plant*, letting everything grow on for a year or so. Then look again!

It won't all be bad. Part may have to be removed and put elsewhere, but what is left will suggest a better idea. Again, when you have finished mourning the loss of some valued plant that has died, either of old age, or unendurable conditions, you can be thankful for the space wherein to try a new discovery.

With my large borders still in mind, I think that even in small gardens bold planting, using few varieties of plants, can be very effective and easy to manage, ideal for someone who has better things to do than forever bothering about the garden.

For those who 'have no time' I'm inclined to think it is a myth that 'putting it all down to grass' is labour saving; certainly I should hate to be faced with an hour's mowing once a week throughout the growing season. I am all for ease of management; why make a hobby of punishing yourself. Half that area of featureless grass could be devoted to a collection of tree(s), shrub(s) and plants which, when established, would cover the ground. Then, the few surviving weeds would make a pleasant excuse for you to crouch down out of the sly east wind, where the view always seems better, the smells most nostalgic. Perhaps that is the danger – one might become a plant addict!

I am aware that there are also grass addicts. Why not? But *they enjoy* their grass.

It might be helpful at this stage to make a little précis of ideas which have helped me in general garden design.

(1) Make an 'outline' plan (it doesn't have to be on paper).
(2) Use only plants that are suited to the conditions you have to offer.
(3) Use plants which rely on foliage and form rather than a mass of flower. Many of these will doubtless provide fascinating flowers, but their habit not only prolongs the lasting effect of the design, but also cuts down on:

   (a) Expense – by remaining there until you decide you prefer something else.

26

(b) Labour – by covering the soil, and so reducing the time you spend weeding.

(4) Try to have one or two spectacular plants to create drama. These will probably be large or variegated.
(5) Do not cram all your spectacular plants into the front garden. Star performers need quiet companions to show them off.
(6) Try to remember that the best overall effect is one of simplicity, even though it may be made up of dozens of interesting plants.
(7) Where space will allow, plants look better planted in groups of odd numbers rather than dotted about singly like hat-pins.

I rarely remember all this at planting time. But when something really looks bad it is because I have ignored too much of it.

5

Borders and Beds:
Dry Sun and Dry Shade

Front gardens can be a nightmare. When minutely small their owners often either struggle with a moth-eaten looking rug of poor grass, or pave the whole thing disastrously with colourful tiles. Larger entrances may have a tatty shrub border edged with fading iris or chrysanthemums. The same street will also contain gardens that slow up the passer-by. These will be of very different styles.

Probably the most popular will be the bedded-out front garden, which can be a really joyous affair. Usually beautifully maintained, it is a riot of colour until the first frost topples its glory, usually in early November. Then the whole thing, except the rose bushes, comes out, and the bulbs and wall-flowers go in. All winter it looks controlled and tidy, albeit a bit severe. Spring provides another display of drilled tulips in a sea of forget-me-nots; then, once again, the whole thing is back to square one, and the garden is naked while the owner, night and morning, carries cans to keep his cherished plants going, sustained by an image of velvet petunias rioting among French marigolds. With admirable perseverance, and no ban on the use of water, he succeeds. We marvel; better even than last year.

Another front garden that takes my fancy is usually much simpler. Probably there is very little planting, but instead a neatly kept area of grass, or an interesting though restrained use of paving. The focal point will be either a spectacular foliage plant, usually evergreen, such as a *Yucca* or *Fatsia japonica*.

A surprise for me was seeing, one autumn, a large isolated clump of common montbretia. This plant is indestructible and not usually remarkable. No doubt this one had survived from a plan long since abandoned. But here it was, alone at the entrance, a beautiful fountain of grassy leaves, shades of russet brown, glinting in the low rays of the sun. I don't remember if there were any other flowers in that garden, but in my mind I enjoy still the contrast of that shape against short cut grass.

Coming back to the small garden, which really has no more than a walled square box beside the front door, I know of two such gardens that give me pleasure every year.

One is against a sun-baked Georgian-type terraced house. It has been filled with two or three Cardoons. (These look almost identical in leaf to the large French artichoke.) Admittedly the space is empty much of the winter, but from spring to autumn these enormous clumps of slashed silvery-grey leaves look spectacular, splendidly in scale with the fine window against which they reflect their sturdy 8 ft/2.5 m stems topped with huge blue thistle-like flowers. So much more successful, I think, than the sparrow-scratched asters in the 'garden' alongside.

Elsewhere I know a row of railway cottages facing north. Several of the occupiers have planted hydrangeas. They are now the proud possessors of immense plants, crowded with flower heads, infinitely better than any of mine! With total simplicity they have achieved total success.

My Entrance Garden

I feel a little hesitant to admit it, but I have several entrance gardens. Originally we came through a farm gateway, passing through a 30-acre field to our house, situated at the far end. As with some of the gardens I have just mentioned, I put off doing anything about the road entrance for some years; it is a quarter of a mile from the house: a case of out of sight, out of mind. But gradually it dawned on me that

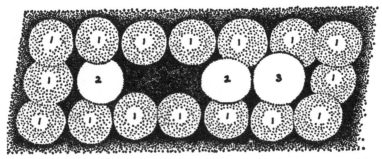

A. A very simple planting for a shady island entrance bed, approx. 5 × 15 ft./
1.5 × 5 m

1. Could be all dwarf vincas or dwarf *Hedera helix* forms
2. *Iris foetidissima*
3. *Fuchsia magellanica* 'Variegata' (not evergreen) or *Lonicera nitida*
   'Baggesen's Gold'

my friends, driving along the main highway to the coast,
with its sundry aids to holidaymakers like eggs and veg.
plentifully displayed, might, with relief, catch sight of that
luminous green unique to *Euphorbia* and realize they had
arrived.

So, Harry – without whom much of this would not have
been possible – and I went up one day and surveyed the site.
On one side was a bank covered with brambles and elm
thicket. The other side was a narrow strip of solid twitch
grass, backed by a fence and garage belonging to a neighbour.
We borrowed a small bulldozer, swept away the brambles
and elm suckers, and levelled the bank. This west-facing
strip was a long winter job for Harry, carefully digging and
throwing out the twitch. The soil in both borders contains
more loam than in the garden proper, so we call it reasonably
good. Still, for good measure we rotavated in a light dressing
of muck.

Then, one spring morning, we took up a trolleyload of
plants to the west border, roughly 45 yd/41 m long, but
nowhere much more than 4 ft/1.2 m wide, only enough
room for one large spreading plant. With my neighbour's
garden offering a few thujas, a pink-washed garage, and a

wooden fence covered with clematis this provided a ready-made background for my cover plants. I chose easy large-growing plants that can look after themselves.

Now, *Brachyglottis* Dunedin Group (*Senecio* Dunedin hybrid) 'Sunshine', robust and always eye-catching, contrasts in texture with the filigree Blue Rue. *Iris foetidissima* between these two makes a startling change in form. Against the pink wall *Artemisia arborescens* pushes a great cloud of finely cut silver foliage into a *Buddleia* which provides height. A good white form of *Clematis montana* tumbles from above into the pink and white flowered forms of cistus. Two shrubby salvias, one purple leafed, the other variegated in tones of green and yellow, have completed a simple border which is now totally filled with soft mounds of foliage all the year round. But the most striking plants which I haven't mentioned are several *Euphorbia characias*, subsp. *wulfenii*. Now over 4 ft/1.2 m tall, and more across, these are seedlings of Mrs Fish's *Euphorbia* 'Lambrook Gold', and magnificent they are. I sometimes grow a few cuttings from her original plant, but I find that seedlings come reasonably true (provided the parent is not too close to a near relative; see Pl. 1). It looks good throughout the year, except for periods of severe cold when the leaves droop and the whole plant looks understandably miserable, but it perks up again as soon as the temperature rises. In February (earlier in mild winters) the flower spike proudly lifts its bent head and gradually opens its massed lime-yellow florets into a huge cylindrical dome shape, sometimes 18 in./460 mm long and 9 in./230 mm across. Although they will stand cold they grow skinny if whirled around by tearing winds. The protection of other shrubs is enough to make them wax fat.

Opposite this exposed sunny border I had to plant a hedge, as a boundary. I set it about 8 ft/2.5 m from my driveway and I chose *Cotoneaster lacteus* because it stands drought, is evergreen except in the severest winters, and holds its berries late. First we erected an easily made supporting fence, consisting of a strong post every 10 ft/3 m, with strong wires strained across, about 18 in./460 mm apart. The young plants were planted 4 ft/1.2 m apart, supported initially by

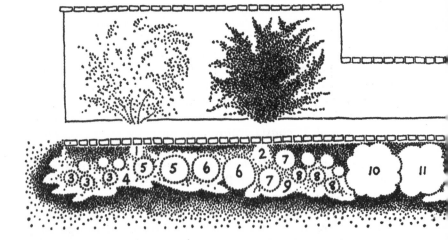

B. Plants for north- or east-facing entrance border, approx. 1 × 30 yd/m

1. *Lonicera* (own choice)*
2. *Hedera colchica* 'Sulphur Heart' ('Paddy's Pride')*
3. *Arum italicum* subsp. *italicum* 'Marmoratum' (A. i. 'Pictum')
4. *Ajuga reptans* 'Burgundy Glow'
5. *Iris foetidissima*
6. *Helleborus orientalis*
7. *Polygonatum × hybridum*
8. *Euphorbia amygdaloides robbiae*
9. *Viola riviniana* Purpurea Group
10. *Helleborus argutifolius* (H. corsicus)

* (N.B. These climbers, growing against the wall, appear to be separated from the border by a path but in fact form an integral part of the planting.)

C. Plants for a south- or west-facing border, approx. 1 × 30 yd/m

1. *Stachys byzantina* (S. olympica)
2. *Yucca* or *Cynara* (Cardoon)
3. *Salvia officinalis* 'Purpurascens'
4. *Ruta graveolens* 'Jackman's Blue'
5. *Euphorbia characias wulfenii*
6. *Cistus hybridus* (C. × corbariensis)
7. *Senecio cineraria* 'White Diamond'
8. *Santolina chamaecyparissus*

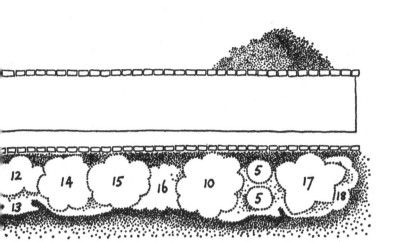

1. Weigelia florida 'Variegata'
2. Hypericum androsaemum
3. Vinca minor 'La Grave' ('Bowles' Variety')
4. Symphoricarpos × doorenbosii 'Mother of Pearl'

15. Hypericum 'Hidcote'
16. Geranium macrorrhizum
17. Bergenia cordifolia
18. Vinca minor 'Argenteovariegata'

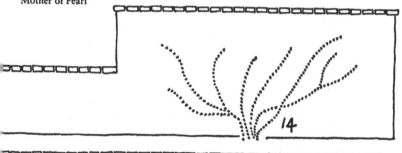

9. Ballota pseudodictamnus
10. Eriophyllum lanatum
11. Foeniculum vulgare 'Purpureum'

12. Euphorbia polychroma
13. Salvia officinalis 'Tricolor'
14. Clematis tangutica

bamboo canes. As they rapidly grew their lax shoots were tied horizontally across the wires. In three years we had a dense hedge over 6 ft/2 m high.

The border beneath this hedge was cooler, being east facing. I made a simple planting of what I had in quantity to cover approximately 40 yd/36 m by about 4 ft/1.2 m – several varieties of *Bergenia* and *Helleborus argutifolius* (*H. corsicus*). I planted both in alternating blocks. The effect would be better, I think, in a shorter length. I have planted a few shrubs of *Lonicera nitida* 'Baggesen's Gold' to try to break up the flat of the ground planting and reach up to the hedge behind, but they look intimidated by their neighbours and haven't made much impression yet.

However, all year this evergreen border looks dressed. I think I like it best in winter when the leaves of the bergenias, burnished by frost, turn all shades of carmine, rose and bronzy reds. Picked up by the car headlights they make a warm welcome on wet winter nights. The hellebores, starting to flower after Christmas, are a spectacular sight by March and continue so till the end of May.

These entrance beds can too easily be forgotten, so far from the house. Before the planting covered the soil weeds could in no time have overgrown the lot. But after the first day spent up there weeding I decided to try a pre-emergence weedkiller which is used when the ground is clean, and can be sprayed over established plants. (Not *all* plants, we are compiling a list from experience of those that will not take this treatment.) This proved a blessing, preventing that rash of seedling weeds, even though a few sturdy perennials ignored it. Now we only go up there about twice a year to tidy up: always after the euphorbias are over, about the end of June, to cut out the old flower shoots to make way for the new, and to prune anything that needs it; and in early spring we prune (not shear) the cotoneaster, and divide the bergenias.

A disadvantage to the herbicide is that one's plants cannot reproduce themselves either. Last year we forgot to spray and as the plants almost covered the soil it was not a disaster. In fact it was a blessing *not* to have used it, for the *Helleborus argutifolius* (*H. corsicus*) have germinated like mustard and cress.

These first two borders illustrate quite different problems in the garden, dry sun and dry shade. There are plenty of dry sunny borders which need little definition – they are found in the bare empty stretches left by the builders, they are the borders we may make at the foot of south-or west-facing walls where plants must sit helpless under the sun. (Lovely for sunbathing, but unendurable when we have had enough. We can get up and walk away.)

The north wall borders are usually cool, which helps but they can also be very dry, especially on poor soils, with low rainfall. East walls are similar, but have morning sunshine. Drier still is the soil under heavy canopied trees, and near the roots of many shrubs. I have in mind lofty horse chestnuts, ancient yews, lilac with its loofah-like root system, and of course its relative, the ubiquitous privet.

The East-facing Long Border

Now, we have arrived at the gate which lets us through the rabbit netting into the main entrance garden leading up to the (small) house. Before us is a broad stretch of grass susceptible to Nature's every whim. There are times when it looks quite impressive. There are times also when I try hard not to look at it. However, cars can always be parked on it, and children can rush up and down letting off steam.

To your right is one of my established borders, 100 yd/90 m long, about 7 yd/6 m wide. Situated on a bank, sloping west, it had been part of a field boundary hedge. I wanted to visually change the slope, and make a border facing east. I planted several more hollies, including a yellow-fruited kind, *Thuja plicata*, *Malus toringo* subsp. sargentii, *Sorbus hupehensis* and a yew. I also planted a wild pear from the mountains of Algeria, grown from a pip (dare I admit?) picked up in Kew Gardens. I'm not sure that it is worth the space, but it has made a handsome shape, a sturdy pillar, 30 ft/9 m tall now, close set with straight branches covered with millions of small bronze inedible pears. A support not to be ignored, I thought, and planted *Ampelopsis glandulosa* var. *brevipedunculata* (*A. brevipedunculata*) nearby, hoping one day in autumn I shall see a cascade of crimson foliage.

Together with the overhanging oaks I now have a partially shaded east-facing border, at the top of a bank, with marginally better soil than some I have, but still very dry. (See Pl. 15.)

Years ago I planted mostly old-fashioned roses in this border, making wooden tripods for the climbers (what a business they were to prune). For about six weeks in midsummer it was an entrancing sight, but for much of the year it was monotonous: a hundred yards of 'Rosa Mundi', even when properly striped, can pall. We kept my favourites, great bushes of *R.* 'Fantin Latour', 'Mme Pierre Oger', 'Reine Victoria', 'Commandant de Beaurepaire' to name a few, then painfully dug out the thickets of *Rosa gallica* 'Versicolor' ('Rosa Mundi'). In 1992 this whole area, about ¾ acre, was converted into the Gravel Garden which, once planted, is never irrigated. It is a horticultural experiment, to help gardeners faced with hosepipe bans.

With most of the roses gone, leaving plenty of space, I aimed to make a border that could be as interesting in winter as in summer. In the most exposed places I planted *Forsythia*, *Weigela* (including the bronze-leafed form), *Philadelphus* and *Hypericum*, to give continuity of blossom throughout the summer. *Hypericum* 'Hidcote' is a wonderful shrub with its perfect saucer-shaped flowers in bright yellow lighting up the border for months, from July to October. A great clump of a chartreuse-coloured *Kniphofia* placed behind one of these shrubs makes a handsome combination. *Hypericum androsaemum* 'Tutsan' I planted under the oaks. It has seeded itself about, very usefully filling in while waiting for more permanent things to take over. The house end of this long border was the most difficult site, completely overhung by an enormous pollarded oak. After struggling unsuccessfully for several years, I hit upon a solution. There is now a background of *Prunus laurocerasus*, the common laurel which sets off a fine golden variegated holly, *Ilex* × *altaclarensis* 'Golden King'. Around these Solomon's Seal

(*Polygonatum* × *hybridum*), *Helleborus argutifolius* (*H. corsicus*), *H. foetidus*, and the male fern, *Dryopteris filix-mas*, grow successfully through a carpet of *Vinca minor* 'La Grave' ('Bowles' Variety').

Dominating the planting are two first-class foliage plants. The first is *Iris foetidissima*, the form known as 'Citrina'. It is a plant I would hate to have to garden without. Much better than our native Gladwin iris, which is smaller in every part and has dingy blue flowers, this splendid evergreen plant makes huge arching clumps of shining dark green leaves. The buff-yellow flowers, smallish but beautifully pencilled in brown, are followed in late autumn by fat pods, bursting with vivid orange seeds.

From October to May two forms of wild *Arum* embellish this stretch. One is *Arum italicum* subsp. *italicum* 'Marmoratum' (*A.i.* 'Pictum' of gardens). Well known, it has long narrow arrow-shaped leaves, conspicuously veined and shaded in green and cream. The other, whose name I do not know, has much larger leaves with only the main veins painted cream. It is no less impressive, however. These lush great leaves dominate the planting. It is easy to miss the pale green spathes of both these arums – they are hidden among the leaves in May – but no one can overlook the foot-high stems of juicy red berries that appear, long after the leaves have faded, in September. Unfortunately for me the ducks don't overlook them either.

Snowdrops have established well among the *Vinca*, aconites still appear, but I don't think many seedlings will push through. However, I have seen areas elsewhere so full of aconites that nothing else will survive, except grass, for the rest of the year.

Vinca minor 'La Grave' ('Bowles' Variety') must take a bow. It is a gem of a plant if you have plenty of dry shade to cover, but it can be tiresome to establish, with grass and chickweed to be picked out from among its runners. Here my first peat mulch was invaluable, no more weeds worth mentioning, and the runners filled in twice as quickly. I have now planted all the different dwarf vincas I can find along the front edge of this border, which is the edge of the driveway. They flower most prolifically in the more open spaces, the band of blue at the gate end, beneath young shrubs of *Potentilla fruticosa*, and interplanted with *Narcissus* 'February Gold', making a lovely sight.

A Persian carpet effect under another oak has been made with *Hedera canariensis* 'Variegata', *Euphorbia amygdaloides robbiae*, *Ajuga reptans* 'Burgundy Glow', and *A.r.* 'Atropurpurea'. Ajugas (bugles) do not like very dry conditions. But I find that with plenty of compost and a mulch of crushed bark they manage very well in shade. (They can be a rampaging nuisance in good soil and the wrong place, e.g. among choice auriculas!) They suffer from two afflictions, mildew and aphis, often both at once. The leaves lose their bright colour, and become grey and rolled. Don't throw them out. A combined spray will kill the aphis, and keep the new growth protected against mildew till moister weather when they take off again, and double and treble themselves in the autumn months.

Colchicums meander through this border. I like their fresh juicy-looking leaves coming so early in spring; I don't have time to bother about them dying down among the mass of other foliage in midsummer, and feel I can never have too many when I see those elegant lilac goblets expanding over the pink and purple carpets of the bugles. Some years they are spoilt by wind and rain which batters them down, but I remember wonderful warm autumn days, when the garden had that special scent of warm wet growth combined with fruit and decay, and the display of colchicums seemed to go on for weeks.

I would not say that they thrive especially well in dry soil. They need rich feeding, with plenty of humus, to make their enormous polished chestnut bulbs. I probably grow them more successfully elsewhere. But it is interesting to see what they will do in dry shade, provided it is not too dense, and you feed them well.

There is a lot of yellow and green in this border. A combination that looks well all the year round has been grouped around three young plants of *Thuja occidentalis* 'Rheingold'. This is a slow-growing conifer, so it will be some years before the three need be reduced to one. The beautiful old gold foliage is set off by the prostrate *Lonicera pileata* planted around it, a modest shrub which is useful for covering indifferent soil. It is more striking in spring when its bright new leaves contrast prettily with the dark of the old leaves which have overwintered.

Hypericum androsaemum adds rosy bronze to this colour scheme with its young foliage, while bold clumps of *Iris foetidissima* stand out as contrast. *Symphoricarpos orbiculatus* 'Variegatus' makes a dainty bush alongside covered with small gold-edged leaves. You need to watch this bush and remove the healthy green-leafed shoots that sometimes appear. Unlike the white-berried form this shrub does not seem to sucker, neither does *Symphoricarpos* x *doorenbosii* 'Mother of Pearl', one of the loveliest berrying shrubs. It makes a small shrub of about 4 ft/1.2 m, and every tip shoot is laden with rose-tinted white berries, big as marbles. All members of this family will tolerate dry shade.

There were plenty of wild elderberry bushes on this bank when left to itself. Removing them made way for the most elegant of golden-leafed shrubs, *Sambucus racemosa* 'Plumosa Aurea'. This European red-fruited elder is not such a rampant grower, although in good soil it will make a big bush. When I remember, I prune mine to keep a sturdy framework. Fresh growth carries magnificent feather-cut foliage, brilliantly gold in spring, cool lemon for the rest of the season. This elder needs shade from the hottest sun to prevent scorching.

On another dry bank I have several more elders, forms of our common elder. *Sambucus nigra* 'Albovariegata' has green leaves with cream margins. *Sambucus nigra* 'Aurea' has rich gold leaves when young, so continues to gleam even though the mature foliage goes green. *Sambucus nigra* 'Guincho Purple' ('Purpurea') behaves the same way with chocolate/purple leaves. *Sambucus nigra* f. *laciniata* looks marvellous when allowed to grow into a huge bush, every leaf cut to dainty ribbons, all topped with heads of frothing cream flowers. But when space is limited all of these elders can be kept in order by hard pruning. (You won't have any flower then, of course.)

Sambucus nigra 'Pulverulenta' is a matter of taste. There are those who cannot rest till they possess it. Others shudder at such a monstrosity. It is an elder so full of virus (as are most variegated plants) that there is more white than green left in the leaves. By late summer the young shoots are almost totally white, very thin textured, hanging from white leaf stalks like lace handkerchiefs. It must be well grown, in shade, to protect and encourage this delicate whiteness. If exposed it scorches and hardens, and the bush looks hideous, covered with distorted, sick-looking leaves.

Philadelphus flourish on this second entrance bank (on poor chalk soils too); flowering with the old-fashioned roses they flood midsummer nights with heavy perfume. Cutting out all the old wood after flowering encourages new shoots and good foliage, and this is what you want to encourage on *Philadelphus coronarius* 'Aureus', the beautiful golden-leafed 'Mock Orange', which also needs partial shade.

A herbaceous plant lighting up this predominantly green border is *Lunaria annua* 'Variegata', which seeds true to type. The crinkled heart-shaped leaves are broadly margined with cream, and as the flower stems elongate the new leaves are sometimes entirely white, and very effective for lighting up dark backgrounds.

Further along a patch of *Bergenia cordifolia* 'Purpurea' is wreathed about with *Vinca major* 'Variegata' ('Elegant-issima'). This *Vinca* could be more appreciated, I think, for it is always in good leaf and cannot be called a menace. A clever idea that I still haven't copied is to plant a big tub of it, and put it near my north-facing glass front door. I have seen such a tub completely smothered in cream and green, lovingly cultivated to produce good foliage to go with the church flowers.

The West-facing Long Border

Turning away from this cool-looking border we cross the driveway and a wide stretch of grass to a more recent addition. Here is part of the east boundary of my land. Four years ago there was only a rabbit-proof fence between us and the icy north-easterly winds from Russia. (See Pl. 2.)

On 12 March 1973, I started to plant a shrubbery. A long strip of grass had been weed-killed the autumn before with Gramoxone. We collected our spades and forks, a barrow filled with compost, another with wet peat, and set off into the most fiendishly cold wind I can remember. We started to dig. Under the top inch or two of dark soil we found red gravel. The spades shot back at us. We had to loosen the stones with forks, then shovel them out. I felt a qualm or two. Was it madness to risk planting in such 'soil'? I was determined to try to make the picture I had in my mind of a wide curving border leading from the gateway to the buildings at the far end. We dug holes wide and deep enough to take one, and sometimes two barrow loads of compost and added soaked peat. In spite of the exercise I had to find a second coat so penetrating was that icy wind.

The trees and shrubs I intended to plant I had been growing on for several years, mostly from seeds and cuttings. It was time they found a home. Covering their roots against the drying wind with pieces of old hessian we spent several days planting, including *Sorbus hupehensis*, *Malus hupehensis* and *Crataegus persimilis* 'Prunifolia' (*C. prunifolia*). My poor gravel is not a very suitable soil for *Sorbus*. They grow wild, high up in mountain woods. However, varieties of *Sorbus aucuparia* will stand acidity, while *Sorbus aria* 'Lutescens', the loveliest whitebeam, which might have been more drought resistant, does well on chalk soils. My *Sorbus hupehensis*, which has white berries flushed pink, are now 8 ft/2.4 m, having grown about a foot a year. They have been heavily mulched, but also have had three dry summers since planting. Certainly they have looked distressed several times, but they stood the 1976 drought quite well, setting a good crop of berries, and it will be interesting to see how they carry on when they get their roots well down.

A form of *Chamaecyparis lawsoniana* similar to *C.l.* 'Triomf van Boskoop', and *Thuja plicata* were planted to make shapes in the winter. These two grow wild in the mountain forests in the coastal belt from British Columbia down into California. *Thuja plicata* needs a better soil I think than the *Chamaecyparis*, but neither really can be said to be ideal drought resisters. However, with heavy mulching they have surprised me. The *Chamaecyparis* are now well over 8 ft/2.4 m, and well furnished, the *Thuja* 5–6 ft/2 m. They were $2\frac{1}{2}$–3 ft/1 m when planted. They have done remarkably well considering there has been very low rainfall since planting.

All these trees were planted in twos and threes. Between their groups I planted *Cotoneaster lacteus* and the common laurel to make bulk. Apart from watering in none of these were watered afterwards and none have died.

During the winter of 1973–4 we started our middle ground. I think I was concerned now more with possibly losing plants from cold, because many drought resisting plants, such as cistus, will not stand very low temperatures for too long. However, in well-drained, poverty-stricken soil they grow tough and are much more resistant. So I took a chance.

I planted *Escallonia* 'Slieve Donard', with small dark green leaves and cascades of pink flowers from red buds. In front of the blue conifer I put *Griselinia littoralis*, whose apple-green leaves have a smooth soapy texture, pleasant to touch. *Genista aetnensis* and *Buddleia alternifolia* were planted to make large fountains of delicate texture against the background of evergreens.

Photinia (Stranvaesia) davidiana makes a large evergreen cotoneaster-like bush. I like to see its oldest leaves turning scarlet in autumn, a vivid contrast against the green leaves that remain. I would prefer to keep these shrubs rather than the laurels. They were slower to get started but made a surprising foot of growth in 1976.

Because I had them I also planted several groups of roses (for colour!!). They include hybrid musks like 'Penelope', 'Buff Beauty' and 'Cornelia', which would be much better on a good stiff clay. They grow well here, and their autumn flowers are usually good, but in high summer with the sun and wind playing havoc they can look pathetic, and will probably come out when I find I need the space for something that will do better. The same applies to *R*. 'Violet Carson', 'Dearest' and 'Iceberg', which look enchanting surrounded by tall candelabra verbascums, their prickly legs screened with lavenders and artemisias – but their blossoms faint in a bad drought.

By now the bed was about 100 yd/90 m long, and 15 ft/4.5 m wide, boldly planted in groups. It was essential that this bed did not make a lot of extra work! I managed to obtain baled straw, and spread it like a thick eiderdown over the whole area. The only weeding we had to do that year was pulling up the odd barley plants that germinated here and there, and digging out a few docks.

I was encouraged to go on. The bed was widened another 5 ft/1.5 m. This stretch was dug and manure incorporated as I intended to make a foreground of large cover plants. I know that many people stick to trees and shrubs as being most labour saving, and in some circumstances that is so. But, for me, such beds look a little as though one was all dressed up for a party but had forgotten to put on shoes and socks. That bare look to the soil worries me. Mulching alone looks better, mulching with plants better still. Yearly forking and stabbing about between trees and shrubs to keep the ground clean (carting off all the weeds and top soil naturally) is not helpful. Roots are either damaged or disturbed. The top and most nutritious layer of the soil is never properly used.

In writing this I feel a little concerned, knowing that many people will be saying, 'It's all very well, but where can I get all that stuff!'. I can only stress the point that my compost heaps are the backbone of my garden, that if one can make a choice between one luxury and another I would take a load of muck every time, and that once applied peat or bark does not have to be put down every year. The cost per week, set against the pure pleasure and peace of mind you will have gained, will not, I think, be considered exorbitant.

Two years ago I planted young home-made plants of *Cupressocyparis × leylandii* 18 in./460 mm high, outside my boundary, immediately behind this border, on the edge of my neighbour's headland. They were planted 4 ft/1.2 m apart, a half-bucketful of wet peat put into every hole, then mulched with straw. They are now as tall as I am, and will be topped at 7–8 ft/2–2.5 m to make a trimmed hedge for a background and wind break. By then some of the laurels and cotoneasters will have been removed, and put elsewhere.

Having taken two years to start off my trees, the most important being the columnar evergreens, and having planted a fast-growing hedge behind them for protection from the cold east winds which blow all spring and half the summer, above which my dominant trees will rise, how did I decide what to plant next?

The length of this border, 100 yd/90 m and now gently curving, may sound intimidating, but it is basically very simple; it is a collection of groups. Each group is planted to make, more or less, a triangular shape, the triangles interlocking, so making heights with gaps between to see through (see Plan D).

In deciding what to plant I first select each plant, tree or shrub for its shape and character, not for the colour of its flowers. (Colour schemes often seem to make themselves!) I try not to dot plants in empty spaces like pins in a pin cushion, but attempt to create a shape that lifts your eye upwards, rather than only paint a picture on the ground. Even among small plants this principle applies. I like to take one dominant plant, then choose others to enhance it. Sometimes, where two long asymmetrical triangles meet, there may be a long low stretch. A stately plant may rise out of this plateau, pin-pointed by isolation.

Now it would be useless to come looking round my garden with a set square. I don't think the principle hits you in the eye, and in plenty of places it is not yet being put fairly into practice. Besides, too rigid planning can be static. But having no principles produces chaos in the garden, as elsewhere.

One of my favourite stratagems for pulling an awkward group together, or adding drama to a sensible but unsensational piece of planting, is the use of a plant with big leaves. It is the change in scale which is a rest for the eye and mind; the more so if you have been walking along a border full of interesting things. Here is a full stop, an interval before the next act. A sense of scale helps. It is no use putting *Crambe cordifolia* into a bed 10 × 10 ft/3 × 3 m, but *Salvia argentea* or one of the bergenias might just make it.

Going back to the entrance gate we will take a look at some of the principal groups along this gently curved,

D. Interlocking triangles with a feature plant (*Kniphofia*) rising out of the plain

exposed border, which gets the sun all day. Several large mounds of *Brachyglottis* Dunedin Group (*Senecio* Dunedin hybrid) 'Sunshine', always good looking, immediately set the scene, intermingled with wide-spreading branches of *Juniperus pfitzeriana* (*J.* × *media*) 'Pfitzerana' (silent P!), a total contrast in form to the pencil-slim column of *Juniperus scopulorum* 'Skyrocket'. Three *Sorbus hupehensis* contribute height to this group, and autumn colour. *Lonicera pileata* sprawls out from the *Brachyglottis* (*Senecio*) to clothe the edge of the border, growing as happily in sun as shade.

An *Onopordum* has seeded itself right on the corner front edge among a group of bergenias; its huge prickly felted leaves make a feature more dramatic than any flower, and will continue to do so as it sends up its 6 ft/2 m flowering stem. Several more are coming up further in the bed, more suitably placed – but the odd giant in the front can be very exciting.

Achillea 'Moonshine', and *A.* 'Taygetea' take the front row, with little *Calamintha nepeta* subsp. *nepeta* (C. *nepetoides*) creating clouds of blue, a-buzzing with bees all late summer. Floribunda roses stand behind these, but they are coming out to make room for *Salvia officinalis* 'Purpurascens', highlighted with *Salvia pratensis* Haematodes Group to harmonize with the *Brachyglottis*.

Red sprawling stems smothered with large yellow funnel-shaped flowers belong to *Oenothera macrocarpa* (O. *missouriensis*), which lies beside large cushions of *Saponaria ocymoides*. Behind these are large airy clumps of *Euphorbia seguierana niciciana*. This is one of the loveliest of recent introductions, flowering for three months, dainty as *E. cyparissias*, but obligingly staying where it is put.

Anthemis cupaniana can do no harm here, flinging its ferny grey-green foliage over several yards, with chalk-white daisies floating above. (One plant only will cover 1 sq. yd!) To halt its progress are several lavender bushes which also cover plenty of space before reaching three fresh-looking shrubs of *Griselinia littoralis*. These may not be very hardy in some districts, but I value them for their evergreen leaves. This combination of greys and light yellow-green is enriched by the blue of a group of *Chamaecyparis* standing behind to cut the east winds. *Verbascum olympicum*, one of my 'full stop' plants, is here. It is a statuesque plant, which is necessary for the scale of this bed. *Onopordum*, Cardoon and *Crambe* are in the same class, adding an element of grandeur to what might be a featureless fuss. The white felted rosettes of *Verbascum*, a yard across when well grown, send up a towering 8 ft/2.4 m high candelabra carrying yellow flowers for weeks. By autumn the winds have whipped the long seed heads into curling shapes, lovely for dried arrangements.

Several cistus form the bulk of another group. *Cistus hybridus* (C. × *corbariensis*) has leathery crinkled foliage which becomes bronze-tinted in winter with reddish leaf stalks. This colouring picks up the rich carmine and bronze-red of the carpet of *Bergenia crassifolia* that edges the border in front of the cistus.

I must digress here to enlarge a little on bergenias. Not all gardeners are aware of the varying types of bergenia. (What a pity it takes so long to learn what thousands of plants, trees and shrubs are available and sound irresistible – a look in Hilliers' *Manual of Trees and Shrubs* shows pages of juniper, holly and sorbus alone, with most of us not knowing more than half a dozen!) For years I was aware of the commonly grown plant called Elephant's Ears by many, also *Saxifraga megasea*, and now *Bergenia × schmidtii*. This plant puts up with, and usually suffers, total neglect, making a small effort much too early in the year as a rule, when the fat pink buds sit in the middle of rather leaden green leaves. A sharp frost usually snubs the poor thing, and the opening flowers dissolve into brown pulp. Unless you like fairly large green leaves it won't turn your head for the rest of the year.

Bergenia cordifolia and *Bergenia crassifolia* are found wild in Siberia. (A large place! Where? Edges of woodland – on mountain slopes perhaps?) Here in East Anglia they flower best in full sun and will tolerate drought surprisingly well if they have been given enough humus. They make rosette-like clusters of large leathery green leaves, which blush most becomingly when touched by frost. I find that those planted on well-drained soil in full sun colour much better than those which are in partial shade and on better soil. These make up in size and vigour, however, for rather less winter colour. Both these plants flower later, missing the spring frosts. (See Pl. 7.)

Bergenia crassifolia is a splendid sight in April on the edge of my dry borders, a mass of slender stems about 15 in./ 380 mm high carrying a profusion of sugar-pink flowers. *Bergenia cordifolia* 'Purpurea' comes later in May, and inter-mittently into the autumn, sending up immense heavy heads of vivid magenta supported on rhubarb-like stalks. Their beautiful evergreen leaves provide much-needed contrast among smaller-leafed plants in summer while they give life to a winter border. For a short while in March they look tatty, their overwintered leaves blackening round the edges, but they are among the first plants quickly to refurnish themselves.

There are several more, both species and hybrids, but coming as they do from sub-alpine meadows and edges of woodland from mountains of central Asia and the Himalayas they will not put up with such poverty as my west border offers, so do not come into this story.

Now, where were we in this border? Among a group of cistus, edged with bergenias which I have tried to explain do not strictly belong to this planting of predominantly drought-loving plants.

Genista aetnensis has been planted to give height eventually to this group, but it has a long way to go to rival the splendid tree I have elsewhere which now falls like a fountain outside the window where I am sitting, filling the sky, 15 ft/4.5 m high and wide. Another smaller group within this framework is made with Bronze Fennel planted alongside silvery pink Oriental Poppies, which in turn are flanked by the imposing clumps of *Centaurea pulchra* 'Major' (Pl. 6), another of my architectural plants; not taking up so much room as Cardoons, it has firm jagged foliage, grey above, white beneath, out of which rise stiff stems topped with silver papery buds which explode into pink thistle-like flowers. *Centaurea pulcherrima* fits lower in the picture, being small and daintier.

Santolinas, dwarf *Cistus*, lavenders, shrubby salvias, Blue Rue and *Ballota* all make medium-sized modest mounds that fit so well into my schemes for this border, filling large dry areas with contented-looking foliage all the year round. Their prime virtue is their ability to survive without undue stress. Then, at various times of the year, they take the stage when more showy neighbours are having a rest.

Stachys byzantina (*olympica*) 'Silver Carpet', and *S. byzantina* have the same virtue at ground level, sprawling their velvet leaves around *Othonna* (*Othonnopsis*) *cheirifolia* which protects its paddle-shaped leaves with blue wax. Beside these *Sedum* 'Herbstfreude' ('Autumn Joy') takes all summer to reveal its two-sided character; being a low mound of pale succulent foliage for months it steps right out in front as it takes the stage in autumn, its great flat-topped heads of brick red blending with the bergenias already turning alongside. If not cut down these make a warm brown feature all winter.

Euphorbias are a continuing theme throughout this border. *Euphorbia cyparissias* runs like a pea-green sea around *Prunus triloba*, a bouquet of pale pink rosettes on long slender wands if it was pruned the year before. *Euphorbia coralloides*, a big seeder, is none the less valued as it never stops flowering from spring till autumn frosts, pushing up new flower shoots through the old if you haven't spared time to snip them out in June. It has seeded among *Bergenia* 'Silberlicht' (white flowers), pushing itself into a bush of the subtle *Phlomis chrysophylla*, whose sage-like foliage has a distinct yellow tint. I think the *Euphorbia* is a bit too bright here. I must think of something darker to show off the *Phlomis*. The *Photinia* (*Stransvaesia*) *davidiana* behind suits it better, while *Malus hupehensis* will lift a great head of branches above them all, loaded with large white cupped blossoms in May, dangling with little cherry-like apples in October. It is tempting to put a clematis over this tree, but I know the soil is too poor.

Crataegus persimilis 'Prunifolia' (*C. prunifolia*) will eventually make a brilliant back stop in this border. I have planted two, well separated, and although not yet very large the small blaze of scarlet and crimson during October has been a delicious anticipation of the conflagration to come.

Perhaps the most surprising plant in the whole border during the drought of '76 was *Penstemon* 'Sour Grapes'. This lovely plant, treasured now, being given to me by Vita Sackville-West (Lady Nicolson), showed not the slightest sign of distress. Its dark green foliage having no felty protection I can only imagine that it had sent its roots very deep beneath the mulch. Beside it, prickly-looking rosettes of aromatic leaves belong to *Morina longifolia*, whose $2\frac{1}{2}$ ft/ 760 mm stems carry jade pagoda-shaped cups, spilling out white and crimson tubular flowers, not easily passed by.

Another fascinating foliage plant behind this group that draws your attention like a magnet is an artemisia given to me by Valerie Finnis (Lady Scott). It is in the same silvery style as *Artemisia ludoviciana*, running about, sending up rather floppy stems.* With me they flop very effectively through low bushes of *Cotoneaster microphyllus*, whose small dark green leaves make the ideal background to set off the large terminal rosettes of startling whiteness, like silvered flowers. The flower stems are indifferent: it is the new shoots which make the show.

With bright green thujas behind them this group attracts me more than the pink and white of roses 'Dearest' and 'Iceberg' further along, although I have to admit that in autumn they too make a very pretty picture, surrounded by foaming grey and silvery white. *Artemisia stelleriana* sprawls a low ground cover, looking like chrysanthemum leaves cut out of white felt. Behind it, making a large soft filigree mound, is another Unknown, labelled *Artemisia* 'Powis Castle': we all await a proper name which no doubt will emerge in time.† Both these artemisias look dejected in winter, losing most of their foliage except the tips, but both break buds from every possible surface in spring and quickly cover themselves anew. *Buddleia alternifolia* has grown well; rising behind the roses it will make a soft cascade of whippy branches, wreathed in June with small, scented clusters of lilac flowers.

I think I have probably muddled you with enough groups. But I hope that one of them, or a combination of them, might help you to plan a large sunny entrance, or main border.

Easily grown feature plants which I hope to add are more eryngiums (*E. giganteum*, 'Miss Wilmot's Ghost', is already there where she can do little harm seeding about), kniphofias, echinops and the verbenas. These last I have only just discovered looking splendid in that 'Well-tempered Garden' of Mr Christopher Lloyd. Of course, I had read about them in his book (that particular one, *T.W.T.G.*) but the trouble is

* This has been identified at Wisley as *Artemisia ludoviciana* var. *latiloba*, but will be known in gardens as *A. ludoviciana* 'Valerie Finnis'.
† Subsequently identified as a possible hybrid between *Artemisia arborescens* and *A. absinthium* to be known in gardens as *Artemisia* 'Powis Castle'.

that you go on reading it, unable to put it down like a favourite novel, and can't possibly remember half the things that struck you so forcibly that you must get, see or do!

The verbenas come from South America, Patagonia and Brazil, so they need sunny places in a warm well-drained soil. *Verbena bonariensis* sends up tall (5 ft/1.5 m) wiry branching stems topped with tufts of mauvish scented flowers. They seed about, so accidentals would probably place themselves ideally among something I have not yet considered. There are dwarfer ones too, most of them fairly violent shades of purple and magenta. They could look jewel-like in the late summer and autumn, rising among *Ballota pseudodictamnus* and Jackman's Blue Rue.

Several groups of *Fritillaria imperialis* are well settled in front of the spring-pruned roses. The only other bulbs are a few scarlet tulips, hybrids between *T. kaufmanniana* and *T. greigii*. I have not introduced more, trying to simplify maintenance. Having said that, I am already imagining galtonias, possibly planted among the frits. to take their applause in late summer.

I cannot leave this border without mentioning grasses as decorative plants. A well-placed grass can make a vivid accent, adding flavour to an insipid mixture. *Festuca glauca* makes low ground cover with the blue of its needle-like leaves intensifying as the drought bites. *Holcus mollis* 'Albovariegatus' ('Variegatus'), although not caring quite so much for severe drought, I have planted to make a carpet beneath *Crambe cordifolia*. Two large groups of this *Crambe* were breathtaking in June '76, their great foaming masses of tiny white flowers standing 8 ft/2.4 m high, and as much across. They were cut down when flowering finished, and the tired leaves removed as well. With a welcome thunderstorm the *Holcus* revived and filled in all the spaces with a shining carpet, more white than green, which catches the eye even in midwinter.

I have a good flowering form of *Leymus* (*Elymus*) *arenarius* whose 6 ft/2 m tall, large headed wheat-like stems would look good in this border, with those rolling wave-like leaves of Sea Kale (*Crambe maritima*). But I don't think I

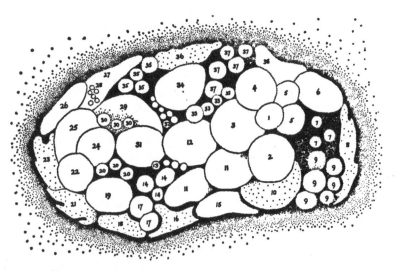

E. Plants for an open sunny island bed, approx. 20 × 12 ft/6 × 4 m

1. *Juniperus scopulorum (J. virginiana)* 'Skyrocket' or *Genista aetnensis*
2. *Cynara cardunculus*
3. *Cistus hybridus (C. × corbariensis)*
4. *Ballota pseudodictamnus*
5. *Santolina chamaecyparissus*
6. *Helianthemum* 'Rhodanthe Carneum' ('Wisley Pink')
7. *Euphorbia seguierana niciciana*
8. *Phlox douglasii* hybrids
9. *Bergenia crassifolia*
10. *Eriophyllum lanatum*
11. *Potentilla fruticosa*
12. *Euphorbia characias wulfenii*
13. *Allium schoenoprasum* 'Forescate'
14. *Euphorbia polychroma*
15. *Hebe* 'Youngii' ('Carl Teschner')
16. *Thymus × citriodorus* 'Aureus'
17. *Thymus × citriodorus* 'Silver Queen'
18. *Diascia barberae* 'Ruby Field'
19. *Rhodanthemum hosmariense (Chrysanthemum hosmariense)*
20. *Iris pallida* 'Variegata'
21. *Silene uniflora* 'Robin Whitebreast' (*S. maritima* 'Plena')
22. *Gypsophila* 'Rosenschleier' ('Rosy Veil')
23. *Thymus* 'Doone Valley'
24. *Foeniculum vulgare* 'Purpureum'
25. *Santolina rosmarinifolia* subsp. *rosmarinifolia (S. virens)*
26. *Penstemon davidsonii* var. *menziesii*
27. *Sedum* 'Ruby Glow'
28. *Allium s.* var. *sibiricum*
29. *Salvia officinalis* 'Icterina'
30. *Asphodeline lutea*
31. *Parahebe catarractae* (garden form)
32. *Nectaroscordum siculum (Allium siculum)* or *Galtonia candicans*
33. *Verbascum chaixii*
34. *Senecio cineraria* 'White Diamond'
35. *Sedum telephium* subsp. *maximum (S. maximum)*
36. *Arabis alpina* subsp. *caucasica (A. albida)* 'Flore Pleno'
37. *Sedum* 'Herbstfreude' ('Autumn Joy')
38. *Haplopappus glutinosus (H. coronopifolius)*

dare. Maybe it should end up in a bed by itself, its invasive habits kept under control by running the lawn mower round it.

Stipa gigantea is ideal in a dry border, placed to catch the sun. It makes a tidy clump of arching narrow-leafed foliage which sends up 6 ft/2 m stems topped with shimmering oat-like flowers fashioned from beaten bronze.

The front 5 ft/1.5 m wide strip of this border was covered with a 2 in./50 mm layer of pulverized bark in spring '75, predominantly around the dwarfer plants where straw would look unsightly. The rest of the border is mulched with straw, which is topped up if needed in the autumn.

These two borders, one facing east, the other facing west, each over 100 yd/90 m long, and around 20 ft/6 m wide are not touched more than three times a year (except for trimming the grass edge). The roses are pruned about March, when the greys also are tidied up if necessary. If *Brachyglottis* Dunedin Group 'Sunshine' (*Senecio* 'Sunshine') has been left for several years it can be pruned well back into the old wood when it will produce much bolder foliage and a neat new shape. The young trees are watched to make sure they keep a good leader.

By July a certain weariness can creep in, so a quick tidy up, dead heading roses, trimming *Ballota*, Blue Rue and santolinas, will encourage fresh new growth which will become mature enough to stand the winter.

A walk over in late autumn, as the odd bale of straw is being tucked into thin places, will be the time to remove the toppling verbascums and cardoons, and any odd weed that has dared to appear.

A Bed to Drive Round

Leaving the two long borders behind you, you arrive at a little circular drive which is in front of the house. In the middle of this is an oval bed, about 15 × 10 ft/4.5 × 3 m. I felt the need of a light screen in front of the house, so I looked for a deciduous tree to make an open fan-like shape, with very simple planting underneath. I chose *Betula pendula*

'Laciniata' ('Dalecarlica'), the graceful Swedish cut-leafed birch, and planted it to one end of this island bed. Originally, I planted two young saplings of *Betula pendula* as well – I suppose I imagined a little grove! But that was stupidly overcrowded, and it was not long before they had to come out. During the first few years the Swedish birch struggled with the poor gravel soil and the usual dry summers, but eventually it settled down, making a stately feature winter and summer. Around its bole on the north side is a great mound of *Cotoneaster microphyllus* which thrives well, making a dark evergreen background for *Rosa xanthina* f. *hugonis* (*R. hugonis*) which now fills the centre of the bed with *Berberis verruculosa*, making another bright evergreen mound at the far end. The floor of the bed is filled with *Helleborus argutifolius* (*H. corsicus*) and *Bergenia cordifolia*

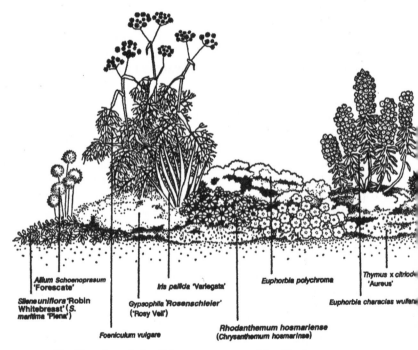

F.   Elevation of plan E for an open sunny island bed

'Purpurea' while the variegated Honesty (*Lunaria annua* 'Variegata') seeds into any empty spaces they may allow. *Alchemilla mollis* came in with the compost and took a long time to establish in this dry open bed, but now over the years has made deep rooted woody stocks which find moisture

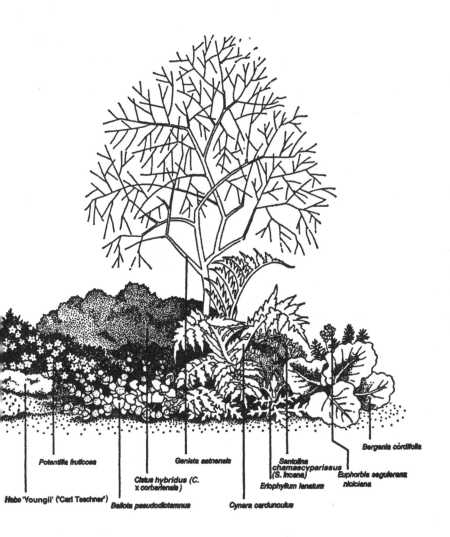

Potentilla fruticosa

Genista aetnensis

Santolina chamaecyparissus (S. incana)

Bergenia cordifolia

Euphorbia seguierana nlciciana

Cistus hybridus (C. × corbariensis)

Eriophyllum lanatum

Hebe 'Youngii' ('Carl Teschner')

Ballota pseudodictamnus

Cynara cardunculus

from somewhere, so prolonging the display of lime green that is the feature of this bed.*

In case anyone is not familiar with *Helleborus argutifolius* (*H. corsicus*) (Pl. 18) I should say that it is, even for a small garden, worth every inch it occupies. It takes the space and importance of a small shrub. In well-prepared soil it sends up every year many strong stems furnished with beautiful jade-green claw-like leaves. All summer these make a firm mound 3 ft/1 m high and as much across. As winter comes the stems fall apart, radiating from the centre point, each head heavy with multiple flower buds. In sheltered places they start to open at Christmas, delicate apple-green cups, with paler stamens and olive-green nectaries. As they continue to open more and more the leaning stem curves upward to lift them above the soil. By April they are a fantastic sight, huge bouquets of luminous green no less startling than the ice pinks and magentas of the late flowering bergenias around them. They will grow almost anywhere, but they are greedy feeders and love a mulch of rotted muck. Cutting icy winds can damage the flowering stem in March. As their glory fades by June the next season's shoots are already standing proud from the centre. I have seen tidy-minded gardeners tie these radiating stems to bamboo canes, being offended that they sprawl about, but ruining to my mind the character of the plant. I do admit, though, that they could take up an excess of room in the very tiny garden.

In some gardens, possibly on cold clay, these lovely plants never seem to thrive, sending up no more than two or three stems, and those afflicted with ugly black blotching, caused by fungus disease. This can be rampant in warm damp weather on all hellebores, eventually rotting leaves, stems and flowers. I grow my *Helleborus argutifolius* (*H. corsicus*) well away from the others, as it will stand drier conditions with more sun and so tends not to become infected. Spraying with Captan or Bordeaux mixture regularly to keep young growth protected until tough and resistant does help to check

* It is interesting, after thirty-odd years, that the underplanting has vanished beneath the birch. It stands isolated and elegant in a simple expanse of gravel driveway.

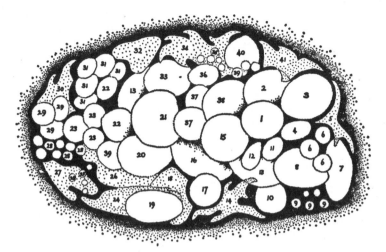

G. Plants for a dry shady island bed, approx. 20 × 12 ft/6 × 4 m
This design is for an area which is in shade, or partial shade, for most of
the day. Shade may be cast by tall buildings or from broadleafed trees further
away.

1. *Taxus baccata* 'Fastigiata'
2. *Euphorbia amygdaloides robbiae*
3. *Acanthus mollis* or *A. spinosus*
4. *Iris foetidissima* 'Variegata'
5. *Hedera helix* 'Manda's Crested'
6. *Tellima grandiflora* Rubra Group (*T. g.* 'Purpurea')
7. *Alchemilla mollis*
8. *Pulmonaria saccharata*
9. *Cyclamen hederifolium* (*C. neapolitanum*)
10. *Epimedium* × *versicolor* 'Sulphureum'
11. *Thalictrum aquilegifolium*
12. *Polystichum setiferum* Acutilobum Group
13. *Milium effusum* 'Aureum'
14. *Vinca minor* 'Aureovariegata'
15. *Lonicera nitida* 'Baggesen's Gold'
16. *Brunnera macrophylla*
17. *Hosta lancifolia*
18. *Lamium maculatum* 'Roseum'
19. *Pulmonaria rubra*
20. *Hosta sieboldiana*
21. *Helleborus argutifolius* (*H. corsicus*)
22. *Iris foetidissima*
23. *Liriope muscari*
24. *Ajuga reptans* 'Burgundy Glow'
25. *Euphorbia cyparissias*
26. *Tiarella cordifolia*
27. *Ajuga reptans* 'Atropurpurea'
28. *Saxifraga* × *urbium* 'Aureopunctata'
29. *Pulmonaria angustifolia* 'Munstead Blue'
30. *Hedera helix* 'Lutzii'
31. *Bergenia cordifolia* 'Purpurea'
32. *Veronica prostrata* 'Trehane'
33. *Iris innominata* hybrids
34. *Vinca minor* 'La Grave' ('Bowles' Variety')
35. *Arum italicum* subsp. *italicum* 'Marmoratum' (*A. i.* 'Pictum' of gardens)
36. *Stipa arundinacea*
37. *Valeriana phu* 'Aurea'
38. *Polygonatum* × *hybridum*
39. *Digitalis lutea*
40. *Geranium endressii*
41. *Viola riviniana* Purpurea Group

this. I confess that we have not made that effort yet. But we do cut off all the leaves of *Helleborus orientalis* and *H. niger* during the winter tidy-up to leave the least possible source of infection when the flowers and young leaves appear in spring. We do spray against aphis for whom the young foliage is caviare – you can suddenly find the undersides of the young leaves smothered in early summer.

A Triangular Island Bed

The left-hand side of this little circular drive is bounded by a roughly triangular bed which leads to my buildings and greenhouse beyond. This bed is about 25 yd/22 m long by 10 yd/9 m at the base of the triangle, and its object again is to be both welcoming and a screen for the work-area beyond it. (Pl. 9).

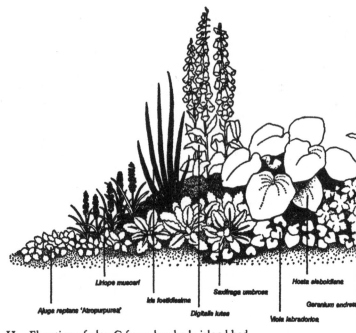

Liriope muscari

Iris foetidissima

Saxifraga umbrosa

Hosta sieboldiana

Ajuga reptans 'Atropurpurea'

Digitalis lutea

Geranium endressi

Viola labradorica

H.   Elevation of plan G for a dry shady island bed

It was planted originally with whatever was available at the time, since when, by natural selection, some things have done well, others have failed miserably. I decided to start again. Fortunately it was the trees and shrubs grouped at the base end which were thriving. *Thuja plicata* and *Chamae-cyparis lawsoniana* 'Triomf van Boskoop', with *Berberis amurensis*, *Rosa* 'Nevada' and *Pyracantha coccinea* 'Lalandei'. *Berberis amurensis* is not one of the showiest

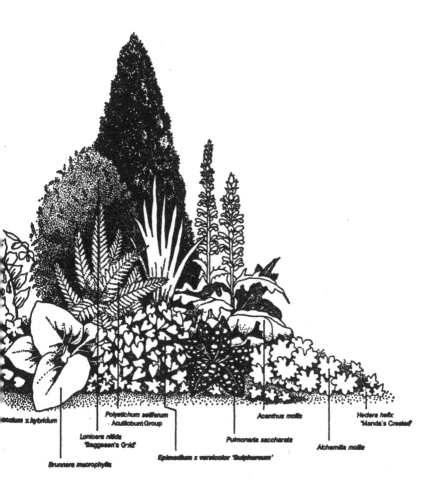

enatum x hybridum

Polystichum setiferum
Aculeolum Group

Acanthus mollis

Hedera helix
'Manda's Crested'

Lonicera nitida
'Baggesen's Gold'

Pulmonaria saccharata

Alchemilla mollis

Epimedium x versicolor 'Sulphureum'

Brunnera macrophylla

barberries, but the two I grew from seed have made a good screen and I hesitate to replace them. Among many which would be preferable are *Berberis vulgaris* 'Atropurpurea', *B. gagnepainii*, and *B. × stenophylla*, all flourishing in similar conditions in other borders. *Berberis darwinii*, and the even more choice *B. × lologensis* are not too happy in very light dry soil, but are doing well where the soil is better.

To add autumn colour to this group I have planted a large *Kniphofia* we call 'Prince Igor'. It is most remarkable in September and October when its great orange-red torches tower over 6 ft/2m high among the thujas.

Here was my vertical, now I had to taper the planting towards the apex.

But before I could attend to that the soil had to be dealt with. One of the reasons too many plants had died out in this bed was because it had been a dumping area on the farm for stones and gravel. It was useless to pile any more good compost on top of that, because it washed through like a colander. So we removed as much as we could and replaced it with a mixture of gravelly soil (all we had!) and our year's supply of compost. It looked a lot more promising, although it would never be good soil.

To repeat the off-centre verticals I planted *Ferula communis*. It took several years, slowly working down its strong tap root, so that this year it was able to send up several flower stems 12 ft/4 m high. These stems, like linen props, emerge from a nest of shining lacy leaves (not scented like the cooking fennel). When young they have a soft bloomy purple colour, and the flower head droops on its way up among the tops of the thujas. As it strengthens, the flowering branches open out straight and wand-like, bearing yellow umbels of flowers starred against the hot summer sky.

Beneath it a Stag's Horn Sumach, *Rhus typhina* is taking the centre of the bed. Probably *Cotinus coggygria* (*Rhus cotinus*) or *Cercis siliquastrum* (the Judas tree) would have been more suitable here, both being members of the foothill maquis, especially in the eastern Mediterranean. However, the *Rhus typhina* slowly makes headway and provides glorious autumn colour. Beneath its open stems, filling the central floor, are mounds of *Santolina chamaecyparissus*, Jackman's Blue Rue, and *Ballota pseudodictamnus*, all ever faithful. *Iris foetidissima* has seeded under *Rosa* 'Nevada', sharp contrast in colour and form with these soft rounded shapes.

Cytisus multiflorus (*C. albus*) also helps make a transition from the columnar evergreens to a group of *Potentilla fruticosa*, and then to the low ground coverers along the edge. A single Cardoon, of great girth, is placed a third of the way down on the edge of the bed, connected visually with the off-central block of vertical planting, making magnificent contrast.

The rest of the bed, apart from two groups of bergenias, are all small-leafed ground covering plants, with occasional soloists like *Nectaroscordum siculum* (*Allium siculum*), *A. cristophii*, and slender verbascums like *V. chaixii* rising from among them. They include *Hebe* 'Youngii' ('Carl Teschner'), helianthemums, *Silene uniflora* 'Robin Whitebreast' (*S. maritima* 'Plena'), *Arabis caucasica* 'Rosabella' (*A. albida rosabella*) and *Penstemon davidsonii* var. *menziesii* (*P. menziesii*). All make sheets of colour at appropriate times, and remain in good foliage for the rest of the year.

A young *Yucca gloriosa* rises from a bed of *Bergenia crassifolia* at the tip end of this bed, echoing the large group that has been planted alone in an island bed just across the driveway in the entrance lawn.

Parahebe catarractae and *Hebe* 'Glaucophylla Variegata' (*H. glaucophylla*) looked very miserable during summer '76, but most recovered in the autumn. They could be seriously damaged by an icy blast out of the north-east, but so far they have not suffered, and cover a wide area.

Again, good growth and weed control have been maintained by a topping of crushed bark. The cover plants have almost entirely filled the bed now after three years planting, and two severe summer droughts.

6

House and Garden Walls

I am not going to write about dry wall gardening, by which I mean the kind of thing you do in those districts that have natural stone walls to keep stock in, instead of hedges or fences, because I have no experience of doing it myself. I am thinking of the beds under the walls round the house which you may feel driven to pave over, to set a chair there and think of other things. With a little planning you might still be free to sit and dream a bit, lulled by evocative scents, occasionally startled perhaps by the sharp pops of bursting seed pods, but overall complacent in the knowledge that you are cradled in a flowery bower and the beds are fairly well looking after themselves.

Much depends on the style of the house, and more on the character of the owner. There is no best way to plant a garden, only what is best for you. Extremes of style, in separate gardens, can be ideal for each – thank goodness for that, else it would be a great bore to go looking at other people's gardens. Of course we all notice first 'our' plants in someone else's garden. (My ... is doing so much better, or worse – how sickening – than that!) More important is to recognize what you do not know. The art is to select, whether from reading or looking, ideas which can be fitted into your own scheme of things like a long-sought piece of a jigsaw puzzle. Suddenly to drop half a dozen species into a well-planned herbaceous border of improved delphiniums, scabious and border phlox may add absolutely nothing. That is not to say that, if carefully selected, some species would not contribute to the beauty of a group of any one of these plants in the right setting.

In principle, however, I personally think that the more perfected cultivars are best kept apart from the species. In no way could I naturalize the improved Dutch hyacinth or gladiolus. Both of these are meant for cutting and should be treated accordingly.

Another digression! What I am driving at is that if you find it easier to fill your house beds with wallflowers and tulips followed by geraniums and lobelia, and you enjoy it, then stick to it. I shall enjoy looking at it. What have you done with the shady sides of the house, I wonder?

Warm Sunny Walls

Walls, especially in areas of low rainfall, tend to have dry borders beneath them, be they sunny or dark. But once you have developed a taste for plants that flourish on or under walls, you quickly run out of space. I find it difficult sometimes not to envy owners of tall houses, and old, walled kitchen gardens! However, much can be done with less. I have both sunny and shady dry borders beneath my house, greenhouse, packhouse and garden walls, and all are crowded with occupants.

Campsis radicans, the Trumpet Vine, is probably the most exotic-looking climber I have. It almost covers the south-facing wall of the house. The last two or three hot summers it has been loaded with huge orange-scarlet trumpets, looking as I have seen it draped nonchalantly over old stone walls in Provence. In cool summers here there is not such an abundance of flower.

Beneath it is a vigorous shrub of *Buddleia crispa*, the baking conditions of the wall in no way upsetting this lovely plant, but causing it to intensify its protective coating. Every leaf becomes veritably white with felt, and its loveliest moment I think is just before the pale lilac flowers open, when it is hung with pendulous clusters of furry white buds.

Sophora tetraptera, the New Zealand national emblem, is

growing beside the buddleia. Grown from seed it took sixteen years to flower! The pretty leaves, made up of many narrow leaflets, contained my impatience, but no photograph I have yet seen conveys the strange beauty of this unusual tree in flower. In April the buds begin to swell, larger and larger till the petals drop down and there they hang, exquisite yellow shuttlecocks. *Not* like laburnum, not like anything else I know!

Something like laburnum is *Piptanthus nepalensis* (*P. laburnifolius*), and in fact it is called Evergreen Laburnum. It is a Himalayan shrub which can be trained against a wall. I have put mine on a south wall, but I'm told it does very well on a north wall. The yellow pea flowers in May are followed by clusters of long pods which can be decorative or unsightly – it depends how you see such things. Incidentally, the *Sophora* has the most curious seed pods, like strings of lumpy wooden beads.

Some people are able to grow the large-flowered clematis on their house walls, but I get nowhere with them on my sunny walls, they become frizzled. *Clematis tangutica*, however, is almost too rampant on the west wall, looking very pretty coming through the bedroom windows. *Adlumia fungosa*, a kind of climbing fumitory, rushes up through it; wisps of pink and pewter intertangled with the lemon bells and silvery feather heads of the clematis look very romantic throughout late summer and autumn, but I think they will be found a more rustic setting over a large shrub or stump perhaps – and let the *Abutilon* x *suntense* have a chance to furnish the wall with its downy vine-shaped leaves. This shrub needs the protection of a wall, but when well grown it is very beautiful in May and June, smothered with large saucer-shaped flowers of soft blue.

Abutilon megapotamicum is likewise tender. It has survived here many years, and flowers, but is a poor effort compared to a barn wall I have seen in Kent where it must be 12 ft/4 m high and enviable, dangling its scarlet and yellow blossoms from every twig high overhead. I have two young plants of a hybrid of it called *Abutilon* x 'Kentish Belle'. Here the corolla is almost apricot, and the calyx soft brick red – I only wish I had the barn wall to go with them.

Clematis cirrhosa var. *balearica* has survived baking summers very well on a south wall, with *Calceolaria integrifolia* shading its roots. The clematis has shining ferny foliage which is bronze tinted in winter. Long sprays garlanded with buds cascade from the wall in January, slowly opening small creamy-green flowers, which are faintly spotted inside. Just below a large sprawling bush of *Daphne odora* 'Aureomarginata' is already opening its carmine buds, filling that corner with heady perfume on the first warm day.

Another partnership that gave me pleasure was in this same spot, at the height of the drought, when *Eccremocarpus scaber* twined itself throughout the clematis, draping the *Calceolaria* and terrace paving below, its orange-red tubular flowers accenting the bright yellow pouches that covered the *Calceolaria*. Both these plants and the *Abutilon* come from Chile.

There are far more jasmines we might grow if only we had walls to shelter them. The variegated form of the common white, *Jasminum officinale* 'Aureovariegatum' is worth building something to support it. Mine is making do with a tool shed, but I have seen it tumbling from the lofty height of a Victorian mansion which it almost redeemed. Even more memorable was the sight of it weaving in and out of the fat round pillars of a balustrade of an earlier period, leading down a flight of steps.

Lathyrus latifolius, the perennial or everlasting pea, has rose-purple flowers which would look very good together with some silvery grey plant like *Artemisia* or *Ballota* that would enjoy a good bake. Less common perhaps is the lovely white form, sometimes called *Lathyrus latifolius* 'White Pearl' which would complement a planting of blue and white *Agapanthus campanulatus*, which survive happily out of doors on warm borders.

The majority of honeysuckles prefer the cool walls of the house or the protection of shrubs to scramble through. In this situation they are a little less susceptible to aphis attacks, which can and do ruin these plants. *Lonicera* × *brownii* 'Fuchsoides' is a refined-looking creature, worthy of a west-facing wall where its sealing-wax red flowers will reward you for a little extra trouble.

Wisteria needs no recommendation. They like sunny walls. But for something that could last several generations I would excavate a large hole and fill it with as rich a mixed diet as I could manage, to give it a good start – if I had the room to start one.

Nothing like so well known are the solanums. The trouble is they are not all that hardy, but for sheltered gardens, especially in the south and west, they are spectacular. *Solanum crispum* is the hardiest, making a scrambling job of getting up some kind of support, for they don't make tendrils or anything useful to help themselves. Solanums are related to the potato. The sight of a potato field in July covered with bands of lilac can cause you to stop your car and get out to have a closer look. Having something similar draping a dull wall with large purple clusters up to 6 in./ 150 mm across from June to September can be quite impressive. There is a white one, *Solanum jasminoides* 'Album', more tender, and tantalizingly desirable. I saw it wreathing a brick pergola at Wisley in October, and determined to have another try.

So far I have not mentioned a wall climber that will make bold contrast and prevent some of these well-loved plants from looking no better than bindweed at times during the summer. Once out of flower, not all climbers have very distinguished leaves – but the great vines do, and they flourish on warm walls. I have planted *Vitis coignetiae*, a Chinese vine, against the west-facing wall where it now runs for about 30 ft/9 m in one direction, and sprawls up over a doorway through the wall onto the toolshed roof. In winter I enjoy the sinuous shapes of its ropey-looking framework fastened against the wall, and emphasize this by hard pruning the laterals back to two or three buds in December. In spring the swelling buds are covered with gold fur, as are the backs of the unfolding leaves. These suddenly blow open till some are the size of dinner plates. Heart shaped, the mature leaves have the texture of embossed leather, light and dark green in colour, retaining the buff-coloured backs. This vine also looks magnificent if you can scramble it over a large tree, something like a *Cupressocyparis × leylandii* which you can spare, from the top of which it will tumble an unrivalled display of autumn glory, crimson, orange and scarlet.

Over the house a less enveloping vine seemed more appropriate. *Vitis vinifera* 'Purpurea' has been planted on the south-west corner. It took several years, and a well-prepared hole, to make a sufficiently stout stock to send out those 10 ft/3 m long shoots which now thrust themselves up under the eaves of the house. Purple scalloped leaves fill the area from ground to roof, making a jungle background for *Commelina tuberosa* Coelestis Group (*C. coelestis*), little gentian-blue jewels dropping out of green hoods, with flamboyant pink nerines justly proud of themselves out in front. In October I love to pick a few bunches of the mouth-drying sour grapes, beautiful to look at, black and bloomy – and arrange them with colchicums, vine leaves (now rich tones of claret wine, especially with the low sunlight behind them), a few nerine heads, and clusters of lime-green hops for contrast.

We have covered a lot of wall space, though not nearly exhausted the possibilities for clothing sunny walls. But we have not done much to cover dusty dry borders beneath. If you have room there is an even larger list of shrubs that thrive with wall protection, provided you make some effort to give them a good start.

Ceanothus, more buddleias, *Callistemon*, the Bottle Brush, the evergreen *Carpenteria* with flowers like single white roses, *Cytisus battandieri*, whose trusses of flowers are pineapple scented and shaped, *Bupleurum fruticosum* with leathery strap-shaped leaves and green umbelliferous flowers, *Cestrum parqui* with clusters of greenish-yellow tubular flowers all along the same season's growth which can be cut down like a fuchsia, *Magnolia grandiflora* if you have a mansion, a small-leafed myrtle if you have not.

To dip into a book like W. J. Bean's *Wall Shrubs and Hardy Climbers* makes you too well aware of what may be far beyond you. You will be tempted all the same.

Tucked into my modest (scorched) borders, filling in the spaces, are the following:

Two coronillas, one plain, one variegated, and both evergreen. The plain one, *Coronilla valentina* subsp. *glauca* (*C. glauca*), is in fact most attractive, making a neat round bush covered with small pinnate bluish leaves, especially in summer. Every axil holds a cluster of buds; they show colour in January – by April you can hardly see a leaf, there is such

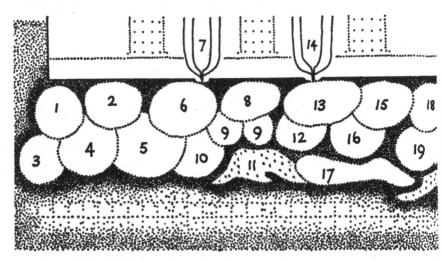

I. Plants for a south-facing Georgian house

Paved walk. Border approx. 20 × 2 yd/18 × 2 m

1. *Cistus hybridus* (*C. × corbariensis*)
2. *Cistus × purpureus*
3. *Crinum × powellii*
4. *Ballota pseudodictamnus*
5. *Helianthemum* hybrid
6. *Senecio cineraria* 'White Diamond'
7. *Senecio viravira* (*S. leucostachys*)
8. *Salvia officinalis* 'Purpurascens'
9. *Euphorbia polychroma*
10. *Euphorbia myrsinites*
11. *Thymus × citriodorus* 'Aureus'
12. *Rhodanthemum hosmariense* (*Chrysanthemum hosmariense*)
13. *Salvia officinalis* 'Icterina'
14. *Clematis armandii*
15. *Euphorbia characias* subsp. *wulfenii*
16. *Helichrysum italicum* (*H. angustifolium*)
17. *Helianthemum* 'Rhodanthe Carneum' ('Wisley Pink')
18. *Strobilanthes atropurpureus*

a mass of bright yellow pea flowers. I wish that *Coronilla valentina* subsp. *glauca* 'Variegata' wouldn't bother, it is too much with all that cream and green to add bright gold as well. I'm tempted to cut the flowers off, which would probably be a good thing and encourage more quickly the new growth which is quite lovely (if you like variegated plants – I know those who don't). Some visitors confuse it with the variegated rue, a plant I have not mentioned for the dry

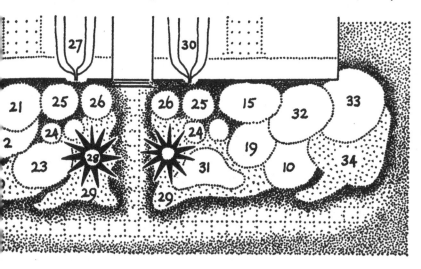

19. *Agapanthus* Headbourne hybrid
20. *Thymus* 'Doone Valley'
21. *Calceolaria integrifolia*
22. *Othonna* (*Othonopsis*) *cheirifolia*
23. *Helianthemum* 'Wisley Primrose'
24. *Euphorbia seguierana niciciana*
25. *Nerine bowdenii*
26. *Iris unguicularis* 'Walter Butt'
27. *Abutilon megapotamicum*
28. *Yucca filamentosa concava*
29. *Stachys byzantina* (*S. olympica*) 'Silver Carpet'
30. *Clematis cirrhosa* var. *balearica*
31. *Helianthemum* hybrid
32. *Artemisia arborescens*
33. *Kniphofia northiae*
34. *Eriophyllum lanatum*

garden. That again can look very indifferent. I had a row of stock plants looking very dejected and leggy, suffering from neglect. Feeling sure they were about to die I took every young shoot off them to make cuttings and left them looking like Brussels sprout stumps. Weeks later I passed by, amazed to see them completely refurnished with the prettiest shoots, ivory-white edged with green. As they mature they become greener, until by the autumn it is difficult to tell them from a non-variegated rue. But obviously they benefit from a bit of hard pruning.

Aster petiolaris scrambles around *Coronilla valentina* subsp. *glauca* into *Buddleia colvilei* which astonished me the first time it flowered.

Our old friends *Ballota*, Blue Rue and santolinas would all do well as cover shrubs but I prefer to use the space for more delicate plants.

Rhodanthemum hosmariense (*Chrysanthemum hosmariense*) starts opening its firm white daisies over neat, cut-leafed grey mounds in late autumn, continuing to do so in mild spells throughout the winter and making a grand finale in the spring.

I have only just obtained *Arctanthemum arcticum* (*Chrysanthemum arcticum*), which makes a bigger plant with dark green leaves to show off its beautiful white flowers in November. I must make a space against my warm west wall to encourage it.

Salvia officinalis 'Tricolor' is not the easiest of shrubby salvias so I keep a plant against a south wall, but an *Abeliophyllum distichum* which looks like a tiny white-flowered forsythia opening pale coral buds on thin purple wands is coming along beside it and will probably swamp it. Will I think the *Abeliophyllum* worth keeping? It is exquisite, but flowers in February so is very liable to be browned by frost. Perhaps I won't keep it, especially if the threatened Ice Age is nearer than we think.

Gypsophila 'Rosenschleier' (*G.* 'Rosy Veil') and *Euphorbia seguierana niciciana* both grace this arid bed in mid-summer with ease and charm. The *Gypsophila* is easy, quickly making a mound a foot high and more across; it is a smother of tiny double pink flowers. It is the kind of plant I pass by in a catalogue, needing to see it to appreciate its worth. Do try to pause long enough to cut it down in July. It will flower determinedly again in October, all through the dead remains of June if you leave it. I must try too.

The *Euphorbia seguierana niciciana* is still the loveliest thing in August, with mats of *Diascia* beside it over which float rose-pink flowers reminiscent of *Nemesia*.

The variegated *Sisyrinchium striatum* 'Aunt May' has survived for several years, a dramatic feature all the year round. But I make sure that some of it is tucked out of harm's way in case we have a really savage frost.

Amaryllis belladonna has just begun to flower, having sat gathering strength for several years, while little rush-like clumps of leaves all year promise the cool white crocus blossoms on long stems of *Zephyranthes candida*. I have had *Zephyranthes rosea* out of doors for two years, but having said so I shall probably be punished for boasting. Perhaps I had better go out and put a bucket of dry peat over it, or, better still, some gravel.

Two companions on another small section of south-facing wall are *Teucrium fruticans*, all silvered leaves and stems with *Tropaeolum tricolorum* floating through it like little scarlet and black fish. Nearby these two, a *Glaucium* species seeds much more handsome rosettes into the gravel path than when I have transplanted it.

Tulipa saxatilis ramps through the stones around a huge bush of *Euphorbia characias* var. *sibthorpii* (an even bigger form of *E. characias* subsp. *wulfenii*). Its massed lavender and gold flowers opening starry flat in April sunshine are compensation for the fact that not much else will survive there after May.

Cistus × *skanbergii* has at last made a bush to cover a lot of scorched groundsel; even sempervivums and sedums have abandoned this site under the *Campsis* and *Buddleia crispa*.

Agapanthus does well here (Pl. 11), *Euphorbia seguierana niciciana*, and a big *Yucca gloriosa* does all I want it to, including flowering most years. So I have decided to remove any small bulbs or treasures surviving to a raised wall bed, specially prepared, and to keep only those larger plants that can endure an oven-like environment. These seem to include all the forms of *Iris unguicularis*: 'Mary Barnard', rich purple, makes good contrast with 'Walter Butt', palest lilac, both smelling to me like primroses. I also have a white form – is there only one? Or is there another with the same beautiful rounded petals as 'Walter Butt'?

Salvia microphylla var. *microphylla* (*S. m. neurepia*) has survived for many years. It has been cut to the ground by frost, but always sprouted larger than ever from the stock. I usually prune it hard back if the frost hasn't done so; by late summer it has made a luscious-looking green bush, tipped with scarlet flowers till winter nips the buds.

Two more unreliables that I would hate to lose, although they take a lot of room, are *Geranium palmatum* (*G. anemonifolium*), and *Osteospermum* (*Dimorphotheca*) hybrids. Again the best geranium plants are sitting in the gravel path, making enormous mounds of lacy green leaves. Provided it hasn't been killed, there it sits in January, looking as though it ought to be an exotic vegetable. Perhaps you should cut off the thick green stalks topped with enormous multi-divided leaves and chop up for a salad the interesting-looking knob at ground level, made up of layers and layers of transparent sheaths, pale green faintly tinged pink. Perhaps not. By May 3 ft/1 m high branching flower stems will have emerged from these sheathed knobs, crowded with bright carmine-pink blooms for weeks. It is a pity there isn't room enough for more of it. But it will seed itself into the *Diascia* or *Dianthus* 'Waithman's Beauty', and like the cuckoo settles itself in. Spreading its great feathery leaves it destroys everything under it.

More lovable is a hybrid *Dimorphotheca*, now called *Osteospermum*. There are several of these South African daisy-like flowers. A white one with metallic blue backs with a navy-blue centre; a deep pink one called *O. jucundum* (*O. barberae*) which is hardy out in the open here, and the one I like best which is, of course, not very hardy, a hybrid which has large soft pink flowers and blue centres, so is called *O.*

72

'Blue Eye'. In the west country it makes huge mounds of apple-green leaves covered with flowers. It can be the most outstanding thing in the garden. Here we sometimes preserve it close against a south wall, but its succulent scented foliage has only to have a whiff of icy east wind to blacken and die.

Those popping seed pods? They come from the *Alstroemeria ligtu* hybrids under the south wall of the greenhouse and the big euphorbias.

A dominating feature on the greenhouse border is *Kniphofia northiae*, making an ascending mound of huge rosettes. This curious poker has 6 in./150 mm wide ribbon-like leaves which cascade out from the centre, curving away for a yard and more to end in a swirl of withered ends on the gravel. This combination of fresh succulence showing signs of mortality upsets tidy gardeners. I confess I hadn't noticed it as a detriment, but I do pull away the oldest leaves in spring so that the new have room for a fresh display.

Crinums have untidy leaves, I will admit. They have enormous bulbs with immensely long necks out of which fall long wrinkly leaves. From the top of stout purplish stalks spill a handful of buds which open, over a period of several weeks, into large trumpet flowers. *Crinum × powellii* is the name. There are both pink and white forms. They need deep rich soil and plenty of manure – so say the books. Nowhere here can they be supplied with deep rich soil, but they grow and flower well, both under walls and in the open in well-manured gravel, with straw cover for winter.

Apart from the general principle of digging large holes, removing builder's rubbish and replacing with plenty of spongy compost, old turves, peat, well-rotted muck, chalk if needed – I do watch newly planted inmates against walls in times of drought and haul up the necessary cans of water until they are established and can fend for themselves. One can per shrub is the dose – not a sprinkling.

Shady Walls

Once you have a taste for foliage plants the shaded border under the house or garden wall can be one of your favourites. This does not mean that you are confined to growing only foliage plants. There are many beautiful flowering plants like honeysuckle, which are woodlanders, and prefer a shaded situation.

However, in areas of low rainfall they will still be dry especially in summer. Sometimes the soil can look green and damp, but in actual fact be very dry underneath. Every effort must be made to conserve moisture here as well as on the dry sunny border.

The width of all wall borders is important. Very narrow borders are best avoided, as often they are in the rain shadow area and rarely get touched by rain, but this does not mean to say that here and there you cannot tuck a fern (if it will thrive) or a narrow bed of arums. But for general planting 3 ft/1 m wide is, I think, the minimum, for effect and efficiency. If you have room, and the scale of your house and walls allow more, then you will have the opportunity for planting on a grander scale, using a few fine shrubs as well as plants and climbers.

On my cooler north-facing walls I am able to grow a few large-flowered clematis, including 'Perle d'Azur'. Good forms of *Clematis montana*, including *C. × vedrariensis* which is a very handsome cross between *C. chrysocoma* and *C. montana* var. *rubens*, do very well. *Clematis rehderiana* is another rampant species and has been removed to chase up an immense *Rosa villosa* 'Duplex', or Wolley Dod's Rose, and on I hope, into an old holly behind. I thought its sweet-scented clusters of little greenish-yellow bells would look delightful in the autumn, with orange hips and the russet and black berries of *Hypericum androsaemun* below. *Clematis potaninii* var. *potaninii* (*C. fargesii souliei*) is another small-flowered species, but it grows so healthily, and its little white flowers, shallow saucers full of stamens, cover it like stars on a winter's night.

There are not enough walls for all the honeysuckles I

would like to grow, but there are two I would hate to be without. *Lonicera x tellmanniana* covers a wall approaching the front door of my house. The fact that it is scentless is of little concern. The dark wall seems bathed in sunlight in June when every shoot carries trusses of large orange-yellow flowers, as showy as an azalea. It is not an easy plant. Aphis torment it, so a constant watch to control them is vital. It also needs more moisture than our sweet-scented, long-suffering *Lonicera periclymenum* 'Serotina' so give it plenty of well-wetted peat, and possibly the opportunity to keep its roots cool under paving.

An attractive companion on this wall is *Parthenocissus henryana* (*Vitis henryana*). Not at all troubled by the dry soil it flings out long thin shoots carrying very pretty foliage. Each leaf is made up of three or five leaflets, green tinted bronze, with silvery-white veins. The undersides are shaded carmine.

The narrow bed below is filled with *Arum italicum*, while *Hedera helix* 'Sagittifolia' and *Hedera helix* 'Buttercup' complete a very simple planting.

The other honeysuckle I like very much may be *Lonicera flava*. Certainly it is perfoliate. The close trusses of creamy-yellow flowers sit in a perfect saucer-shaped leaf. In the autumn every saucer is full of transparent orange-red 'currants', even more attractive than the flowers.

There are so many ivies, all of which can be grown in dry shade, provided they are given a good start. As with vincas your life will be less fraught if you well mulch them also. They will respond by growing so much more vigorously, and you will not keep pulling up the long rooting shoots as you fiddle to fork out the grasses rooted between them.

Hedera colchica 'Sulphur Heart' ('Paddy's Pride') is not so well known, I think, as *H. colchica* 'Dentata Variegata'. The variegation is in reverse. The broadly ovate leaves have a central golden heart dissolving into shades of yellow and pale green before it reaches the dark green margin of the leaf. With both these forms every leaf is different, as though painted by hand. Both these ivies make very effective ground cover as well as climbing walls or old tree stumps.

The smaller non-variegated ivies I use in wall borders are *Hedera helix* 'Manda's Crested', and *H. helix* 'Invalace'. These completely cover a little north-facing corner bed (including a manhole cover now obliterated, but available), with winter jasmine behind them, also *Iris foetidissima* 'Variegata' and *Helleborus argutifolius* (*H. corsicus*). *Alchemilla mollis* flourishes a froth of lime-green among them in mid-summer.

Another ivy admired for its curious shape is *Hedera helix* 'Parsley Crested' (*H.* 'Cristata'). The leaf margins are even more curled than those of 'Manda's Crested', as though they had been crimped by a minute goffering iron. The plant looks most attractive in the autumn when its abundant new shoots carrying fresh pale leaves show up against the background of mature leaves.

Beneath the clematis and honeysuckle wall is my *Primula auricula* bed. Still the same poor gravel, it was prepared with old well-rotted muck well dug in with a little wet peat. I planted the auriculas ('them Reckless plants', as an old country man called them who brought me one) in this border as a last resort, having found nowhere else suitable. They need summer cool, but simply won't tolerate having their leaves wet and soggy in winter. I have some good velvety blues, old rose pink, bright yellow, pale citron yellow, and one we call 'Cherry' which almost vanishes beneath its clusters of small but abundant cherry-red flowers.

'Old Red Dusty Miller', and 'Old Yellow Dusty Miller' are there, with their flour-dusted foliage, almost more beautiful without flowers, especially when the new leaf rosettes unfold like petals of pale cream suede. They are less vigorous than some of the others, but have increased since being moved to the shade of this wall. They have plenty of light, but do not suffer from drought. Even in the 1976 drought they looked well, protected by the mulch.

I planted ajugas in the gaps between the blocks of *Primula auricula* – *Ajuga reptans* 'Burgundy Glow', *A. reptans* 'Variegata', and *A. r.* 'Atropurpurea' to make ground cover, but in spite of dry soil they have flourished too well among such fastidious companions. Barely in time I discovered the threat. Already some auriculas had died in the dark embrace of overwintering *Ajuga* foliage. Someone will be commenting that ajugas are pestilential weeds anywhere – when suited they do run like mad – but *not* in full sun on dry gravel, nor on the matted roots of shrubs with a rainfall of 20 in./500 mm.

Polystichum setiferum Acutilobum Group is one of the most elegant ferns which, while it will be probably twice as tall in better conditions, nevertheless looks well among the auriculas. It makes a slowly increasing stock, with delicate narrow fronds about 2 ft/600 mm long. They overwinter well, finally dying down as the new fronds uncurl from a soft brown scaly 'nest'. Young fernlets are borne along the mid-ribs of the old discarded leaves, which in moist situations would probably sink down into damp leaf mould, enabling the youngsters to put their feet down. If you pin one of these leaf ribs onto a box or pan of peaty compost and keep it sheltered and shaded, the young ferns will root down and can be potted on, ready for planting out.

Making a splash of gold at the base of the clematis are some plants of *Valeriana phu* 'Aurea', whose foliage competes with the display of daffodils for a few weeks in early spring, but becomes green with maturity. The tall branching stems topped with bunches of small white flowers create an intermediate height for a long while in summer. (See Pl. 19.)

A statuesque plant to place on one of these dry shady borders (but *not* anywhere near small treasures) is *Acanthus mollis*, or for a smaller space *Acanthus spinosus* (Pl. 4). I have planted *Acanthus mollis* outside the bathroom (ground floor) window, and its soaring flower heads, white and maroon, pass out of sight, unless I am lying flat in the bath. It is the frontispiece to a tangle of *Lonicera japonica* 'Aureoreticulata', *Hedera* 'Parsley Crested' ('Cristata'), and massed *Arum italicum*. It will always be the dominant feature of this particular patch, whatever other ideas I may have. Once established it is next to impossible to eradicate. I suppose a really savage attack with a systemic weedkiller would do it, if it became a necessity, but it is such a proud sight all the year round, except when really harsh conditions reduce its large shining leaves to pulp. Large-leafed bergenias would also make a welcome change in scale in these shady borders, and so too would hostas.

Hostas are deservedly honoured plants among gardeners today although there was a time, not so very long ago, when they were considered coarse, suitable only for the back of the shrubbery. While they really do need rich deep soil to develop into the truly magnificent plants they can become, they will grow tolerably well in poor soil, suitably enriched in shady borders.

Hosta sieboldiana with its corrugated glaucous blue leaves will add grandeur in such a position. The longer the plants are allowed to settle down, with occasional inducement in the form of a good dressing of muck, the larger the leaves will become. There are other forms of *H. sieboldiana*, bluer of course, and they are very desirable. But if you do not possess *H. sieboldiana* itself you deprive yourself of one of the noblest garden plants. I find it does well where its improved forms tend to miff; *they* will only accept the best. Its only drawback perhaps is its rather short flower spike of crowded, almost white flowers – but they in turn make lovely seed heads, stems of straw-coloured wooden stars.

Hosta lancifolia is not overpraised (because it is not variegated I imagine), but to my mind it is a lovely plant with a most useful form. Robust and healthy, it makes good clumps of narrow shining green leaves, useful where it would be too dry for *Asplenium scolopendrium*, the Hart's Tongue Fern. It flowers in the back end of the season, slender trumpets of deep lilac hanging from tall graceful stems, a joy for weeks.

There are several more trees, shrubs and climbers that can be grown against dry shady walls where there is room. I have not mentioned *Garrya elliptica*, *Fatsia japonica*, the mahonias, *Pyracantha* spp., *Akebia quinata*, and winter jasmine. These are a few that I grow and can recommend as they are all doing quite well here, and would no doubt be better still on heavier soil.

Fixing plants on walls can be an expensive and bothersome performance. All kinds of trellis can be obtained and erected.

Not all of it is admirable. The cheapest and least obtrusive I have found is this: we drill the walls at 3 ft/1 m square intervals, plug the holes with Rawlplugs and screw in ring-headed vine eyes. I have been able to obtain from ex-Government stock old Post Office telephone wire, sometimes ex-Army I think. This is insulated with a kind of dark cotton which prevents plants cutting themselves. (I don't like that thin, bright green plastic-coated kind!) Threaded through the rings it makes a 3 ft/1 m square pattern over the wall, very strong and not unsightly.

7

Dry Shade under Trees and Shrubs

A rather different and more difficult situation for plants is the dry shady area to be found under trees and shrubs. Again I must remind you that we are not in wet Wales, or along the west coast of Scotland. There, much heavier rainfall and frequent mists will provide growing conditions totally unrealizable here. The competition for moisture among tree and shrub roots is fierce and unmerciful in my garden, so I have, over the years, and not always with the wholehearted approval of others, ruthlessly rooted out any tree or shrub which I did not consider was making a worthwhile contribution to the planting. When renovating an old garden, I personally think it is a waste of time to try to add a few newcomers, poked in among hoary old pensioners. They rarely succeed. Take the old boys, often mangled, cut-back stumps, out. Keep only what justifies the space. You can then make a really good job of deep digging, aerating the compacted soil, and replacing with new, if necessary. The newly planted shrubs and plants give pleasure from the first weeks of planting, and by the end of the season you will have forgotten how it looked before.

But if you are the possessor of some rare antique which at all costs should be spared I hope you will know enough to recognize it before it is too late. No amount of easily grown cover plants can compensate for the lifetime's growth of a rare tree.

I have described already a planting along the old hedge

bank that became my east-facing main entrance border. I have another farm boundary hedge, where the soil may be a little less stony, but it is if anything drier. It is partially shaded by half a dozen ancient oaks. The following plants are growing in this area now, all of them having been given a good start.

Paeonia delavayi var. *ludlowii* (*P. lutea ludlowii*), and *P. delavayi* have both made great leggy bushes (modestly screened by lower plants), more valued by me for their handsome foliage than their rather small flowers. The blackish red bosses of *P. delavayi* shaded beneath the washed-pink blossoms of *Prunus* 'Taihaku', look down onto the reflexed petals of *Geranium phaeum*, finding their colour almost repeated in miniature.

Cotoneaster 'Rothschildianus' with creamy-yellow fruits, and a *Pyracantha* with really showy yellow berries (both of which have to be wreathed with black cotton) have been planted to help form a wind break beneath the oaks, the west wind coming uninterrupted across a 30-acre field. (To ease this situation and give my young shrubs a chance we have not only erected a rabbit-proof fence here, but have fastened a close-netted wind break over it.)

Prunus laurocerasus 'Otto Luyken' I have used as cover; I like its narrow shining leaves, and its compact habit makes it a useful filler between larger shrubs.

Beneath an immense oak which I thought would never really look as though it belonged to the garden I planted the Portugal laurel, *Prunus lusitanica*. Now after seventeen years planting it has made the most handsome evergreen shrub, 12 ft/4 m high, and as much across. It has glossy oval leaves, with red leaf stalks, and in autumn is hung with chains of red and purple fruits. It is so much better for us to be able to grow well this impressive if not spectacular evergreen which furnishes a difficult site than struggle with rhododendrons which make poor showing. I added *Hamamelis mollis* to this group, with *Euphorbia amygdaloides robbiae*, *Iris foetidissima*, *Vinca minor* 'La Grave' ('Bowles' Variety)', *Polygonatum* × *hybridum* and *Viola labradorica* to make ground cover. Now an area which defeated me with sorrel and Annual Meadow Grass is a permanent carpet of interesting foliage, with snowdrops, aconites, wood anemones and foxgloves, all of them contributing to a scene over which the old oak presides.

I put *Hydrangea anomala* subsp. *petiolaris* (*H. petiolaris*) at its foot but although it is well up the trunk it is still rather lost, so I have planted another piece over the stump of an ancient crab-apple where I hope it will make a mound and sprawl over the bank with *Clematis* × *jouiniana* 'Praecox' which has already established there.

Viola labradorica spreads by seeds and runners between the stems of *Euphorbia amygdaloides robbiae*, both so attractive in winter. April brings *Anemone nemorosa* 'Robinsoniana' peeping out shy lavender-blue flowers among the small purple leaves of the violet while the euphorbia lifts expanding heads of lime-green flowers above. Overtopping them are the arching stems of Solomon's Seal contributing graceful form to this area right to the end of the year, when they suddenly lighten the scene with a blaze of gold as they prepare for their winter sleep.

Everyone's favourites are the wild cyclamens. These exquisite little plants are found in the woods of southern Europe. They are easy to establish in a dry shady border, but do give them a good start; they are used to a rich leaf-mouldy soil. Probably one of the reasons why so many 'do not come up' is because they have been thrown out with a large tuft of grass or mat of chick-weed. Certainly when dormant they do look like a smooth round stone. Look carefully when you plant them to make sure you do not put them in upside down. They are no trouble at all if you can mulch them after planting. Their silvery marbled leaves stand out against the warm brown mulch, be it peat, bark or leaf mould. This will also stop you poking about with a fork and lessen the risk of stabbing them. (See Pl. 16).

Epimediums are woodland dwellers from Europe to Japan. The choicer Japanese forms need more moisture, but *Epimedium* × *versicolor* 'Sulphureum', with possibly the toughest constitution, is no less lovely than the others. Still

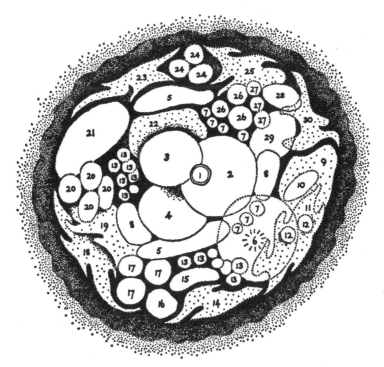

J. Plan round an oak tree, approx. 24 × 24 ft/7 × 7 m

On the plan, the clump formers or slow spreaders are white, the quick spreaders are dotted

1. *Quercus robur*
2. *Prunus lusitanicus*
3. *Ilex × altaclarensis* 'Golden King'
4. *Viburnum tinus*
5. *Polygonatum × hybridum*
6. *Hamamelis mollis*
7. *Lunaria annua variegata*
8. *Iris foetidissima*
9. *Lamium maculatum* 'Roseum'
10. *Euphorbia cyparissias*
11. *Vinca minor* 'La Grave' ('Bowles' Variety')
12. *Geranium endressii*
13. *Euphorbia amygdaloides robbiae*
14. *Viola labradorica*
15. *Polystichum setiferum* Acutilobum Group
16. *Dicentra formosa alba*

17. *Helleborus orientalis*
18. *Vinca minor* 'Argenteovariegata' ('Variegata')
19. *Melissa officinalis* 'Aurea'
20. *Epimedium × versicolor* 'Sulphureum'
21. *Hypericum calycinum*
22. *Symphytum ibericum* (*S. grandiflorum*)
23. *Hedera canariensis* 'Variegata'
24. *Dryopteris filix-mas*
25. *Vinca major* 'Variegata'
26. *Geranium phaeum*
27. *Aquilegia vulgaris* or hybrids
28. *Arum italicum* 'Marmoratum' (*A. i.* 'Pictum' of gardens)
29. *Symphoricarpos × doorenbosii* 'White Hedge'
30. *Hedera helix* 'Pedata Heron'

in the rain shadow of a great oak I have planted them with *Iris innominata* hybrids, *Dryopteris filix-mas*, the common male fern, with *Digitalis lutea* for height. The white form of *Digitalis purpurea* I try to keep pure, so any young plants showing a touch of purple in the leaf stalk are rooted out if seen in time.

Lamiums tolerate quite a lot of drought, but in very dry 1976 I lost some of my lamium carpets beneath larger trees whose roots were pumping daily the gallons needed to keep huge canopies alive. I think I shall replant the driest spots with small-leafed ivies.

The pink and white flowered forms of *Lamium maculatum* have survived in all but the driest conditions. *Lamium galeobdolon* 'Florentinum' ('Variegatum') can be a rampaging nuisance in the wrong place but it would be hard to beat for effectiveness and performance under the shade of large trees. I have also seen it completely covering a hedge bottom on heavy Norfolk clay, looking most attractive, especially in winter with its frosty silver leaves. (See Pl. 21.)

Symphytum ibericum (*S. grandiflorum*) I find useful among big shrubs, where choicer plants would not be seen, nor would they survive. It makes creeping carpets of rough dark green leaves. In early spring little croziers of cream cowslip-like bells tipped with orange buds unfold themselves. *Brunnera macrophylla* is reputed to like the worst bits of soil. I think it prefers really heavy land. It does not thrive here on poor gravel, but certainly has looked better nearer the clay with additional humus. (See Pl. 20.)

The scented leaves of *Geranium macrorrhizum* cover yards of poor soil between shrubs and colour better for being a bit starved. *Geranium endressii* also tolerates dry soil, with its little salmon or rose-pink flowers floating over apple-green foliage all season through. In fact I find it needs a rest, and when I think of it, or stop to make time, I cut it down in July, when it is a tangled mass of stems, whereupon it makes neat tidy mounds to show off its autumn crop of flowers. *Tellima grandiflora* Rubra Group (*T. g.* 'Purpurea') and *Tiarella cordifolia* both grow in the shrubberies. They love leaf-mouldy soil, and will tolerate quite dry conditions. If too extreme *Tiarella* will wither away, especially if exposed, but it is always possible to find protected pieces tucked under the shelter of hosta leaves, from where it will run out again as soon as the weather becomes kinder.

Bowles' Golden Grass (*Milium effusum* 'Aureum') fills in the odd spaces between all these plants, looking in March and April like patches of sunlight dropped through the leafless branches. It will stand dry at its roots, but it will not put up with bright sunlight or exposure to drying winds. (See Pl. 24.)

Looking up into an old cob nut can also be a bit dazzling when the Golden Hop (*Humulus lupulus* 'Aureus') has twined up and around the many trunks, dropping again to the ground, and forming a vivid carpet there, its bright leaves contrasting with hellebores and hederas.

One of the best smotherers I have found to grow under the dense shade of trees is *Rubus tricolor*. It sends out long runners which root down in autumn, eventually making total cover.

Hedera hibernica (*H. helix* 'Hibernica'), the Irish ivy, I am also using in the same way, having seen the magnificent circular carpets it has formed fitting exactly under the canopies of great trees at Kew Gardens, standing isolated in mown grass. Apart from hostas there are a few other large-leafed plants to provide relief among these smaller, sometimes fussy-looking carpets.

Pachyphragma macrophylla is a plant I value highly. It starts the season very early. Long before *Tiarella* has thought about it this plant has sent up bunches of small white cress-like flowers dotted between the shrubs, their startling whiteness embroidering the bare spaces between dormant hostas. They are followed by shining, very round green leaves, puckered with radiating veins, some of which grow to the size of a tea plate, forming dense overlapping mounds. I have seen it in a shrubbery in Yorkshire where it makes total cover in deep shade.

Trachystemon orientalis can produce a lush effect under trees – it is much too coarse for small gardens but can be splendid where something elephantine is needed. The flowers come before the leaves; rather naked-looking pink stems of blue borage-like flowers in early spring are followed by huge hairy leaves, handsome in the right setting.

8

Raised Beds

I do not have a rock garden. Living in an area where we have no natural rock it seemed inappropriate, although I do grow many plants that come from dry, stony mountain sides. Originally many of these, the smaller sedums, sempervivums, achilleas and encrusted saxifrages I had planted around the edges of my original 'Mediterranean' garden. But gradually, as the garden grew and I had less time to tend them, some of the smaller plants became overlaid, or if not, were overlooked.

So I decided to make a raised bed, thinking it would be easier to manage, with my small plants grouped together. We surrounded an area 15 ft/4.5 m long by 5 ft/1.5 m wide with 4 in./100 mm wide concrete blocks, laid two blocks high. This meant that we could have 2 ft/600 mm of prepared soil instead of the shingle most of them had been putting up with. (This might also be the answer to anyone struggling to grow alpines on heavy clay – to remove the clay and put in a layer of coarse stone for drainage and then fill up with improved soil.) We had no need to worry about bottom drainage, but straightaway filled up with a half and half mixture, our own vegetable compost and reasonable top soil. For the last 6 in./150 mm or so we changed to a three-part mixture of compost, sharp sand and well-wetted peat.

Because this mixture would have germinated a flourishing crop of weeds, and as I was trying to cut down all the weeding I could, we sterilized the bed. To do this the soil mixture must be really damp long enough for hard-coated weed seeds to soften and be on the point of germination. A powder called Basamid is then sprinkled over the surface at the recommended rate and incorporated to a depth of about 6 in./150 mm. The bed is then sheeted down with polythene, secured at the edges and left for two to three weeks. The result is impressive: not 100 per cent free of weeds perhaps, but near enough. This material is recommended also for the control of eel-worm. How it manages to avoid destroying valuable soil bacteria (or if it does so?) I do not know. But I do know that my plants flourish after its use.

To help create the scene on the flat surface, and provide some shade for roots, I used a few large pieces of ragstone. This is found locally when deep sub-soiling is being carried out. Gravel and sand have been 'cemented' together by iron deposited from the water which has lain over a bed of clay, the cause of bad drainage. These stony lumps are a reddish colour which looks right with the gravel we use to top the beds. Moss grows over them, and so too do creeping plants like thyme and *Raoulia*, so giving a natural effect.

I hasten to say that as yet I am not a prominent member of the Alpine Garden Society, and know little or nothing of the mysteries and intricacies of growing really awkward high alpines. Most of the plants I used on this first raised bed are ordinary and very easily grown. At the end of the first season it was almost covered, and has been a surprising source of pleasure and interest from the moment it was planted. A good thick layer of sharp grit helped to prevent too much loss of water, and worked wonders in setting off small plants. Being nearer to hand and eye (and a novelty), nothing suffered from lack of attention.

I made one disastrous mistake, when I put in the plant known as *Geranium orientalitibeticum* (*G. stapfianum* 'Roseum'), enchantment personified in a pot. No book had warned me that pretty as its dainty speckled leaves and constant succession of pink flowers are, I would find it making its exuberant way from one end of my bed to the

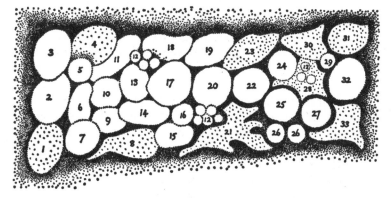

K. Plants for a small sunny island entrance bed, approx. 5 × 15 ft/1.5 × 5 m

This plan could be planted directly into reasonably good garden soil. If the soil is very heavy, or very poor sand or gravel, then it would need to be prepared as for a raised bed. The height of a raised bed is not important; it will probably depend on what is available to build it. The mixture inside is more important. For a heavy clay soil excavate enough to put in a layer of stone, broken pots, whatever you can find to aid drainage. Then add a mixture of peat, good top soil, grit and leaf mould if available.

1. *Silene uniflora* 'Robin Whitebreast' (*S. maritima* 'Plena')
2. *Onosma alborosea*
3. *Haplopappus glutinosus* (*H. coronopifolius*)
4. *Euphorbia myrsinites*
5. *Armeria maritima* 'Alba'
6. *Arabis alpina* subsp. *caucasica* (*A. albida* 'Variegata')
7. *Achillea rupestris*
8. *Phlox douglasii* hybrids
9. *Sedum spathulifolium* 'Cape Blanco' ('Capablanca')
10. *Iris* 'Green Spot'
11. *Sedum kamtschaticum* var. *floriferum* 'Weihenstephaner Gold' (*S.* 'Weihenstephaner Gold')
12. *Sempervivum* hybrids
13. *Hypericum olympicum* f. *uniflorum* 'Citrinum'
14. *Azorella trifurcata*
15. *Sedum spathulifolium*
16. *Limonium bellidifolium*
17. *Hebe* 'Youngii' ('Carl Teschner')
18. *Antennaria parvifolia* (*A. aprica*)
19. *Chiastophyllum oppositifolium*
20. *Helichrysum italicum* subsp. *microphyllum* (*H. angustifolium* 'Nanum')
21. *Thymus serpyllum* 'Minimus'
22. *Sedum populifolium*
23. *Phlox subulava* 'Temiskaming'
24. *Dianthus* 'Sops-in-Wine'
25. *Pterocephalus perennis* (*P. parnassi*)
26. *Geranium einereum* var. *subcaulescens*
27. *Crepis incana*
28. *Raoulia australis*
29. *Sisyrinchium californicum* Brachypus Group (*S. brachypus*)
30. *Artemisia schmidtiana*
31. *Gypsophila repens* 'Dubia'
32. *Achillea ageratifolia*
33. *Cerastium tomentosum* var. *columnae*

other. After two years I found its roots, looking like strings of beads, everywhere. So it all had to be pulled to pieces and started again. The geranium I have banished among the roses on the big entrance border where I can't believe it will do harm! – it *is* very pretty.

I often think that instead of the six lop-sided rose bushes planted in a narrow strip leading to many a front door, giving colour for a comparatively short while and nothing but discomfort and bare stems for the rest of the year, something of this kind of planting could be so much more enjoyable, whether raised or planted flat.

It really does not matter what is used to support the bed, as after a couple of years it can be almost smothered. Obviously if you live in an area of good stone you will create something infinitely more beautiful. The thing to avoid is a mixture of the real thing and man-made blocks. Railway sleepers act and look very well if obtainable.

Among some of the things I planted (less damaging than the geranium) were several fairly fast-growing plants to drape themselves over the rather severe concrete blocks. *Silene uniflora* 'Robin Whitebreast' (*S. maritima* 'Plena'), *Gypsophila repens* 'Dubia', and *Haplopappus glutinosus* (*H. coronopifolius*) were all very obliging. *Gypsophila* 'Rosenschleier' ('Rosy Veil') was planted and removed, as in one season it made a frothy cloud that took more than its share of space. However, I still have plans for it to grace a larger bed. Many different kinds of *Sempervivum* and *Sedum* found their way here with tidy cushions of dwarf achillea and non-invasive geraniums like *Geranium cinereum* 'Ballerina' providing all the colour you could wish for. Really prostrate mat-formers to run between and over rocks were thymes and raoulias, with *Azorella trifurcata* making a tight hard mound of solid green, irresistible to touch. *Arabis procurrens* 'Variegata' (*A. ferdinandii-coburgii* 'Variegata') proved its worth by spreading its clustered cream and green rosettes through the grit, while a minute daisy, a miniature Sea Lavender and a coral-coloured *Oxalis* caught your attention if you thought of rushing past.

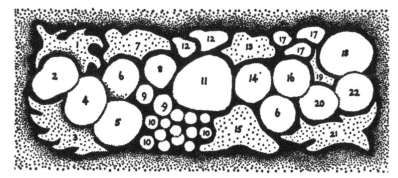

L. Plants for a small shady island entrance bed, approx. 5 × 15 ft/1.5 × 5 m

1. *Vinca minor* f. *alba* ('Alba')
2. *Alchemilla conjuncta*
3. *Vinca minor* 'La Grave'
   ('Bowles' Variety')
4. *Hosta fortunei albopicta*
5. *Geranium renardii*
6. *Tellima grandiflora* Rubra
   Group (*T. g.* 'Purpurea')
7. *Ajuga reptans* 'Burgundy Glow'
8. *Primula* 'Guinevere'
   ('Garryarde Guinevere')
9. *Digitalis grandiflora*
10. *Saxifraga* 'Aureopunctata' (*S. umbrosa* 'Variegata')
11. *Euonymus* 'Emerald 'n Gold'

12. *Veronica prostrata* 'Trehane'
13. *Ajuga reptans* 'Atropurpurea'
14. *Fuchsia magellanica* var.
    gracilis 'Tricolor'
15. *Viola cornuta* 'Alba'
16. *Hosta lancifolia*
17. *Tanacetum parthenium*
    (*Chrysanthemum parthenium*)
    'Aureum'
18. *Carex morrowii* 'Variegata'
19. *Waldsteinia ternata*
20. *Iris foetidissima*
21. *Hedera helix* 'Marginata'
22. *Helleborus orientalis*

My interest in raised beds already aroused, I had the good fortune to find my way to the garden of Valerie Finnis and her husband, Sir David Scott. I was immediately lost. What a wealth of lovely things, spilling out of wall beds like cornucopias, and all looking so well. There was no room to put a label between them; but at the same time the plants had room to grow. I have seen alpine collections that reminded me of continental war cemeteries, so full of white labels in straight rows. Not a bit of that here. Helianthemums and dianthus draped over the edges while treasures like *Omphalodes luciliae* and *Potentilla nitida* 'Rubra' looked as though they could not help growing like weeds. With mellow old walls and roofs to set them all off, here was everything you would love to possess, growing in abundance – not without infinite care and attention to achieve such apparent nonchalance I might add.

I could not wait to start my second raised bed! Along the west-facing wall of the garden I had made originally a narrow bed for species bulbs in particular, with anything else that would survive very cruel conditions. The spring display was always deceptively good. Walter Butt's ice-blue iris, followed by the Juno irises and *Anemone pavonina* and then the fritillaries surrounded by dwarf sedums and sempervivums, all looked quite encouraging. But after the bulbs it was difficult to find dwarf-growing plants to follow on. Thyme mats shrivelled, and even the sempervivums shrank into themselves. There had been crocus until the mice ate the flowering bulbs, leaving millions of bulbils to produce untidy grassy wisps. A tiresome allium, not at all remarkable in flower, proliferated and produced the same unkempt look. Interest flagged, weeds crept in, something had to be done. If we made a raised wall bed, we could remove all our problems with the top spit (including that appalling menace *Campanula rapunculoides* which went down feet – *do* hope we have got out the last bit) and make up some really good soil for treasures.

So, in July 1976 with the heat so great we could have coddled eggs in the soil, I dug out everything worth retrieving. Then Harry did all the hard and heavy work, removing the infected soil, building the new walls, and infilling with a well-drained but water-retentive mixture. That always sounds contradictory, but I hope you know what I mean. Before he began, we had to decide the width of the new bed, standing there with blocks propped before us to see what was the most comfortable stretch to reach the bed at the back of the wall. Now I look forward to planting special treasures that will enjoy this warm site. I hope I have learnt to avoid too invasive trouble-makers, but there will be plenty of the less common easy doers. A long expanse of grit and labels signifying microscopic difficulties are not for me. But *Iris sari* is one of my treasures waiting to go back under the wall with the sloe-bloom *Fritillaria tuntasia* to keep it company – and of course many others.

9

My 'Mediterranean' Garden

Now I come to my original 'Mediterranean' garden, which has been the nucleus for some of my later extensions.

In 1960 it was a bare gravelly slope, lying to the south-west of the single storey, split-level house which had just been built. It covered an area of about 36 yd/32 m long and 20 yd/18 m wide, protected from the north by the house, and from the east by a 5 ft/1.5 m wall built of concrete blocks. Off centre there had been a badger's set, an enormous mound of fine silver sand piled up over the years from much tunnelling and many spring cleanings. The decision had to be made, and when the bulldozer arrived to make a series of platforms in the bank on which the house would rest, the badger's set was levelled. I did not see it happen. But I feel sure that he had already moved out. Like cats, badgers are aware long before events take place. He did not go far. There is now another colony developed at the far end of my land, protected by a bit of oak scrubland.

We were left with the fine dry sand spread thickly over already poor gravel soil. It was a little daunting, even with Mediterranean plants in mind.

We decided there could be no grass walks here. Paths and steps were laid out to fit the slopes, paved where essential and gravelled elsewhere. We were lucky that we were moving from only seven miles away, but it took a year (with other things to do) to ferry over our stocks of bulbs, young plants and rooted cuttings. I had made a small nursery area where

I could grow them on for a while until their new homes were prepared. Digging out bracken roots took weeks and weeks (like old tarry ropes, milky white inside). Today I would use a weedkiller called Azulox, but that takes a year's treatment. You cannot rush these things.

I collected up all the leaf-mould I could find and dug it in. We also bought a load of mushroom compost. This contains a lot of chalk which many of the plants going here would not mind at all. (One has to remember, however, when applying chalk that it may be washed out lower down the slope into areas where you might wish to plant lime-haters.) These applications of humus were pathetically inadequate for the poverty-stricken soil, but they were better than nothing.

The planting had to begin. Running across the slope, from north to south, I planted the backbone of my beds – trees and shrubs to make a framework, a setting for sub-shrubs and plants. These included *Cupressus arizonica*, *Cupressus sempervirens*, *Juniperus communis*, *Calocedrus decurrens*, and a beautiful columnar yew, *Taxus baccata* 'Fastigiata' and *Chamaecyparis lawsoniana* 'Ellwoodii' which is reminiscent of Gothic cathedral pillars. These are my verticals. Grouped near them are the larger shrubs, *Genista aetnensis* now 15 × 15 ft/4.5 × 4.5 m, *Spartium junceum*, *Cytisus battandieri*, *Buddleia fallowiana*, and *Cistus ladanifer*.

The eye is carried downward from these to the infilling mounds of *Ballota*, salvias, *Ruta* (of course), smaller cistus and helichrysums.

And so to the small bays and openings that have been made to provide cosy homes for smaller plants, cushions and mat formers, in a setting whose scale becomes them. The grouping here was designed on a much more intimate scale than some of my later beds, where maximum effect with least effort and little subsequent maintenance has been a necessity. The original planting was to make homes for as many interesting plants as our soil would allow, for as many days in the year as possible. There was no thought of planting in large groups. Single plants, three at the most perhaps to run together, were sufficient. But individual though they might be they were set with neighbours that enhanced them. If the boundaries of my garden had remained here there would have been no problem of maintenance. But I have to admit that at this moment my 'Mediterranean garden', like its makers, is a little the worse for wear. Like the long wall border it has been somewhat neglected while other projects have had priority.

The main furnishings are there. The trees and shrubs have made height and shelter, but a little replanting of the floor is essential now. The low areas need to be cleaned out, and plenty of compost dug in, before being replanted. Some areas have become impossible with seedling bulbs whose long grassy remains spoil cover plants and look untidy for weeks. I do not belong to the 'backcombed and lacquered' (to borrow a phrase) school of gardening – tidiness does not as yet come before creativeness. But I am trying to make a garden where working shall be a pleasure, not merely repetitive boredom. This must largely be achieved through the planting, so anything which damages that has to be reconsidered.

I think crocuses, especially *Crocus tomasinianus*, are my worst offenders. I grow *C. sieberi*, several forms of *C. chrysanthus*, *C. imperati*, *C. angustifolius* (*C. susianus*) and *C. flavus* subsp. *flavus* (*C. aureus*), while in autumn the grey garden is rekindled with *C. kotschyanus* and *C. speciosus*. I love them all in flower, but their great thick bunches of foliage are a worry. I have planted out many of them on a reserve border, and am planning to plant them in drifts by themselves under shrubs, either mulched or in mown grass. Will that work? Or will the mice clear the lot? I have learnt to put mouse bait in screw-top jars with a mouse-sized entrance hole. It will be a question of remembering in time to put the jars down I expect.

Then there are plants like *Sedum album*. 'Only to be allowed on crumbling walls on the roadside, *never* inside the garden gate,' should read the inscription in the books. It is charming, filling in one season yards of dusty-dry soil: every minute piece that has dropped off has made a healthy green cluster in a matter of days. But it has put itself into everything, thyme mats, hearts of helianthemums, alyssum, dwarf phlox – everything! Annual Meadow Grass too has joined in this sabotage. This must all be removed now by the spadeful; it is beyond fiddling about with hand weeding. As with the wall border, valuable bulbs will be marked and removed when their foliage has died down, so these troublesome edges will have almost everything removed. The remaining shrubs will be well manured, not digging too close to their roots.

The small plants that merit and need regular attention will be on the new raised wall bed. Then the old 'Mediterranean garden' will have its groups rejuvenated.

The great plants of *Euphorbia characias* subsp. *wulfenii* which are a feature of this garden for months in spring and early summer will tower above silvery helichrysums, including *H. italicum* (*H. angustifolium*), filling the air with its spicy scent. Velvet mounds of purple sage will make a setting for small-flowered *Dianthus* 'Sops-in-Wine', and *D.* 'Waithman's Beauty' which, in my soil, make so much denser cushions of neat bluish foliage than the larger hybrid pinks. The brilliant little *Dianthus deltoides* will seed with kind permission into wide sheets of *Thymus pseudolanuginosus* (*T. lanuginosus*) or *T. polytrichus* subsp. *britannicus* (*T. drucei*) 'Albus'.

I have two forms of *Thymus herba-barona*. The first is well known and smells strongly of Caraway seed. The second we collected in Corsica, with the sharpest lemon scent of any thyme. Both make low wiry mounds covered with very small leaves and pale lilac flowers. Both contribute to the aromatic atmosphere that causes many visitors to recall gardens, or hill sides, in the south.

Three different forms of *Yucca* add to this southern feeling (even though they come from the south-east United States!) while their splendid architectural form adds drama in winter as in summer. (See Pl. 13.)

Slim columns of juniper rise out of the planting, casting no shade, their formality repeating the confined outlines of the house.

I have already started replanting a small section backed

by a bay, some cistus and juniper. Unusual plants here now include *Parahebe perfoliata* whose stems of glaucous circular leaves are reminiscent of some *Eucalyptus* species. This plant comes from Australia which does not surprise me. *Salvia candelabrum* flings up stems of dark indigo-blue flowers, from behind a sunburst clump of slim-leafed *Libertia grandiflora*. Around these are dwarf achilleas, the feathery *Tanacetum densum* subsp. *amani*, carpets of mountain phlox and golden cushions of *Thymus vulgaris aureus*. This flat area is broken again with rosette plants like *Carlina acaulis* and *Carduncellus rhaponticoides*.

Another of my favourite plants, *Crepis incana*, makes slowly increasing clumps of greyish-green toothed leaves from which rise, in late summer, 'bridesmaids' bouquets' of powder-pink dandelion flowers on many branching stems. I have never found a seedling but they divide and come from root cuttings. If you had a terrace large enough for a few dot plants (as opposed to crevice plants) and not being in the way of garden furniture or walkways, then this would be a perfect setting to show off this delightful plant.

The back door of my house opens into a little paved yard, surrounded by tool shed and part of the west wall, both draped with *Vitis coignetiae*. This warm corner was the place for my herb garden. I do not want to go far on a wet night for a sprig of rosemary. So, very simply planted together, are my rosemary bush, golden marjoram, coloured sages and various bush thymes, some plain, some variegated. They all taste good, whether penny plain or twopence coloured. *Artemisia dracunculus*, the true French tarragon, is here. What a difference between this and the other, almost unscented, plant that one sometimes meets in gardens, and also finds being sold in herb bunches. When dried the true form retains its strongly pungent scent, invaluable for chicken or fish stocks.

The lemon balm, *Melissa officinalis* 'Aurea' likes a little cool and shade, so it is tucked on the shady side of a lavender bush. I have two forms now of this *Melissa*; my original one has vivid marginal variegation till it sends up its dreary little flower heads, when the whole thing looks drab, and needs to be cut down. The other one has totally gold leaves, which it keeps throughout the growing season, a lovely thing. But like many gold-leafed plants, including marjoram, *Origanum vulgare* 'Aureum', it needs a little shelter from the hottest glare of the sun which is inclined to scorch these delicate leaves.

Garlic I grow elsewhere, individual cloves lined out in early October, in well-enriched soil. Chives, too, need better soil, as does edible sorrel, *Rumex acetosa*; I grow a delicate French form with large spinach-like leaves. These we also grow in rows, well fed.

A large *Spartium junceum* dominates my herb garden, with euphorbias and fennel adding to the scene, all part of my 'Mediterranean' garden.

Other useful cover plants include three different forms of *Alyssum saxatile*, the invaluable *Stachys byzantina* (*S. olympica*) 'Silver Carpet' and perhaps the most lovely of silver plants, *Senecio cineraria* 'White Diamond'.

I planted a Judas tree (*Cercis siliquastrum*) many years ago, thinking how suitable it would be here, but it has never thrived. I suppose the soil really is too poor. I must try it again. There are several fine examples of this tree in the neighbourhood.

Artemisias of all kinds make clouds of silvery foliage among the bitter greens of *Cistus* and *Iberis* (Candytuft). The largest, *Artemisia arborescens*, fills a great space where nothing else would thrive. It might be devastated by a prolonged hard frost, but the various cistus and *Phlomis fruticosa*, grown so starved, have never been affected.

Many species bulbs have prospered in this warm soil. I have already mentioned fritillaries. Added to these are several iris, including *Iris histrioides*, *I. reticulata*, *I. magnifica* and *I. korolkowi*. *Iris pumila* makes early colour too with *I.* 'Blue Pet' among the many colour forms, and best of all *Iris* 'Green Spot', whose firm petals are marked with bruises, shaded green on white.

Iris pallida 'Variegata' is probably one of the loveliest foliage plants we grow (Pl. 3). Completely hardy, growing anywhere the ordinary summer flowering iris will tolerate, it makes handsome fans of smooth bluish leaves, vividly striped. There are two forms, one banded with silvery-white, the other with cream and gold. Well grown they provide a focal point throughout the summer until the frosts, when they die down; they are not evergreen.

Species tulips, various forms of grape hyacinths, nerines, galtonias and sternbergias all come and go, their brilliant colours set off by the scale and tone of planting around them. While I have had to remove troublesome alliums planted inadvertently, those that remain are an important part of the design, adding as nothing else can elegance and mathematical beauty. This applies especially to *Allium cristophii*. This allium sends up a short stem, not more than 18 in./460 mm which carries a perfect globe of glistening stars, all radiating from a central point.

Allium aflatunense and *A. rosenbachianum* stand on tall slender stems, their lilac heads poised above the mounds of grey beneath them. Among the most striking alliums, whether fresh or as dried heads for winter decorations, is *Nectaroscordum siculum* (*Allium siculum*). On a thick smooth stem 3 ft/1 m tall a pointed papery case splits open to release waxen bells curiously tinted greenish-blue with a maroon central stripe. *N. s.* subsp. *bulgaricum* (*Allium bulgaricum*) is very similar, without the maroon stripe, its greenish bells faintly tinged with cream and apricot.

Among the small alliums, *A. flavum*, *A. carinatum* subsp. *pulchellum* (*A. pulchellum*), *A. senescens* and *A. tuberosum* add their individual themes from spring to autumn. I should not forget to commend for its decorative effect, as well as the good use we may make of it in the kitchen, that splendid large flowered form of chives, *Allium schoenoprasum* 'Forescate'.

It would be untrue if I gave the impression that all the plants I have described have never shown signs of distress. A few have, in very prolonged droughts. In some cases leaf rosettes have reduced themselves to the innermost hearts, and leaves themselves have shrunk to half their normal size in an effort to preserve the plant. But very little has died, and nothing has been watered, except at the time of planting.

To help reduce transpiration and tidy up any drainage, I prune many grey-leafed plants and shrubs in July. Pruning is necessary in any case to keep the plants sturdy and dense with healthy foliage. If they are left several years they grow leggy and fall apart from the centre, letting weeds grow up in the gaps. *Ballota, Santolina,* the helichrysums and Blue Rue can all be reduced by half in July. They quickly break new shoots from below, remaking firm mounds, with plenty of time ahead of them to toughen up for the winter. If you miss this opportunity then the time for a good trim is in late March or early April, after the worst of the winter weather. On heavier soils, provided there is adequate drainage, grey plants rarely show distress in dry weather. The problem there may be winter wet. Every effort must be made to ensure that water drains away quickly, and does not lie in puddles on the surface. Plenty of humus to encourage the worm population, plus grit both on the surface as well as mixed into the soil, will help these plants to overwinter in heavy soils where they will reward you by their ability to survive whatever the summer may bring.

Pot Gardens

Finally, to set off my 'Mediterranean' garden I make an effort to keep a few plants which are not hardy protected during the winter. These plants are sheltered, when space can be found, either in a small corner of a greenhouse which is kept just above freezing, or tucked up with straw wrapped round the pots and put in an unheated plastic tunnel. Only the toughest survive this. So far these have included the big agaves, both green and variegated, which look so splendid in large containers.

Pots of geraniums can take all summer to look generous. By tucking in a plant or two of *Helichrysum petiolare* (*H. petiolatum*) you can have a flamboyant display in no time at all, as this lovely foliage plant grows with great speed, not forsaking elegance, so that by August your tubs will be hidden beneath its silvered stems through which will thread themselves your ivy-leafed geraniums. There is a form with smaller leaves, called *H. p.* 'Microphyllum', which might suit some situations or containers better.

I have besides these many succulents and cacti (for the most part their names are unknown to me) of all shapes and sizes, some making tall columnar pillars wreathed in silky hair, others succulent rosettes the size of a wine tray. Of subtle colours and varied textures – some may be smooth as marble, in tones of blue, bronze, green or grey; others, like the prickly pear, are armed with wicked prickles which, if you approach them without thought, you may find embedded in inexplicable places for days afterwards. Some time early in June they all emerge from hibernation, and I enjoy myself creating groups in strategic places on the paved areas. They are in all kinds of pots, some raised on bricks, creating height and breadth to the group, with perhaps the variegated or gold-leafed form of *Helichrysum petiolare* (*H. petiolatum*) wreathing its way around to unite them, and the odd geranium to add a little dash of colour; they remind me of many little pot gardens I have seen, both in France and Spain.

10

Alphabetical List of Plants

This is not intended to be a comprehensive list of all garden-worthy plants that could be termed 'drought resistant', but a selection of those I have personally been able to grow reasonably successfully in my own area of low rainfall and predominantly gravelly soil.

I have included only a few of the larger and more striking bulbous plants. The myriads of species *Crocus*, *Chionodoxa*, *Tulipa* and *Scilla* are but a few among many less familiar but no less desirable bulbs that utilize the spring moisture to flower prolifically and remake their bulbs before heat and drought burn up their foliage. This vast and fascinating subject has been presented comprehensively and infectiously by Brian Mathew in his book *Dwarf Bulbs*.

ACANTHUS. These are large-scale plants, valuable for adding a dramatic accent to a group. They will grow in sun or shade, but are not suitable under dripping trees. They have long searching thong-like roots, difficult to eradicate if you change your mind later, but ideal in the right place, their large mounds of overlapping leaves keeping the ground weed-free. They flourish in any soil, provided it is well drained. They are best planted in spring. It might be necessary in cold districts to protect them with a mulch until established.

mollis latifolius is found from Spain to Greece and North Africa, in cool and rocky, or shaded hills, often with *Arum italicum* and *Vinca major*. These three look well together in the garden, while a shady corner protects the large soft foliage, which is inclined to wilt in full sun. Deeply cut, glossy green, the beautiful leaves are a feature all the year round except in very severe winters. Most imposing are the flower stems, more than 5 ft/1.5 m in prepared soil, they carry large and curious flowers. A white frilled lip emerges, from a stiff greenish-purple hood. The flower withers, but the hood remains to hold a cherry-like shining seed pod.

spinosus is found in Italy and Turkey, on dry hills and rocky places. The dark green leaves are much more finely cut, better adapted to heat than *A. mollis*. Planted in full sun it also flowers more freely, but with shorter stems (4–5 ft/1.2– 1.5 m). Both make a show for months in late summer and autumn. Both species dry well, either when the flowers are at their freshest, when you hang them upside down in a dry room, or when they are sere in late autumn. Then the stiff hoods of *A. spinosus* are edged with needle-like spines, extensions of veins, like very fine fretwork.

ACHILLEA. Familiar to us as yarrow, one of our roadside weeds, most are easily grown in well-drained soil. They can show distress in the severest drought, but usually recover. Most achilleas produce flat heads of little square-petalled daisies, often with buff-coloured centres. In those which have hard close-packed flower-heads the petals are almost absent.

ageratum 'W. B. Child' (*A. decolorans*), is of Swiss origin. With its finely cut green leaves it prefers a fairly cool site. Not invasive, it makes tidy clumps. The chalk-white flowers on rather lax stems have noticeable petals, making an open lacy head, attractive when picked. Midsummer. (18 in./ 460 mm.)

filipendulina (*A. eupatorium*) from the Caucasus, probably in dry brush woods with *Dictamnus, Lathyrus rotundifolius* and *Anchusa azurea (italica)*. *A. filipendulina* 'Gold Plate' is well known with its tall stiff stems bearing large flat heads of tiny yellow flowers. Picked at the peak of freshness they dry well, retaining colour. Summer. (3 ft/1 m.)

millefolium 'Lilac Beauty' is a very lovely form of our common yarrow. Making creeping mounds of fine feathery green leaves it sends up large heads of soft lilac flowers in midsummer and again in autumn when this colour is valued. (2 ft/600 mm.)

'**Moonshine**' is a splendid hybrid introduced by Alan Bloom. Makes large mounds of soft silvery feathery foliage above which graceful branching stems carry flat heads of light yellow flowers for weeks. Good with the shrubby salvias. Midsummer. (2 ft/600 mm.)

'**Taygetea**' is sometimes preferred by those who find bright yellow too much. This *Achillea* appears two-toned. When fresh it is primrose-yellow, fading to cream as it matures. The grey foliage is not so attractive as *A*. 'Moonshine'. Both these achilleas dried when fresh produce a pale effect, sometimes more useful than the brighter yellow of *A. filipendulina* 'Gold Plate'. (18 in./460 mm.)

Apart from those larger border achilleas there are several dwarf types invaluable as edging or rock garden plants.

In recent years hybrids have been made introducing more colour forms.

ageratifolia from northern Greece makes low cushions of silver-grey rosettes with narrow leaves, saw-edged. In May the plant is buried beneath the profusion of white petalled flowers. Occasionally trimmed the pretty foliage makes a feature for the rest of the year. (4 in./100 mm.)

argentea makes a closer tuffet of narrow silvery leaves, again covering itself in early summer with flat heads of chalk-white 'daisies'. (6 in./150 mm.)

tomentosa is found all round the Mediterranean and further east, on dry slopes, rocky places and walls. It quickly spreads a carpet of woolly filigree foliage over the poorest soil. Flat heads of bright yellow flowers on 6 in./150 mm stalks make a gay show for weeks.

AETHIONEMA. Species are found on calcareous stone and rockfields at the crests of mountains in Armenia. Drought loving, they are suited in walls, crevices or well-drained limy soil.

grandiflorum is superbly better than Pulchellum Group if you can find it, with larger and deeper pink flowers. Midsummer. (8 in./200 mm.)

grandiflorum Pulchellum Group (*A. pulchellum*) makes wiry little bushes, smothered with clusters of light pink cress flowers among blue-grey foliage. One of the loveliest of rock garden plants. Midsummer. (8 in./200 mm.)

AGAPANTHUS. It is enough to know in this context that there are several perfectly hardy species of the lovely African Blue Lily which do well in gardens and do not need to be lifted in winter. They all like rich feeding and a warm site in full sun. A bucketful of peat or leaf mould tipped over the crowns before winter would probably be wise in very cold districts. Here the leaves collapse with the first frost, but old-established clumps are never damaged.

campanulatus forms clumps of strap-shaped leaves from which rise in August (most welcome) tall stems bearing round heads of tubular blue flowers. They make handsome seed heads, green or dried. (2–3 ft/600 mm–1 m.)

campanulatus 'Albus', the beautiful white form, also lasts well in water.

'Profusion' (*A. patens* 'Profusion') has light blue open-faced flowers, abundantly produced.

AJUGA reptans is our native woodland bugle, so tolerates fairly dry shade. But in light soil, albeit shady, it will show distress in severe drought. Plenty of humus will help. In heavier soil it thrives, sometimes too well, but where there is room the coloured forms make attractive ground cover. As with the vincas it does help if you can mulch the first year to spare weeding between the runners which quickly fill in. Two problems can beset ajugas, ruining the effect of their shining leaf rosettes: aphis and mildew, often both together, cause the leaves to curl and look grey. A mixed spray will deal with both, when you must wait a short while for new foliage to replace the damaged leaves.

– 'Atropurpurea' can vary in intensity, but the form with darkest purple shining leaves makes a good companion for *A. r.* 'Burgundy Glow'. (4 in./100 mm.)

– 'Burgundy Glow' is the most colourful form, its fresh leaves suffused rose and magenta, edged with cream. 3 in./ 80 mm spikes of blue flowers in early summer make vivid contrast.

– 'Multicolor' shows its best colour in autumn when it resembles tortoiseshell with its purplish-brown leaves speckled and mottled with pink and cream. (4 in./100 mm.)

– 'Variegata' will do well in deeper shade where its mats of pale green and white leaves can enliven a dim patch. (2 in./ 50 mm.)

ALCHEMILLA. The alchemillas tend to be mountain plants, found in cool, rich soil in mountain meadow grassland. They have a curious habit of reproduction. They have no fertilizing male sex cells; neither do they reproduce from the eggs of the female part of the flower, but from an ordinary cell of the flower – you could call it a kind of 'cutting'. There are thousands of minute variations in these plants, but for gardening there are two outstanding species.

conjuncta is a relative of *A. alpina* found wild in a few places in Scotland, as well as France and Switzerland. The leaves are much smaller than those of *A. mollis*, neither are they entire, but deeply cut, to the base in *A. alpina*, only partially so with *A. conjuncta*. Dark green above, the backs are lined with gleaming silk which forms a shining rim on the top side. This exquisite leaf is much used by creators of dried flower pictures. The flower is not particularly interesting. It will grow anywhere, in sun or shade. (4 in./100 mm.)

mollis, makes a deep-rooting woody-based clump from which in spring velvet-soft young leaves open into circular pleated capes, edged with finest curving hooks. The early riser will see, on a still warm morning, gleaming drops like quick-silver held around the borders of the leaves. In midsummer long foaming sprays of tiny lime-green starry flowers are flung around in great profusion. This plant will grow in sun in good soil, but looks better in part shade among trees and shrubs where it will stand drought reasonably well. Its strange mode of reproduction does not prevent it, in some people's eyes, from being all too prolific, but when there is room nothing is more lovely than a billowing sea of this loveliest of all colours, luminous green. (18 in./460 mm.)

ALLIUM. The ornamental onions carry the bulb season on from spring to late autumn, with an amazing variety of shapes and sizes. They make very apt appearances, rising up above surrounding cushion plants, or making low drifts of colour long after crocus and tulips have vanished. Like the vegetable onion they prefer good living. They will grow in very poor soil, but a rich diet of well-rotted muck or compost produces their best efforts.

Their only fault, not applicable to more restrained members of this lovable family, is a tendency to over-produce themselves. Some, like *Allium roseum* bewitch you with a meadow of pale pink heads, but not only do they shower their seeds into everything around them, they also make bulbils in their flower head, while underground the mother bulb seems to proliferate into millions of bulblets. These, and the like, I have learnt to avoid. But the following I value.

aflatunense comes from northern China, probably from the rich loess region. Tall stems (3–4 ft/1 m+) carry heads the size of small oranges, packed with deep lilac flowers in May. The straw-coloured seed heads continue to lift the eye above the mounds of *Santolina* and Blue Rue beneath them.

atropurpureum. 2 ft/600 mm stems carry an upturned cluster of blackish-purple flowers, wonderful among silver filigree foliage in June.

bulgaricum, see *Nectaroscordum siculum* subsp. *bulgaricum*.

carinatum subsp. pulchellum is another seeder, pretty and harmless in cracks in paving. In the dead season of July and August among fine bluish foliage it sends up quantities of slender stems (15 in./380 mm) from which dangle myriads of dusty lilac bells, lovely among the whitened greys. They are found from the Mediterranean to the Caucasus.

– f. **album** is a lovely white form. Each hold their flowers in tall pointed cases before splitting open.

cernuum comes from the Great Plains and the foothills of the Rockies. Smaller, about 18 in./460 mm, it is an elegant little flower with its nodding heads of deep amethyst, lovely massed beneath old-fashioned roses with purple-leafed sage.

cristophii (*A. albopilosum*) is found in the Kopet Dagh mountains on the borders of northern Iran, probably in mountain steppe. It is a marvellous design of strength and delicacy. A shortish stem (18 in./460 mm) carries an immense head of metallic lilac stars in which the petals touch tip to tip, forming a huge airy globe almost as large as a football. It dries in perfect shape, the delicate spoke-like stems which support the bleached head remaining purple.

flavum is distinguished by its tight little clumps of almost blue foliage set off by heads of small citron-yellow bells. It grows around the Mediterranean in arid places, preferring calcareous rock. (9 in./230 mm.) Flowers in early summer.

karataviense is found on the West Tien Shan ranges of central Asia in mountain steppes. It is the combination of flower and foliage that commands attention in this allium. In early spring the leaves emerge tightly rolled, showing maroon edges. They open broad and curving, a dark pewter green that sets off the pale beigy-pink head that sits large as a tennis ball clasped between them. The leaves gone, the interest is maintained as the fleshy seed capsules gradually dry, and open into translucent 'wooden' petals. (6 in./150 mm.) (See Pl. 10.)

moly, wild in Spain on limestone rubble, has clusters of upturned yellow flowers on 12 in./300 mm stems, fine for naturalizing and not a nuisance.

neapolitanum, found around the Mediterranean in fields and olive groves, is valued as a cut flower. Its slender stems carry dainty heads of pure white flowers. It is a spreader, enchanting where it can do no harm. Early summer, height 2 ft/600 mm.

oreophilum, from sub-alpine meadows in the eastern Caucasus, is fine for rock gardens. It has small heads of comparatively large deep rose-pink flowers, which dry into pale papery seed heads. Midsummer. (4 in./100 mm.)

The Dry Sunny Garden   1. One of the main feature plants of the dry, sunny garden, *Euphorbia characias* subsp. *wulfenii* has huge cylindrical heads of luminous yellow-green, surmounting stiff stems of sea-green foliage

Above
2. The west-facing entrance border to White Barn House after three years' planting

Left
3. *Iris pallida* 'Variegata'. There are two forms of this striking plant: one has soft grey-green leaves striped with gold, the other with ivory

Right
4. *Acanthus spinosus,* stately in flower and handsome in foliage

Below
5. The bright yellow daisy-like flowers of *Eriophyllum lanatum* smother its low mounds of soft woolly foliage, whitened by drought

The Dry Sunny Garden 8. West-facing steps at White Barn House decorated by *Parahebe catarractae* with a large potted *Agave* set out for the summer. A hardy *Yucca* could be substituted

Above
9. *Genista hispanica,* helianthemums, *Artemisia* and
Ballota fill part of the island
bed approaching White Barn
House

Left
10. *Allium karataviense,* ideal
for placing on the front edge of
a hot sunny border

Right
11. The hardy *Agapanthus campanulatus* always gives a handsome display of blue in late summer. There is also a white form

Below
12. *Senecio cinerea* 'White Diamond' is the hardiest and the whitest of the varieties of this species

13. *Yucca filamentosa* 'Concava Variegata', showing its fascinating filaments peeling from the edges of its leaves

14. Crumpled tissue-paper petals of *Cistus × purpureus*

The Dry Shady Garden

15. Part of the east-facing entrance border at White Barn House, with a glimpse of the sunny west-facing border in the distance

16. In autumn the hardy *Cyclamen neapolitanum* produces endless variations of marbled green and silver leaves with dainty flowers in pink or white

17. The large handsome leaves of *Hosta fortunei* var. *albopicta* rest the eye among more fussy foliage

18. From the New Year until early summer the large clusters of pale apple-green flowers of *Helleborus argutifolius* (*H. corsicus*) illumine shaded borders

Right
19. *Valeriana phu* 'Aurea' has light yellow leaves, bright as daffodils in spring, maturing to green by midsummer

Below
20. When the airy sprays of forget-me-not-like flowers have faded, the heart-shaped leaves of *Brunnera macrophylla* will grow larger to form an imposing, weed-smothering mound

Left
21. *Lamium maculatum* weaves among *Phlox stolonifera,* backed by *Iris foetidissima* var. *citrina*

Below
22. Dry shade under an old oak completely carpeted with *Bergenia cordifolia* and *Vinca minor,* highlighted with *Helleborus argutifolius* (*H. corsicus*) and *Digitalis*

The Dry Shady Garden

23. The small north-facing courtyard at White Barn House

24. *Milium effusum* 'Aureum', whose soft yellow leaves provide contrast of form under trees

Left
25. *Epimedium × youngianum* 'Niveum' with small white columbine-like flowers floating over heart-shaped leaves

Below
26. *Hosta fortunei albopicta,* whose beautiful variegated leaves light up shady places in early summer

27. *Euphorbia amygdaloides robbiae* (*E. robbiae*) with dark evergreen rosettes of leaves, topped by loose heads of yellow-green flowers. *Liriope muscari*, also evergreen, can be seen in the background

28. *Tellima grandiflora* Rubra Group (*T.g.* 'Purpurea') makes soft, rounded clumps of leaves tinted bronze and carmine in winter

29. *Alchemilla mollis* and *Hosta sieboldiana* make elegant partners for a north-facing entrance border

schoenoprasum, known to us as chives, is found in damp rocky pastures throughout the cooler parts of the northern hemisphere from Europe to Japan. The best form is *A. s.* 'Forescate' which is much more robust than the commonly grown chives, with plenty of bright green foliage for the kitchen and masses of pinky-mauve flowers like large thrift blossoms. It does not do well in the driest parts of the garden. (6 in./150 mm.)

senescens (*A. montanum*) makes flat vigorous clumps of twisting grey-green leaves. The cool lilac heads on 6 in./ 150 mm stems are welcome in late summer.

sphaerocephalon is found in dry places from Germany to Persia. Its small bulbs divide freely so it is not difficult to have a mass of slender leafless stems (18 in./460 mm) topped with small egg-shaped heads packed with wine-purple flowers; most effective in the grey garden in late summer.

tuberosum, from India to China, carries the season well into autumn being the last allium to flower. In September and October its white green-eyed flowers on 18 in./460 mm stalks look surprisingly fresh.

ALSTROEMERIA, the Peruvian Lily, comes from Chile.

aurea (*A. aurantiaca*) is easily grown in any soil, in sun or part shade. It makes dense clumps of fleshy running roots which throw up many stems set with narrow green leaves topped with large heads of small lily-shaped orange flowers. Summer. (3 ft/1 m.)

ligtu hybrids in shades of rose and salmon pink, with occasionally a cream one, all have interesting throat markings. They can be awkward to establish, so are best planted in a sunny well-drained position using young container-grown plants so that the thick, white wax-like roots are not damaged. Summer. (3 ft/1 m.)

Both these alstroemerias spread freely when pleased, taking up a lot of room. They make handsome seed pods which need to be picked before the seeds are exploded into surrounding plants.

ALYSSOIDES utriculata (*Vesicaria utriculata*) would probably not be considered as a garden plant; in fact, it has been known to have been cast out as Charlock. A little more patience would have been rewarded when the long sprays of mustard-like flowers were replaced with curving stems of round pea-sized seed pods, lovely for arrangements, green or dried. Summer. (12 in./300 mm.)

ALYSSUM montanum is such a pretty, dainty thing, its bright yellow flowers are most welcome on the rock garden. It is widely distributed in central and southern Europe, being found on dry sunny hills on both sand and limestone slopes. It forms a wiry little shrublet clothed with bluish-grey small narrow leaves, while every tip carries a thimble-sized cluster of tiny yellow flowers in early spring. (6–8 in./150–200 mm.)

ANAPHALIS triplinervis is found in the west and central Himalayas at above 10,000 ft/3,000 m with such plants as *Delphinium brunonianum* and *Papaver nudicaule*. In spite of its small neat foliage being felted with white it dislikes the driest of soil, but will stand full sun. In late summer it carries clusters of pearly-white everlasting flowers on 12 in./ 300 mm stems.

ANEMONE fulgens, probably a hybrid between *A. hortensis* and *A. pavonina*, is found in Greece and Turkey, in open places in deserted fields and olive groves, often in sandy soil. It has intensely scarlet flowers with navy-blue centres, wonderful contrast with lime-green *Euphorbia polychroma*. (9 in./230 mm.) *A. pavonina* is similar, but has soft shades of cream, pink, mauve and plum red.

blanda is found in mountain woods from the eastern

Mediterranean through Turkey to the Caucasus. Spring flowering, its large many-petalled flowers come in shades of blue, over purplish-green fine-cut leaves. There are also pink and white forms. (4 in./100 mm.)

nemorosa is our own wildwood anemone. There are several lovely forms, all of which will grow in dry soil among shrubs if helped with leaf mould. Probably the best are *A. nemorosa* 'Vestal' (6 in./150 mm), which has tightly double white flowers, and *A. n.* 'Robinsoniana' (7 in./180 mm), with large flowers of soft lavender-blue filled with gold stamens.

sylvestris is a lovely thing in dry shade, running easily through light soil. Its quite large nodding white flowers are a delight among species daffodils, or *Hepatica nobilis*. Its clumps of seed, atop each stem like balls of creamy cotton wool, are attractive too. (8 in./200 mm.)

ANTENNARIA makes flat-spreading mats of silver-grey rosettes, useful as edgings on rock gardens, in sinks or paving cracks.

dioica var. rosea has heads of small ruby-red buds opening into pink chaffy flowers on slender 5 in./130 mm stems.

parvifolia (*A. aprica*) has pretty foliage to trail over the edge of a trough, palest pink flowers in spring on 5 in./130 mm stems.

ANTHEMIS punctata subsp. cupaniana is invaluable for new dry sunny gardens. It makes a loose mound of finely cut silvery-grey foliage covered in May and June with large white daisies. In winter the leaves are green. (18 in./460 mm.)

marshalliana (*A. rudolphiana*) makes neat clumps of silver filigree leaves, enhanced with smallish flowers of bright orange-gold. Not a spreader, it comes from rockfields and alpine turf mats in the Caucasus. (6 in./150 mm.)

ARABIS alpina, found on cliffs and rocky places in south-eastern Europe, Caucasus and Iran.

– 'Flore Pleno' makes wide-spreading mats of greyish-green rosettes. The 9 in./230 mm stems of double white flowers look like tiny double stocks. Attractive with the old double wallflower, *Erysimum* (*Cheiranthus*) *cheiri* 'Harpur Crewe', both flowering in May.

– 'Variegata' has leaf rosettes edged creamy yellow, and single flowers. (10 in./250 mm.)

ferdinandii-coburgii is found in Macedonia. The variegated form makes a fine feature plant. Tiny rosettes of shining 1 in./25 mm leaves splashed with more white than green, slowly spread out a flat carpet over gritty soil. 4 in./100 mm stems of single white flowers would not be missed.

ARMERIA. There are thirty-six species in Spain and Portugal. The thrifts make tight mounds of grassy leaves, preferring light sandy soils. Valuable ground cover, either as edgings or for planting between rocks.

alliacea (*A. plantaginea*). The garden strains, when grown from seed, vary considerably in form, indicating possible hybridity. Makes large tussocks of grassy foliage, sometimes very narrow, sometimes broader. The tall flower stems (15 in./380 mm) carry large knobby heads of pale pink to deep rose-coloured flowers. Foliage is sometimes burnished red in winter. Summer.

corsica (of gardens) makes low neat tuffets with small brick-pink heads on 3 in./80 mm stems in summer.

maritima, universal on seashores and tops of some mountains. Makes ideal ground cover. The white flowered form (*A. m.* 'Alba' is most effective. Summer. (6 in./150 mm.)

ARTEMISIA. A huge family of mostly aromatic plants, with beautiful ferny silvered foliage, varying in form from trailing mats to woody sub-shrubs. They are all splendidly adapted to stand drought. In winter they tend to look sad and bedraggled, but provided they have really good drainage, topped with plenty of grit for the crawling types, they are reasonably hardy.

absinthium (Wormwood or Absinth), is found on waste, rubble and rocky places in the eastern Mediterranean. The best form is 'Lambrook Silver', introduced by Mrs Fish. It is a superb foliage plant. Making a woody base, it throws out long much-divided leaves of silvery grey, overtopped with cascades of tiny pale mimosa-like flowers. After cutting back the flower shoots more leaves appear, stronger and finer. They shrivel under winter frosts, but the tip shoots remain alive and new buds break with warm spring weather. The only pity is that this plant is so reluctant to be propagated. (18 in./460 mm.)

alba 'Canescens' (*A. canescens*) (of gardens). Distinctive in form, this artemisia makes low bushes of upturned woody stems covered with finest filigree foliage, standing out in the autumn as whitest and laciest of all the greys when it sends up narrow spires, clothed in curling silver wisps bearing insignificant little yellow flowers. (18 in./ 460 mm.)

arborescens comes from the south-west European coasts, on stable dunes and maritime rocks. Hence, although perhaps the showiest of all silver plants, it needs a very warm site in perfectly drained soil. For those who can grow it, it quickly makes a large lacy bush (4 × 4 ft/1.2 × 1.2 m) covered with fine silky foliage.

dracunculus comes from Russia and Siberia. Growing in meadow steppe with *Filipendula vulgaris* (*hexapetala*) and *Anemone sylvestris*. Though not interesting to look at, with dull narrow green leaves, the strongly scented form called French tarragon is desirable, delicious cooked with fish or chicken, or lightly sprinkled over the first spring salad. Not very long lived in cold clay, it flourishes in warm light soils. (2 ft/600 mm.)

glacialis is a high mountain creeper from the south and central Alps, growing on exposed rocky slopes. Completely prostrate stems clothed in silvery-white thread-like foliage look well tumbling over a rock or wall. It will not stand wet cold, so on the flat must have sharp drainage and dressings of grit or gravel. Pretty among small bulbs. (1–2 in./ 25–50 mm.)

ludoviciana is found over a wide area from the prairies of Nebraska to the foothills of the Rockies. This invasive plant can be a pest among more choice herbaceous plants, but in rougher situations or in openings among shrubs it makes useful ground cover once established. Tall stems (4 ft/1.2 m) clothed with willow-shaped silvery-white leaves make a graceful accent. The small yellow flowers are insignificant, but if the flower head is hung upside down to dry in bud it makes a very good spire shape.

purshiana is very similar to *A. ludoviciana*, with shorter stems, but larger, whiter foliage (2 ft/600 mm.)

schmidtiana comes from northern Japan, both high on the mountains and from the seashore. It makes low hummocks of silky silver thread-like foliage, an interesting contrast among dwarf sedums. (4 in./100 mm.)

stelleriana comes from the sand dunes of northern Japan and Korea. Bold and handsome foliage, looking like chrysanthemum leaves cut out of white felt, it sprawls on lax stems to make a very effective carpet in front of a big border.

(8 in./200 mm high × 24 in./600 mm across.)

ASPHODELUS. Throughout southern Europe from Spain to Greece the elegant white asphodels can be seen, isolated, or in drifts on dry hillsides. From a cluster of fleshy, moisture-conserving roots they produce a huddle of long narrow leaves above which their flower stems proudly stand.

albus has smooth strong stems sparely branched, topped with spires of long narrow white buds held in brown calyces which open into starry white flowers with a soft brown vein down the centre of each petal. (3 ft/1 m.)

AURINIA saxatilis (*Alyssum saxatile*) the rock cress, grows wild in southern Europe and into Turkey, adapted to hang over rocky slopes and cliffs. The screaming bright yellow form is all too often seen with rose-pink tulips and mahogany wallflowers. With quieter companions, perhaps bordering a warm shrubbery or carpeting a rose bed, or ideally, cascading over a wall or large rock, it can be appreciated as a very beautiful plant.

– **'Citrina'**. I think I prefer this form which flings out coolest lemon sprays of tiny flowers.

– **'Dudley Nevill'** has flowers of faded apricot. Both this and 'Citrina' can make mounds of mealy grey leaves 3 ft/1 m across, about 10 in./250 mm high, flowering in spring.

– **'Flore Pleno'** makes a more compact plant with prim bunches of tightly double flowers, clear bright yellow and long lasting. (15 × 6 in./380 x 150 mm.)

BALLOTA. I have two species of this valuable genus. The first was labelled *B. pseudodictamnus*. It makes a woody base from which spring 2 ft/600 mm curving stems clothed in round leaves so that the tip forms a rosette, pretty as a flower, specially when a well-formed plant is covered with close-packed rosettes. In poor soil and full sun these are heavily felted white, of a smooth suede-like texture. The other I bought as *B. acetabulosa*, at first sight very similar, but in effect daintier, whiter, and less dense, each leaf appearing smaller and crinkled along the edges.

The flowers of both are minute scraps of mauve, scarcely noticeable, but they are carried in curious flat-faced green bobbles beneath every pair of leaves. With *B. acetabulosa* the bobbles are considerably larger and showier. If the leaves are removed when these curiosities are still fresh green, and the stem is placed for two or three days in a mixture of glycerine and water, and then hung up to dry, the bobbles will turn to soft beige, the texture of velvet, and will remain so until you tire of them.

Investigation has produced these facts: *B. acetabulosa* is found wild in Greece, on dry rocky ground up to 3,000 ft/ 900 m. *B. pseudodictamnus* is found in Crete, has smaller leaves!! Do I have my names misplaced?

BERGENIA. I have already sung the praises of this family on page 47.

cordifolia has large rounded leaves with markedly crinkled edges. The large showy flower heads are soft pink on 18 in./ 460 mm stalks. This form remains green in winter, and grows wild in Siberia.

– **'Purpurea'** has large rounded wavy leaves. Odd ones die off slowly in summer and autumn, gradually turning brilliant red or yellow. In winter, especially in poor soil, they become burnished purplish-red. The flower stalks, thick as rhubarb, and the same cherry colour, support dangling sprays of vivid magenta flowers, a fine contrast with the lime greens of euphorbias or *Helleborus argutifolius* (*H. corsicus*). (18 × 24 in./460 × 600 mm.)

crassifolia is found in the Altai mountains, in open spaces in the fir forests at 7–8,000 ft/2–2,400 m. Smaller than

B. cordifolia the leaves are smooth and spoon-shaped, held upright in rosettes, so that the backs, richly carmine, contrasting with the polished green and bronze fronts, can be seen. In summer the leaves are fresh green. The pink flowers emerge in May, making a fine display on 15 in./380 mm stems.

There are many more species, forms and hybrids of bergenias.

BRACHYGLOTTIS compacta (*Senecio compactus*) is a dense little shrub from New Zealand, similar to *B. greyi*, and *B.* (Dunedin Group) 'Sunshine', very useful where the latter would be clumsy. It has small oval leaves, grey above, white beneath, the edges conspicuously crimped showing the white lining. (12 in./300 mm.)

'Sunshine'. I refer to a shrub which is ubiquitous, long known as either *Senecio greyi* or *S. laxifolius* (two rather rare New Zealand shrubs). Both these plants are uncommon in English gardens. The plant we commonly grow originated as a hybrid in the Dunedin Botanic Gardens, New Zealand, and has now been given the new name *Brachyglottis* (Dunedin Group) 'Sunshine'. Treated properly this shrub can furnish the garden elegantly all the year round. Too often it is never pruned, or if it is, it is just chopped about. No matter how neglected and gawky, if it is pruned hard back in spring, cutting out the old wood, and leaving a compact but spaced woody frame, it will completely reclothe itself with graceful wands of grey and white felted leaves. The following summer these will produce sprays of silvered buds opening into bright yellow daisies. If the stems are reduced in number after flowering and the remaining ones halved you will have started a programme which will keep it shapely throughout the year. (3 ft/1 m.)

BRUNNERA macrophylla (*Anchusa myosotidiflora*) is found in mountain forests on the Black Sea side of the Caucasus. In spring it sends up long sprays of tiny forget-me-not blue flowers which are followed by robust clumps of basal leaves, each huge and heart shaped.

macrophylla 'Langtrees' was given me by Dr Tony Rogerson, and named after his garden. It is handsomely marked with a distinctive border of metallic silver spots. (18 × 24 in./460 × 600 mm.)

Both of these plants need plenty of humus but will stand drought much better than *B. m.* 'Variegata' which will not.

CALAMINTHA grandiflora has pale green aromatic leaves making small clumpy plants, which cover themselves with small pink sage-like flowers. Sometimes I think they look a little spotty, but they keep up such a continual display, both of fresh foliage and flower, that I am forced to admire them, decorating the border edge, among *Sedum telephium* subsp. *maximum* (*S. maximum*) and *Euphorbia seguieriana niciciana*. They are found wild throughout central France, the Pyrenees and Corsica. (12 in./300 mm.)

nepeta subsp. nepeta (*C. nepetoides*) is found in the Alps, Cévennes and eastern Pyrenees, on rock debris. It makes wiry little bushlets, covered with small, dark, scented green leaves. In late summer it starts, and continues well into autumn, to produce clouds of tiny pale blue labiate flowers. Bees love it. It needs to be massed on the edge of a border, to see, smell and hear it. (12 in./300 mm.)

CARLINA acaulis is a mountain thistle found throughout central Europe, the Vosges, Jura, Alps and Pyrenees, on poor rocky soil where grass is thin. It prefers a chalky soil but does well enough in lighter soil. It makes a smallish rosette of prickly leaves in the middle of which sits the flower on a short stalk. When newly opened the centre is full of typical blue fuzz, but it is as a dried flower that this plant has great appeal. The centre now is a pale cream disc surrounded by many glistening silver strap-shaped petals, so that it looks like a brilliant daisy, sometimes 4 in./100 mm across. Behind the 'petals' springs a ruff of wickedly prickly jagged leaves, brown and twisted. It is like nothing else in the centre of a dried arrangement.

CARYOPTERIS x **clandonensis** is a small dainty shrub, best grown in full sun and well-drained soil, excellent on chalky soils. It adds colour to the grey garden in late summer with its clusters of soft blue fluffy flowers followed by attractive greenish-blue seed heads. (2 ft/600 mm.)

CATANANCHE caerulea grows in dry places, in the southern *garigues*. A clump of hairy strap-shaped leaves send up thin stalks topped with translucent paper buds which open into square-edged blue-petalled 'cornflowers' in mid to late summer. (18 in./460 mm.)

CENTAUREA. This is the family of Hard Heads, Cornflower or Knapweeds, certain of which we recognize as roadside plants, especially on chalky soils. Their characteristic feature is their hard knobby buds, often covered with gauzy scales. On opening they often have fluffy thistle-like centres, surrounded by narrow tubular flowers with frilly edges, producing an airy sun-ray effect, as in *C. nana* 'Rosea', or *C. pulcherrima*. Others, like *C. macrocephala*, dispense with the showy surrounding florets, but are no less effective. Many have interesting foliage, cut leafed, woolly or felted, all helping to conserve moisture.

macrocephala is a large strong plant for the backs of large borders, or semi-wild places where there may be competition from tree or shrub roots. It makes great clumps of coarse long leaves which throw up stout stems topped with large brown glistening scaly buds. These open in midsummer to a mass of golden fluff, actually tightly packed fertile florets. Cut before the flowers burst open and hung upside down, the brown crackly knobs dry well. These plants deserve good soil preparation when they will stand 5 ft/1.5 m tall. They come from sub-alpine meadows in the Caucasus, where they are found with *Geranium* x *magnificum* among others.

nana 'Rosea' is a charming little dwarf. It creeps through light soil, making little cut-leafed rosettes of silvery whiteness above which quite large pink 'cornflowers' float on short stalks. (3 in./80 mm.)

pulcherrima is another Caucasian Cornflower, growing with the familiar *Papaver orientale*, the big scarlet Oriental Poppy. This is a choice plant, not too large for the edge of a border where you can appreciate the complete effect of silvery fine-cut leaves, and slender branching stems carrying large cyclamen-pink flowers. *C. hypoleuca* 'John Coutts' is very similar, perhaps a little more robust, not quite such delicate charm, with less silvery foliage and deeper pink flowers.

ruthenica chooses to be very different from any I have described. A much more delicate-looking plant, it has beautiful dark green finely cut leaves, with very slender branching stems, about 4 ft/1.2 m tall with heads of pale lemon-yellow flowers, most uncommon. It comes from eastern Europe, in the grassy steppe lands of Russia where it grows with *Limonium latifolium* and *Gypsophila paniculata*. Mid to late summer.

CENTRANTHUS ruber is the unfamiliar name of that old-fashioned plant, Valerian. It always seems strange that such a lush-looking plant (it has fleshy green leaves and large branching heads of minute rose-pink or red flowers in mid-summer on $2\frac{1}{2}$ ft/760 mm stems) can do so well on brick dust or rubble. In nature it grows on rocks, around the Mediterranean and Atlantic coasts.

CERASTIUM tomentosum var. columnae is found wild in southern and eastern Europe, including Italy and Sicily. Less rumbustious than the well-known 'Snow in Summer' which usefully covers many a dry sunny bank where little else would survive, this plant is irresistible. During hot sunny weather its low mounds, covered with narrow leaves are of an incredible whiteness. The saucer-shaped white flowers, which come in early summer, are good too. It does spread, but not objectionably. (3 in./80 mm.)

CHAMAMAELUM nobilis (*Anthemis nobilis*) 'Flore Pleno' is the double-flowered form of lawn chamomile. The rich green flat carpet of ferny foliage is starred for weeks with little pom-pom blossoms, green centred. (7 in./180 mm.)

CHIASTOPHYLLUM oppositifolium (*Cotyledon simplicifolia*) can be useful on the rock garden, or grouped to make a low edging to a border, not necessarily sunny. It makes creeping rosettes of succulent round green leaves touched with bronze. In midsummer it has small yellow flowers like threads of beads, drooping from 6 in./150 mm red stems. This plant grows wild on calcareous rocks on the Black Sea side of the Caucasus mountains, up to 7,000 ft/2,100 m.

CISTUS. The Rock Roses are natives of western and southern European countries, well adapted to stand drought but inclined to be tender in cold districts with heavy soil. They grow much tougher and hardier in poor sandy soils. I lost none here during the 1962 winter on my poorest gravel soil, whereas those elsewhere in the garden, which had grown much more luxuriantly, were cut to the ground. Although their flowers last only one day they are produced so abundantly, of such butterfly charm scattered over the bushes in drab July, the garden would be bereft without them. Even more I value their leaves, evergreen or grey, creating the backbone of my warm dry borders all the year round. Here are some that I grow.

albidus is the best of the felt-foliaged cistus, very pale, almost white in hot summer with pale lilac flowers. But it is one of the least hardy, needing a very sheltered site. It is found in the garigue, the rockfields of the western Mediterranean, preferring calcareous soils. (3 ft/1 m.)

hybridus (*C.* × *corbariensis*) This hybrid seems very hardy, making compact bushes, eventually about 4 ft/1.2 m tall, with close crinkly foliage which takes on attractive bronze tints in winter. The flowers have conspicuous red buds, opening to small white cups with yellow centres.

ladanifer is hardier, and one of the best, eventually making a large shrub 6 ft/1.8 m high and across, its tacky, dark green narrow leaves forming good background relief for all the greys and silvers around. The large white flowers, big as the palm of your hand, open crumpled and creased till the warmth of the sun irons them smooth to show off the purple-black blotch at the base of each.

× **pulverulentus** (*C. crispus*) is a dwarf shrub, about 2 ft/ 600 mm tall. It has sage-green leaves with crimply edges, and shocking magenta-pink flowers.

× **purpureus** has similar flowers, rich pink petals instead of white, equally large. The leaves are smaller of a dull sage green which sets off the brilliant display of blossom. Definitely needs shelter, but has thrived here on poorest gravel for many years. (4 ft/1.2 m.)

'**Silver Pink**' is very popular, and seems very hardy. It has narrow felted leaves, and very pale pink flowers with paler centres. (3 ft/1 m.)

× **skanbergii** I grow under the south wall. It makes a thin bush covered with narrow sage-like leaves, smothered in midsummer with small rose-pink cupped flowers. The poorer the soil the more crowded with blossoms it is, and the more likely it will survive a cold winter. (3 × 3 ft/1 × 1 m.)

COMMELINA tuberosa Coelestis Group (*C. coelestis*) is one of the joys of autumn. Intense blue three-petalled flowers fall from green hoods. It comes from Mexico, so needs a warm site. Looks superb with nerines under a wall backed with *Vitis vinifera* 'Purpurea'. (18 in./460 mm.)

CRAMBE cordifolia is the great Kale from the Caucasus. It is a plant for large gardens, for rough places, or as a feature in a very big border, preferably not too exposed to wind which smashes the immense flower head. It makes a mound of large crinkled green leaves, from which soar airy branches up to 8 ft/2.5 m, carrying a great cloud of small white 'cabbage' flowers. The effect on a hot day in mid June is breathtaking.

maritima (Sea Kale) is a native of our shores and the shingle beds of the European Atlantic. Known as a vegetable, more in books than practice I suspect, it is a treasure where there is room. As a vegetable it is delicious. The young shoots must be blanched under large pots or old buckets. Don't cut and throw away the crumpled peach-coloured leaves before you cook the delicate stems: chop them with chives and add a few tarragon leaves to make a unique spring salad. Decoratively there is no leaf more beautiful – huge, waving, sea-blue and waxen – and unaffected by drought. Why don't we plant it at the base of *Echinops*, *Onopordum* and perhaps *Eremurus*. Finally, it makes a handsome head of white flowers in June, about 2 ft/600 mm high.

CREPIS incana from south-eastern Europe is another exquisite plant, probably underestimated. Neat rosettes of greyish-green jagged leaves send up thin stiff branching stems making a bouquet of powder-pink dandelion flowers with deep rose centres. As a feature among mat plants it is unique in late summer. (18 in./460 mm.)

CROCOSMIA, montbretia. These South African bulbous plants add useful spire-like shapes to the autumn garden. All have blade-like leaves which, with their knobbly seed heads, make graceful shapes for the dried flower arranger. They will grow in any soil (unless it is very heavy and wet), appreciating some feeding if very light.

x crocosmiiflora is the common montbretia which, though inferior in flower to the many fine hybrids now available, is valued in some gardens for its graceful clumps of arching foliage which are totally weed resistant. ($2\frac{1}{2}$ ft/760 mm.)

masoniorum is superior in every way to the familiar montbretia it resembles. It has large upturned fiery flowers in shades of orange and scarlet. ($2\frac{1}{2}$ ft/760 mm.)

paniculata (*Curtonus paniculatus*). Its dark red flowers are rather small, but it is the stiff sword-like pleated leaves, up to 4 ft/1.2 m high which, when established, can make a very imposing clump, valuable contrast in a mixed border, or set on the edge of a shrubbery. Very lovely coppery shades in autumn; useful dried.

Alan Bloom has made splendid hybrids between *Crocosmia* and *Curtonus*.

CYNARA cardunculus (Cardoon). If the Sea Kale is outstanding as a horizontal decoration, the Cardoon is second to none as the supreme vertical foliage plant, hardy in dry gardens. Great arching leaves of silvery whiteness divide and redivide, combining a filigree effect with great architectural strength. As the stout flower stalks emerge, this combination is carried ever upwards (6 ft/2.8 m), culminating in large spikey buds which burst into luminous blue thistle-like heads. This plant differs ornamentally from the edible artichoke in that its leaves are whiter, more finely divided, and the flowers are smaller, never opening fully when dried, whereas the dried artichoke head opens out into a golden-hearted 'sun flower' when you have removed the blackened flower remains. The Cardoon is usually placed at the back of a sunny border, but I have a fine clump on the edge of a gravel drive where it forms a focal point, surrounded by *Thuja*, *Cytisus* and *Ferula* while *Ballota* and *Santolina* carry the eye down to *Euphorbia myrsinites* and *Helianthemum*.

Found wild in the garigue of the Mediterranean it is well adapted to stand drought. In very cold districts, on heavy soils, it might be advisable to put a little protection over the crowns, but they are no trouble once established.

DIANTHUS. I find the wild pinks and some of the old-fashioned single pinks do better on my sandy soil where they are long lasting and make tight clumps of foliage which do not fall apart.

carthusianorum grows in arid stony places in central and southern Europe. It is like a dainty 'Sweet William' on tall stems – it has several flowers of velvety red close set in an upturned head. (12 in./300 mm.)

deltoides is a native and is found throughout Europe and western Asia in dry pastures and open woods. Abundant little starry flowers of rich carmine red stand over close mats of dark green foliage. Self seeded into thyme mats or crevices in the rock garden it is enchanting. There is a white form with a pink eye, over pale green foliage. (8 in./200 mm.)

'Sops-in-Wine'. The plant I grow under this name has very neat blue-grey foliage with single wine-red velvety flowers with a white spot on each petal. (8 in./200 mm.)

'Waithman Beauty' is more delicately pencilled – the petal edges are more frilled. Sometimes called 'The Clock-face Pink'. (8 in./200 mm.)

DIASCIAS come from Basutoland. They like a warm sheltered spot where they quickly make loose mats of small round green leaves. They produce a succession of nemesia-like flowers, tiny twin-spurred hoods in shades of pink, mid to late summer.

– **'Ruby Field'** (*D. cordata* × *D. barberae*) is a hybrid completely hardy in well-drained soil and full sun. Standing a little taller, the rich salmon-pink flowers carry the colour later into October. (9 in./230 mm.)

Both these plants do better with the addition of a little well-wetted peat, in a warm site. Several others have been introduced.

DICTAMNUS, from eastern Europe and western Asia. Sometimes called 'Burning Bush', it is said that on warm, still days, when the seed pods are ripening, if a match is held near this plant it will ignite. I have never tried it, nor met anyone who has. But that it contains volatile oil I believe, for the whole plant is strongly perfumed with a rich citrus-like scent.

albus (*D. fraxinella albus*). Each plant sends up several straight stems, about 2 ft/600 mm tall, carrying dark green divided leaves. Above the leaves are slender spires of almost lily-like white flowers, with remarkably long curving stamens.

albus var. purpureus is identical, except that the flowers are soft mauve with darker veins. This plant makes an interesting feature above some of the smaller geraniums, like G. *renardii*, G. *sanguineum* var. *striatum* (var. *lancastriense*) or G. *himalayense* (G. *grandiflorum*).

DIERAMA pulcherrimum, the Wand Flower, or Angel's Fishing Rod, comes from South Africa, the East Cape Province, on mountain sides in rich moist soil, part shaded. I find it doing very well in my well-drained soil in full sun, provided that we have dug in plenty of humus. I think it could be killed here in heavy wet soils if deeply frozen. It is an elegant plant; the tall wiry rod emerges in midsummer from stiff grassy foliage, the tip weighted gracefully with large pink bells, which develop into bead-like clusters of seed. There are varying shades of cyclamen pink, from palest silvery pink to deep foxglove, and pure white. There is also a dwarf species, *D. dracomontanum* (*D. pumilum*), with foliage about 12 in./300 mm, flower stems a little taller.

DIGITALIS. Our own native foxglove, *Digitalis purpurea*, springs up immediately in disturbed soil on the edge of woodland, where there is always plenty of root competition. The white form is most effective in shadowy places. Two exquisite forms, creamy primrose and soft apricot pink, are sometimes found in seed catalogues.

ciliata I obtained from Harlow Car Gardens. It grows as tall as *D. lutea*, but has handsome large flowers of cool lemon. A useful perennial.

ferruginea has smooth narrow dark green leaves, makes large rosettes, with flower stems 3–4 ft/1 m+ bearing close-set rounded buds which open to small short trumpets of coppery yellow, veined brown. Good seed heads.

grandiflora (*D. ambigua*) is a splendid perennial from Greece and the southern Alps, with good sized flowers of soft yellow, and slightly hairy leaf rosettes. (2½ ft/760 mm.)

lutea makes a vigorous plant, sending up tall spikes set with small narrow pale yellow flowers. (4 ft/1 m+.)

DIPLARRHENA moraea is a member of the iris family from Tasmania and south Australia. Hardy in the south in well-drained, well-fed soil, it is a plant of unusual charm. Close-set fans of narrow dark evergreen leaves make a permanent feature, setting off 18 in./460 mm stems which bear remarkable flowers. Not large, each has three rounded white petals, with three little central standards, one yellow and two purple.

ECHINOPS, the Globe Thistles, are lovers of hot sun and poor soil. They make tall statuesque plants, clothed in shiny leathery leaves, with grey or white undersides, deeply cut with sharp spiny tips. Round drum-stick heads of hard blue flowers, sometimes white.

bannaticus (*E. ritro*) is the most familiar form seen in gardens, found wild in Europe, from Spain to Palestine, in dry rocky places. (4 ft/1.2 m.)
    There are several others with larger, whiter or more prickly foliage, with varying shades of blue or white flowers.

EPIMEDIUM. There are many species and varieties of these lovely woodland plants, all tolerating shade but not excessively dry conditions. All have dainty heart-shaped leaves on massed wiry stems, many marbled in bronzy-reds and green in spring. Sprays of tiny columbine-like flowers in shades of yellow, pink and white are obtainable, slowly making wide-spreading clumps. All appreciate plenty of humus, including peat.

x versicolor 'Sulphureum' I find the easiest in the poorest conditions. Beautiful marbled spring foliage, pale primrose-yellow flowers in March. If you have not cut off the bronze overwintered leaves in February you may well miss them. (12 in./300 mm.)

ERIOPHYLLUM lanatum comes from dry sunny hills in California. It makes vigorous spreading low cushions of blunt-cut foliage which becomes whiter and woollier the drier the conditions. Masses of bright yellow daisies on slender stems provide colourful contrast for weeks in mid-summer. Immensely useful for quick cover where its wandering roots will do no harm. (12 in./300 mm.)

ERODIUM. These are members of the geranium family, mostly dwarfs, suitable for sunny well-drained places, preferably calcareous, on rock gardens or troughs. They make attractive hummocks, many with fine ferny foliage, a few with little round crinkled leaves. Innumerable small flowers in pink, white and palest yellow embroider them for weeks in summer.

guttatum has soft ferny foliage with delicate pink, almost white flowers, each lower petal blotched with chocolate. (6 in./150 mm x 9 in./230 mm.)

x **hybridum 'Roseum'**, a hybrid of *E. reichardii* (*E. chamaedryoides*), has rosy-pink flowers, veined crimson. (1 in./25 mm x 6 in./150 mm.)

There are others.

ERYNGIUM. A large family known to us as Sea Holly after our own native which grows on sand dunes. Many other members are to be found in Europe and America, often on mountain slopes. They thrive in full sun, in light well-drained soil, whether it be lime or sand and gravel.

agavifolium from Argentina makes large striking rosettes of broad blade-like green leaves, each conspicuously serrated. The sturdy flower spike can be 5 ft/1.5 m with a closely branched head of thimble-sized flowers of a dull white, not beautiful in themselves, but the whole plant making an interesting form.

alpinum is one of the gems. It has heart-shaped light green leaves, slightly toothed, sending up a bluish stem carrying the largest lace-like ruff of exquisite metallic blue. It is not prickly – you can draw the head through your hand without suffering. Needs better, deeper soil than some, coming from rocky alpine meadows of the European Alps, preferring calcareous soil. ($2\frac{1}{2}$ ft/760 mm.)

bourgatii is found in Spain and the Pyrenees, among rubble, rock slides and pebbly pastures. It has beautiful foliage: the thistly, prickly grey-green rosettes are heavily veined, and white short stems carry silver-blue heads of flowers. (2 ft/600 mm.)

bromeliifolium, a doubtful name, possibly a form of *E. agavifolium,* but has survived and seeded here for many years. It makes a basal rosette of long, very narrow serrated leaves, sending up tall narrow branches of small greenish-white heads, very effective rising out of mounded plants. (5 ft/1.5 m.)

giganteum 'Miss Wilmott's Ghost' is a biennial – 2 ft/600 mm stems carry stout branches of large silvered cones surrounded by metallic silvery-green bracts. Needs to be planted where its freely produced seedlings will not be a nuisance. One of the loveliest things in the dry garden on dusty days in July.

maritimum, our own native, is among the best of these fascinating plants. It likes to loll about in hot gravelly or sandy soil, the whole plant being in shades of waxen grey and blue. (12 in/300 mm.)

× oliveranum is one of the darkest blues. It makes a thick clump of fresh green leaves which send up dark blue stems accentuating the blue of the flowers. (2½ ft/760 mm.)

planum makes airy branching heads of small blue flowers. Some forms are a poor dull blue, the best has strong blue flowers, almost dock-like leaves. (3 ft/900 mm.)

proteiflorum (sometimes labelled 'Delaroux') is outstanding. Comes from Mexico. Needs a warm site and well-prepared soil; it has long narrow leaves armed with widely spaced barbs. The central cone of fertile flowers is surrounded by long petal-like bracts, similarly armed, all of a satiny silvery whiteness. Autumn. (2½ ft/760 mm.)

tripartitum, probably another hybrid, possibly the best of the small-headed types. Wide branching stems are crowded with deep blue cones surrounded by blue spiny bracts. (2 ft/600 mm.)

variifolium makes a striking rosette of fan-shaped green leaves, not prickly, boldly marked with white veins. The flowers make a total contrast, small grey-blue cones enmeshed in aluminium spines and prickles. It is found high in the Atlas mountains in Morocco, on screes and rocks in the snow zone. (18 in./460 mm.)

ERYSIMUM (*Cheiranthus*). Wild forms of wallflower are found in Greece. They grow on rocks and cliffs, especially near the sea. If I had crumbly old walls I would let the sweet-scented wallflowers seed into the odd crevice where they would make hard woody specimens and live for years. As it is I grow two forms of wallflower, both with small but interesting flowers.

'Bowles' Mauve'. This plant makes a bold handsome bush of dark green foliage, topped with lengthening stems of rich mauve flowers for months. In fact it will not stop, and when I can bring myself to do it I like to shear off the remaining burden from the exhausted plant in July so that it can gather strength to produce a show for the autumn. It needs a sheltered place; sitting in the teeth of an icy wind it will shrivel and die. It makes a bush about $2\frac{1}{2}$ ft/760 mm high.

cheiri 'Harpur Crewe' is a very old plant. I like to think of it coming direct to us from Elizabethan times, preserved by love and care, as it can only be produced from cuttings. It makes spires of tiny golden double flowers, blooming with deep blue *Muscari latifolium* or double white *Arabis*. It will last several years, gradually becoming rather leggy, when it is time to start a few new ones, from cuttings, like our ancestors did.

EUPHORBIA. Native forms are known as Spurge or Milkweed because of the milky sap which spurts out when the stem is cut. This can blister delicate skins, so care needs to be taken. The family contains many forms, some of which have become great favourites, both in the garden and as cut flowers. (When cut, if they are stood for a few seconds in very hot water the milky sap will not seal the end.) From March to September it is possible to have, somewhere in the garden, the brilliant lime green peculiar to euphorbias which brings a freshness and vivacity not obtainable with any other plant. Three useful garden species, *E. sikkimensis*, *E. griffithii* and *E. palustris* will not flourish in poor dry conditions, so do not come into this book.

amygdaloides, our native Wood Spurge (also found in Europe and western Asia) can still be found in copses and sometimes roadside hedges. There is an attractive form whose tip leaves and flower buds are strong maroon-red in spring, very effective when the flower buds open yellowish-green, but fading as the leaf matures. Handsome when healthy, this plant is very susceptible to mildew, which has to be controlled by spraying. Needs to be grown in part shade. (2 ft/600 mm.)

– robbiae is named after Mrs Robb, an intrepid lady plant collector, known also for her bonnets. She found this plant growing in oak woods in the central Balkans with *Hypericum calycinum*, and preserved it in one of her hat boxes. It makes invaluable cover among shrubs, spreading through leaf mouldy soil (it would go wild in peat!) by means of underground runners, and sending up many dark green rosettes. From the centre of these leafless spires unfold flat lime-green flowers, gradually making a large head. These start in spring and remain into winter, sometimes becoming copper tinted by the autumn. Not all remain attractive – those dying off brown should be removed. (2 ft/600 mm.)

characias, including *wulfenii* (*veneta*). These two plants are separate forms, probably from the same ancestor. *E. characias* is the western Mediterranean form, its place being taken in the eastern Mediterranean by *E. characias* subsp. *wulfenii* (*veneta*). In gardens they are much interbred and it is not easy to be definite about naming them. However, *E. characias* when found fairly pure is a much tougher, more sinister-looking plant, with short narrow leaves, red stems and narrow cylindrical heads of dull green flowers with baleful black 'eyes'. *E. characias* subsp. *wulfenii* makes a much more generous plant (*E. c.* subsp. *wulfenii* var. *sibthorpii* the largest form, up to 6 ft/2 m in good soil) and has enormous heads, more rounded, although the flowers still spiral cylindrically; the colour is bright lime green, almost gold in the case of Mrs Fish's splendid plant *E. c.* subsp. *w.* 'Lambrook Gold'. Crosses between these two can produce interesting forms, some with chestnut 'eyes'. They can be used in the garden as sub-shrubs. Being evergreen they are a permanent feature. They start to flower in March, continuing to illuminate the planting until the end of June. Then the old flower stem should be cut out at the base, making way for the new shoots already thrusting from the base.

cyparissias can be either a menace or a blessing, depending how much room you have. It makes quantities of underground runners, all sending up 12 in./300 mm) stems covered with ferny grey-green leaves topped with lacy heads of brilliant lime green. Attractive in spring, billowing around small shrubs, it is a menace among small treasures.

dulcis 'Chameleon'. Soft oval leaves totally wine-purple all summer. Then, in late autumn, they turn to shades of orange, scarlet and plum, a splendid contrast amongst silvers and greys, by the edge of the border. (1 ft/300 mm.)

myrsinites. From a central point radiate prostrate stems, clothed in waxed blue leaves, each terminating in large heads of lime-green flowers. A delight in early spring and for the rest of the year, placed on the edge of a border, trailing over a low wall or rock face. Grows wild in Corsica, Sicily, Italy and Greece, in stony rocky places. (6 in./150 mm.)

nicaeensis flowers later in the season, from May onwards and can be seen in flower in September. Heads of strong flowers, more green than yellow, but good against its very blue foliage on sprawling stems. (2 ft/600 mm.)

polychroma (*E. epithymoides*) follows *E. myrsinites*; starting in March as low tight rosettes embracing greenish clustered buds, the plant gradually expands throughout the spring into a dome of 12 in./300 mm stems completely covered with golden-yellow heads, rivalling the yellow clumps of daffodils elsewhere. The seed capsules are furry red, while in some gardens the whole plant makes lovely autumn tints.

rigida (*E. biglandulosa*) is found in the eastern Mediterranean, from Greece to Palestine, including north Africa. Also in Armenia and on steep rocky slopes near Mount Ararat. It is the aristocrat of a noble family, but does need a sheltered site with well-drained soil. It makes a large stiff clump of sprawling stems, not so lax as *E. myrsinites*. The leaves, set spirally round the stems, are more pointed, glaucous grey-blue, while the large flat heads showing colour in February continue to expand for weeks, a marvellous combination of olive and gold. A well-grown plant can be 3 ft/1 m across, by about 2½ ft/760 mm high.

seguieriana niciciana, one of the best, introduced from Turkey by Jim Archibald. Following *E. polychroma* it is in fine fresh flower for three months, into September, no matter how hot and dry the weather. A single clump sends up more than a hundred stems clothed in narrow blue-grey leaves topped with dainty heads of lime yellow. It does not run and looks lovely with agapanthus, any greys or large border sedums. (18 in./460 mm.)

FERULA communis is found all round the Mediterranean Sea, on dry stony sites, by roadsides and on waste cultivations. It makes a noble plant. From a huge mound, 2 × 2 ft/600 × 600 mm of dark green, finely cut, unscented foliage rises the vast flower stalk, thick as a linen prop. A bloomy purple colour when young, it eventually reaches as much as 12 ft/4 m, lifting fairy wands of yellow umbel flowers into a blue sky. Young plants only can be set out and time is needed for the great tap root to delve deep down, making firm anchorage for such a spectacular sight.

FOENICULUM vulgare again comes from all round the Mediterranean, from dry stony places. It has become naturalized in Britain. The green form is both useful and ornamental. Delicious chopped into salads, or mixed with butter and lemon to stuff fish. (5 ft/1.5 m.)

– 'Purpureum', the bronze-leafed form, makes soft mounds of mahogany brown silky hairlike foliage. Deliciously scented of aniseed, like the green form, it is also edible. The tall (5 ft/1.5 m) stems carry ochre-yellow flowers, making a filmy pillar above mound plants, or the tumbled stems of Oriental Poppies.

FRITILLARIA. These unusual bulbs, flowering in spring and early summer, are found wild in Europe, Asia and North America. Too large a subject to deal with here in detail, several can be grown in Britain, especially in warm, well-drained soil. Elsewhere some might need to be treated as cool greenhouse plants. I grow the following without difficulty.

acmopetala, tall graceful stems (15 in.–2 ft/350–500 mm) droop greenish bells with chocolate markings. Inclined to make innumerable offspring which are slow to make flowering bulbs.

imperialis. The Crown Imperial, well known in gardens, needs a sunny spot in well-prepared, freely drained soil. Left to settle down it will make bulbs the size of a grapefruit. One of the first bulbs to emerge in spring, the curious pungent scent drifting across the garden in early March brings nostalgic feelings to some, while others find it offensive. Shining, lightly twisted leaves spiral round the thick stem, ending halfway up when the stem becomes purple, topped at about 4 ft/1 m+ with a crown of downturned orange bells, each carrying a plume of narrow green leaves. There are several forms, with larger bells, deeper colour and, rarely, variegated leaves. There is also a form with cool yellow bells and green flower stems. If you tip up the large waxen bells you will see a tear, a pearl drop of liquid, at the base of each nectary.

messanensis, from Greece, Crete and Sicily, has chestnut coloured bells, two or three to a stem, a subtle colour to stand above bronze and red rosettes of sempervivums and tight plum cushions of *Sedum spathulifolium* (12 in./300 mm.)

137

persica slowly makes a clump of leafy stems from which emerge a spire of drooping bells, their soft purple colour overlaid with glaucous bloom reminiscent of grapes. It likes a warm site, under a wall, and barely seems to have the strength to support the flower head, but tying it up is ruinous to its character. I let mine lean against *Euphorbia biglandulosa*. (2 ft/600 mm.)

– **'Adiyaman'** is similar, but taller and stronger with flowers more closely set, very handsome indeed. But I am not sure that I like it better. (2½ ft/760 mm.)

pontica has large glaucous leaves with fat bells of shaded green with pale chestnut markings, one or two on shortish stems. (12 in./300 mm.)

pyrenaica carries two or three bells of matt chocolate colour. The bottom edge curls over a little modestly, showing the shining yellow-green lining. (6–12 in./150–300 mm.)

sewerzowii (*Korolkowia sewerzowii*). I have one fat bulb grown from seed which every March rapidly sends up a leafy stem with coppery-coloured open bells hanging in the axils. If we are lucky and don't have a frost there is occasionally seed. (15 in./380 mm.)

tuntasia has narrow twisted grey leaves whirled around short stems which carry several small open bells of darkest purple, almost black overlaid with silvery bloom like a sloe plum. Choice and lovely for a raised bed, grows wild in Greece, probably endemic to Kythnos in mica schist soils. (12 in./ 300 mm.)

verticillata found wild from central Asia to Japan. Tallish (2 ft/600 mm) stems are clothed in very narrow leaves which become clinging tendrils at the flower end of the stem, possibly to lift the flowers up to the light among surrounding grasses. The open bells are creamy-green, very lightly chequered with brown inside. The seed pod is fascinating, being large and angular, surrounded by bone-dry curling tendrils.

GALTONIA candicans, the Summer Hyacinth, is another late summer flowering plant from South Africa. It is found on the slopes of the Drakensberg in Natal, Orange Free State and North-East Cape Province. Like most bulbs they need to be well fed to flower well. A lot of energy is needed to produce the stately pale green stem (4 ft/1.2 m) with its heavy head of large drooping white bells. Flowering at the same time as the hardy agapanthus they look well together, but I also like to see groups of them rising out of my mixed foliage borders. They make good seed heads, scattering very fertile seed liberally into neighbours if you let them.

princeps is a smaller version, with pale green flowers. There is a much better form called *Galtonia viridiflora* which has larger, better shaped green bells. (3 ft/1 m.)

GAURA lindheimeri flowers in the autumn, when there are few flamboyant neighbours to detract from its modest charm. Palest pink flowers, held out from the stem in a tubular calyx, float for weeks among the open branches of this slight plant. It thrives in full sun in light, well-drained soil, and comes from Texas. (3 ft/1 m.)

GENISTA aetnensis, the Mount Etna Broom, makes a large elegant shrub or small tree. It casts practically no shade, and scents the air all July when dripping with golden flowers. (10 ft/3 m.)

hispanica forms a low dense mound of dark green prickly foliage which can eventually cover several yards. Completely covered in early summer with bright gold gorse flowers. ($2\frac{1}{2}$ ft/760 mm.)

lydia, from the eastern Balkans, makes an open springy dome-shaped mound of seemingly leafless branches, smothered with yellow pea flowers in mid-summer. (12–18 in./ 300–460 mm.)

sagittalis, a native of central and southern Europe, makes a prostrate mat of curiously winged stems, producing a dense evergreen carpet, enlivened with bright gold in midsummer. (9 in.–1 ft/230–300 mm.)

All of these forms of broom will tolerate full sun and very dry conditions.

GERANIUM or Cranesbills, the name referring to the shape of the long beak-shaped seed case which splits and catapults out the large seeds. Perfectly hardy (and not to be confused with bedding or greenhouse geraniums, which are pelargoniums), they are invaluable garden plants, bettered by none for attractive and weed-proof ground cover. Their parasol-shaped foliage, often deeply cut, is always attractive and often scented. Their flowers are jewel-like in intensity of colour, produced over a long period, and in great profusion. They are easy to grow in almost any soil provided it is well drained. On very poor sand or gravel they will appreciate additional humus. I have not included those which I consider too choice to put on the poorest soil, such as some of the double forms, and *G. maculatum* to which I give my best.

clarkei 'Kashmir White' (*G. pratense* 'Rectum Album') is a very beautiful form from Kashmir. It makes large mounds, about 2 ft/600 mm of very finely divided foliage with large, slightly cupped white flowers veined with lilac.

endressii has more dainty foliage, making a mound of light green prettily cut leaves from which spring elongating sprays of rose-pink flowers. (15 in./380 mm.)

– 'Wargrave Pink' is similar with light salmon-pink flowers. Both these plants make spreading clumps which can be divided. In a neglected garden they hold their own, never beaten by native weeds. They come from the Pyrenees. (15 in./380 mm.)

himalayense, long known to me as *G. grandiflorum*. Found in Sikkim this lovely plant makes wide-spreading carpets of finely cut leaves which colour well in autumn, especially on poor soil. The large flowers are a rich violet blue with darker veins. I grow *G. h.* 'Gravetye' (*G. h. alpinum*) which has a dark reddish heart, intensifying the colour. I also have G. 'Johnsons' Blue' which is very similar without the dark centre, the flowers produced in such abundance the mounds of vivid colour draw you like a magnet. Although they love full sun I find they are more impressive in improved or better soil when they will stand more than 1 ft/300 mm.

macrorrhizum from southern Europe is probably the best for weed-proof ground cover. It can be broken up in spring whether the pieces are rooted or not, and provided the weather is not against it every bit will root. Left to itself it creeps about on rooting stems covered with round frilly leaves, strongly scented. In autumn many are tinted bronze and scarlet, but the youngest remain throughout the winter. The flowers held just above the leaves come in shades of magenta pink. Perhaps the prettiest is *G. m.* 'Album', of the faintest pink set off by soft brownish-mauve calyces. (1 ft/ 300 mm.)

– **'Variegatum'** has richly variegated leaves in cream and green. I grow it among shrubs in semi-shade. (12 in./ 300 mm.)

× **magnificum,** again wrongly labelled by many as *G. ibericum*. In fact it is a sterile hybrid known in gardens for nearly a hundred years. It makes clumps of dark green woolly foliage with long, rather floppy stems of deep violet-blue flowers. Usually seen with scarlet poppies or paeonies, but better I think with cool lemon achilleas. (2 ft/600 mm.)

malviflorum (*atlanticum*) is similar to *G. tuberosum* in that it runs underground and disappears after flowering. The dark green cut leaves start appearing in autumn, continuing to emerge fully by early spring. Large bright blue flowers appear in May, along edges of shrubs or among roses, and the whole plant vanishes by midsummer. But the other plantings will have overlaid any gaps. (12 in./300 mm.)

nodosum has smooth, lobed leaves of a glossy green, with unremarkable little flowers of lilac-mauve. It will make cover in very dense shade under trees, but can be troublesome to eradicate if you change your mind. It is a European native (12 in./300 mm.)

× **oxonianum 'Claridge Druce'** is a hybrid of *G. endressii*, even more vigorous, making rampant ground cover in the shade of trees and shrubs, or in full sun. Large creeping mounds of grey-green (evergreen) leaves set off bright mauve-pink flowers for weeks in summer. (Up to 3 ft/1 m.)

phaeum, called the 'Mourning Widow' because of its sombre-coloured flowers which can vary in seedlings. I try to keep the deepest purple-maroon forms, easily propagated by division. This plant thrives in really shady dry places, lit up with a few plants of honesty. (2 ft/600 mm.)

pratense, a British native, is found wild in woods and clearings throughout northern Europe and Asia. Tall stems bearing heads of clear blue flowers are to be seen, often with bright pink campions. There are a number of selected forms grown in gardens; among them are:

– **'Mrs Kendall Clark',** an especially free-flowering good blue form. (2 ft/600 mm.)

The double forms I could not commend for really dry gardens, they are worthy of really good soil, and are too scarce to risk losing.

All forms of *G. pratense* die down completely in winter.

psilostemon (*armenum*) from Armenia is a gorgeous plant, distinctive from the moment its cherry-red buds start to peep through the soil in early spring. It makes a large mound

(3 × 3 ft/1 × 1 m) of elegant foliage, large frilled parasols on tall stems which are often brilliantly coloured in autumn. Above them wide-branching stems are crowded with blossom for weeks in midsummer. Few flowers have such intensity of colour, the brightest magenta pink, each with an indigo eye, marvellous with silvers and old-fashioned roses.

renardii comes from the Caucasus. Low mounds of round sage-green leaves with scalloped edges, finely quilted. The almost white flowers have a network of delicate purple veins. It makes a neat edging plant. (10 in./250 mm.)

– **'Russell Prichard'**. This hybrid is a joy. Planted in a warm sunny site (not too poor), it keeps up an inexhaustible display from June to the November frosts. From a central tuft it sends out ever-lengthening sprays of rich pink flowers lying flat against the surface or thrown into surrounding plants. (6 in./150 mm high × 3 ft/1 m spread.)

sanguineum. The Bloody Cranesbill makes woody stemmed hummocks of small divided leaves, some of which have good autumn colour. In midsummer it is covered with vivid magenta flowers, lovely contrast for *Origanum vulgare* 'Aureum' planted nearby. Odd jewel-like flowers will continue to decorate it until the first frost. (1 ft/300 mm.)

sanguineum 'Album' is a more leggy plant with paler leaves, but the pure white flowers are very fine. (2 ft/600 mm.)

– **var. striatum** (var. *lancastriense*) makes a much lower plant, a sprawling carpet with pale salmon-pink flowers, veined crimson. (6 in./150 mm.)

Rock Garden Types

cinereum 'Ballerina' makes a neat mound of cut greyish foliage with large crinkled lilac flowers, heavily veined purple, with dark centres. (6 in./150 mm.)

– var. subcaulescens is an arresting sight, its neat mounds of fine-cut leaves covered with vivid carmine flowers, intensified by dark eyes. (9 in./230 mm.)

– – 'Splendens', without the dark eye, of a lighter, even more startling shade of carmine-pink. (6 in./150 mm.)

dalmaticum has small shining leaves, bronze tinted, making low spreading mats sprinkled with clear pink flowers for weeks in summer. (6 in./150 mm.)

sessiliflorum 'Nigricans' makes low rosettes of small, soft brown, round leaves, highlighted with the occasional orange leaf. The small white flowers are hardly noticeable, nor missed. (4 in./100 mm.)

tuberosum spreads slowly through the soil by underground tubers, so could be too invasive in small rock gardens, but ideal on the edge of the border, as its finely cut foliage is up all winter marking bulbs. In early summer it is an airy mass of tiny floating pink and white flowers, on 12 in./300 mm stems, but everything disappears by midsummer.

GLADIOLUS. I grow several species here which have survived cold winters in well-drained, well-prepared soil.

communis flowers about the same time, in early summer, but is not so tall, has softer, lighter colouring, and the flowers are more widely spaced. It is found throughout southern Europe from Spain to Greece, in grassy heaths and meadows. (15 in./380 mm.)

– subsp. byzantinus from the central and southern Mediterranean, from Corsica to Palestine, and also north Africa, in old fields and wasteland. The vivid flowers are a strong mixture of purple and magenta with touches of copper and cream, but surrounded by 'cooling' muted foliage like the greys, or shrubby salvias they can make effective accents. Increases rapidly in light soils, less so in heavy soils. (3 ft/1 m.)

illyricus is the smallest, standing about 12 in./300 mm, with grassy foliage, and little flowers almost iridescent in shades of pink, magenta and purple. Has attractive seed heads too. It grows in heaths and stony places throughout the European Mediterranean to Turkey and Palestine. (15 in./380 mm.)

papilio from Natal is a very curious flower. Late in September slender stems appear above the stiff grassy foliage carrying a spire of downturned hooded flowers of a strange greyish lilac. Inside the under lip is pale creamy-green with soft brownish 'eye' markings, like the 'eye' on a butterfly's wing. In a quiet way it has an exotic orchid-like charm. Not very free flowering, except in very hot summers. It needs to be dug up, and only the best bulbs planted back in revived soil. It tends to make far too many offsets crowded together. (4 ft/1.2 m.)

tristis, also from Natal, is not reputedly hardy, but has lived here for seventeen years under south and west walls, more recently further afield in very light soil. It sends up quantities of bright green rush-like foliage, overtopped with slender stems carrying the most delicate creamy-primrose flowers in late spring. (18 in./460 mm.)

GLAUCIUM, Horn Poppy, so called because of the long curving seed pods. There are many kinds. The yellow-flowered form, G. *flavum* grows still on dune areas of our own east coast, but it is not considered a long-lived perennial.

A better plant is one I used to call G. *phoenicium*, now called G. *flavum f. fulvam*. My plant is very definitely a perennial; I have a hoary old specimen with a gnarled woody stock, many headed, each head carrying a live rosette of leaves. Each leaf stem is red at the lower end, gradually elongating until it is about 10 in./250 mm long. For the best foliage younger plants make the most handsome rosettes, each one composed of fine-toothed leaves so heavily felted with hairs, and curled to show both back and front, that they appear silvery blue. The shallow cup-shaped flowers are a unique flame colour, of translucent silk texture. Finally, the branching stems (18 in./460 mm) are hung with 5 in./130 mm long curving seed pods, unusual decorations themselves. The seeds sown directly into well-drained or sandy soils make the best plants, but they can be transplanted if sown into pots, and planted out when still small. Some people prefer to use this plant entirely as a foliage plant by not allowing it to flower, which does preserve its perfect symmetry. But I must confess that I like to see my plants reproduce themselves, to know and enjoy every stage of their development.

GYPSOPHILA. Probably best known as the large cloud-like mass of tiny white flowers on tangled stems which used to be put with sweet peas. There are others, all needing well-drained, preferably limy, soil. They do not last long in heavy wet soils.

paniculata is the familiar white 'cumulus cloud', standing about 3 ft/1 m. It is found wild among the large tufted *Stipa* grasses of the steppe in southern Russia, and also on dry hills in central Europe. In the garden it is usefully employed in a midway position in a border, possibly filling the gap left by some early flowering plants, like the Oriental Poppies, or *Fritillaria imperialis*.

repens 'Dubia' (*G. dubia*) is a rock garden form, from southern Europe. It makes completely prostrate trails of small grey leaves touched with maroon, on red stems, so looks interesting when not in flower. It is probably evergreen in its natural habitat, though here all the leaves are sered in winter except the tip shoots. But the whole plant breaks new shoots in spring, smothered with tiny pink single flowers in early summer. It is a delight draped over a rock or wall. (3 in./75 mm.)

146

'Rosenschleier' ('Rosy Veil') is, I think, more attractive. Too large except on the larger rock garden, it is a joy on the edge of a dry border, or spilling over a low wall. From neat cushions of grey glaucous tufts springs a foaming mass of tiny palest pink double flowers, 12 in./300 mm high and 2 ft/600 mm+ across. If this first flush is cut down as it begins to look untidy a fresh bouquet will be equally fine in September–October.

× HALIMIOCISTUS sahucii (*Cistus salvifolius × Halimium umbellatum*) comes from the open maquis and garigue of southern France. It makes a low, wiry, spreading bush bearing small narrow dark green leaves tinged bronze, almost covered every June morning with an abundance of small saucer-shaped white flowers; by afternoon every one has dropped. (4 × 4 ft/1.2 × 1.2 m.)

HALIMIUM is related to *Cistus* and *Helianthemum*, but on the whole is more tender.

calycinum (*H. libanotis*) has narrow leaves and bright golden flowers, unblotched; it also has been here many years on a sandy bank, sheltered from the worst of the north east winds. ($2\frac{1}{2}$ ft/760 mm.)

halimifolium is a small, erect, grey-leafed shrub with bright yellow flowers. Each petal has a dark maroon spot at its base. ($2\frac{1}{2}$ ft/760 mm.)

lasianthum, from Spain and Portugal, is more spreading and hardier. Has survived here in gravel soil. Flowers as above. ($2\frac{1}{2}$ ft/760 mm.)

HAPLOPAPPUS glutinosus (*H. coronopifolius*). There are thirty species of haplopappus in the Rockies. I have not yet discovered exactly where this one was found. I first saw it hanging like a soft cushion over a low wall, studded with little orange-yellow daisy flowers. It makes a loose mound of bitter-green deeply toothed leaves, good contrast for its gay little flowers in late summer and autumn.

HEBE. An enormous and very varied genus from New Zealand, where it takes the place of heather. They are sun-loving evergreen plants for well-drained soil, associating well in gardens with both heathers and with many Mediterranean plants. The smallest leafed forms seem to be the hardiest; some of the larger forms with large soft leaves and showy flowers like *H.* 'La Séduisante' are definitely not hardy in East Anglia although, being tempted of course, we sometimes keep them for a while in very sheltered corners. The small-leafed kinds all make tidy compact hummocks, especially valuable in borders close to the house where tidy furnishing is valuable.

Although they are reasonably drought-resisting on very light soil, they benefit from some wet peat dug into the soil, plus a mulch to guard against the severest drought.

'Amy' makes a medium sized bush, remarkable for its beautiful purple young growths, with dark blue flowers in late summer. (4 ft/1.2 m.)

× andersonii 'Variegata' is splendid for really warm gardens. It has survived here several years, tucked well under a west wall, but would be killed by a really severe winter. A strong growing shrub, with long narrow leaves broadly margined and lined with creamy-white; long racemes of palest lavender-blue flowers in September. (4 ft/1.2 m.)

armstrongii is one of the dwarf 'whip cord' hebes, having no proper leaves but overlapping scales on many divided and redivided cordlike stems of lovely shades of olive green. In winter the bushes glow golden bronze, outstanding among dark green heathers. There are several other whip cord hebes, all interesting individually. Possibly *Hebe hectori*, which has thicker, rounder branches looking as though they had been emulsioned bright fern or moss green, is one of the best. (18 in.–2 ft/460–600 mm.)

'Glaucophylla Variegata' is a small upright shrub with slender wiry stems carrying narrow grey-green leaves, margined with white. Splendid as a special vertical among low growing plants. Does not need its white flowers. (18 in./ 460 mm.)

'Great Orme' has grown well here for several years, although one of the large leaf, larger bush types. It has bright pink flowers in long tapering racemes for weeks in late summer. (4 ft/1.2 m.)

hulkeana, although tender, has survived several years here under a south wall. The loveliest of all hebes, it makes a loose woody bush of glossy dark green leaves from which cascade long racemes of lilac-blue flowers in May and June. (2 ft/600 mm.)

'Midsummer Beauty' makes a strong growing bush (4 × 4 ft/ 1.2 × 1.2 m) of large, lance-shaped leaves, the young ones tinted purple underneath. Long racemes of lavender flowers all late summer and autumn (colchicums beneath). Sometimes damaged by severe wind frost when it catches a northeast wind, but always recovers.

pinguifolia 'Pagei' (*Veronica pageana*) makes widespreading mats of small, very blue-grey rounded leaves which are handsome all year round. White flowers in May. Inclined to die off in the centre – dig it up when ground is still warm and moist in autumn, refresh soil, replace in clumps – it rots easily from the stem. (8 × 15 in./200 × 380 mm.)

recurva does not sprawl, but makes a very compact prim little shrub, also with very glaucous foliage, but larger, more pointed leaves than *H. pinguifolia* 'Pagei'. The clusters of white flowers are preceded by most attractive pinky-brown buds. (2 ft × 2 ft/600 × 600 mm.)

'Youngii' (*H.* 'Carl Teschner') is a splendid hybrid. Small dark green leaves, bronze tipped when young on purplish stems, make first-class evergreen ground cover, or an ideal low shrub for rock garden or raised bed. Violet flowers, white eyed, are close-packed on short stems. The tidiest of plants, it is lovely among helianthemums with *Euphorbia seguieriana niciciana* to complete the group. (6 × 18 in./ 150 × 450 mm.)

HEDERA. With its many variations ivy is one of the most valuable of garden plants, capable of surviving and flourishing in dark and difficult places where few other plants will grow. In hedge bottoms, under the dense canopy of large trees, on north and east walls of buildings, especially ugly ones, ivy will grow and create a feeling of abundant vitality. (Ivy does not harm well-built brick walls, and careful pruning and observation will prevent any damage to trees.) Once established as a total ground cover no weed will grow through it.

When grown up a wall of a building I find that every two years or so I need to cut the plant down to a few feet above the ground to force the production of the new runners which carry the most attractive leaves. Most ivies benefit by being pruned back occasionally; the fruiting branches carry different shaped leaves and do not throw out long trails.

canariensis, 'Canary Island Ivy', is found in the Azores, Portugal, Canary Islands and north-west Africa. The form most often seen is *Hedera canariensis* 'Variegata' ('Gloire de Marengo'). It has medium to large leaves, softly variegated, with an ivory margin surrounding a shaded grey-green centre. Many leaves are tinted crimson in winter, with leaf stalks crimson also. Young leaves can be damaged in very severe weather, but the plant itself is hardy.

colchica is found wild, making immense entanglements in the oak and beech woods of the Caucasus.

– **'Dentata Variegata'** is the form most generally grown, on walls, patios or over old tree stumps. Has large, broad, triangular and oval leaves, every one differently 'painted', a broad irregular margin of cream, the centre shades of deep and lighter green as though brushed on with a wet paint brush. Sometimes in deep shade a leaf is entirely parchment yellow.

– 'Sulphur Heart' ('Paddy's Pride') has equally large leaves, the colouring reversed, a pale primrose and green-washed centre, strengthening out to a broad irregular deep green margin. Quite outstanding.

helix, our native Common Ivy. While its many forms are hardy, some, especially the heavily variegated forms, suffer some leaf damage in severe frost. Very young plants not properly established could benefit by having a little bracken tucked round them for protection. Once established all will break new leaves in spring.
    There are very many variations. Here are a few of the more distinct:

– 'Buttercup' has small new leaves, entirely gold. It is slow to establish, and must be placed in part shade or it will scorch (east or north walls are suitable). Mature leaves are pale green.

– 'Erecta' has wedge-shaped leaves upturned on the stem, very rigid growth. Can be fan-trained against a wall, or if trained around a stout stake, and kept well pruned, it makes an unusual vertical in place of a juniper.

– 'Invalace'. Not quite so rampant as H. 'Manda's Crested'; has small dark green incurved leaves ribbed with pale veins. Both of these I use to conceal manholes.

– 'Lutzii' has smallish leaves, prettily speckled cream, green and primrose. Makes attractive ground cover.

– 'Manda's Crested' differs from H. 'Parsley Crested' in having wavy leaves without the crimped edges. The vigorous new shoots in autumn carry pale green leaves, copper tinted, making contrast with the mature leaves of summer. Makes quick ground cover.

– 'Marginata' has triangular leaves, broad margined with creamy white which becomes flushed carmine in winter.

– 'Minor Marmorata' ('Discolor'). Tiny triangular leaves, so heavily stippled with white that we nicknamed it 'White Lace'. Best in shade.

– 'Neilson' is very like the ivy in the hedge, except for the tiny shoot of wee leaves set in the leaf axils which grow out, making the plant provide excellent ground cover.

– 'Oro di Bogliasco' ('Goldheart') is a very showy plant, growing well on a north or east wall with plenty of young trailers. Dark green leaves with a large central zone of gold.

– 'Parsley Crested' ('Cristata') is more vigorous than the variegated forms, useful for quick cover. Sends out long sprays of pale green geranium-shaped leaves with heavily goffered margins, especially lovely with lots of new growth in autumn.

– 'Pedata Heron' has very finely divided leaves, closely packed on curving stems, to make a neat lacy mound, charming on shady corners.

hibernica (*H. helix* 'Hibernica') 'Irish Ivy'. Very vigorous, with large dark green leaves making runners up to 10 ft/3 m when established. Most valued as ground cover in large shrubberies, under dense canopied trees, or on difficult banks at the drive entrance.

HELIANTHEMUM, Sun Roses, make quick, excellent ground cover in dry sunny situations, more liable to frost damage on cold heavy soils. Most of the kinds we grow in gardens are hybrids, with grey or green leaves, and flowers in many shades from white, cream, primrose, orange, apricot to crimson. Summer. (6 × 18 in./150 × 450 mm.)

HELICHRYSUM. A large genus, distributed over the warm and temperate regions of the Old World. While the greatest concentrations are to be found in South Africa and Australia, the small shrubby types found around the Mediterranean area are most suited to English gardens, in open sunny situations on well-drained soil. They can, I think, be too easily overlooked, among the more glamorous shrubs like broom and cistus. But in fact I value them highly. They stand drought better than most small shrubs, becoming whiter and more aromatic as the rainless days pass by. Their soft rounded shapes make a useful link between low plants like helianthemums and thymes and the taller cistus, always providing a good background for temporary performers like alliums or verbascums. It is probably the combined perfumes of various helichrysums, cistus and thymes that cause visitors to pause in my 'Mediterranean' garden, recalling the scents of the sun-baked hillsides of the warm south. The following are the most distinct kinds I grow:

italicum (*H. angustifolium*). We collected our original plant in Corsica. It is found throughout the eastern Mediterranean on arid hills, on rocks and cliffs. Commonly called the 'Curry Plant' it is the most strongly scented kind we grow, being pleasantly similar to that combination of cooking spices. It makes a dense dwarf shrub, with short narrow leaves of a silvered sage green. A background plant more valued for its perfume than its appearance. (2 ft/600 mm.)

– 'Nanum'. Under this name I have a delightful little bush, ideal to plant as a choice feature among low thymes and sedums. Very upright, it has tiny narrow silvery-white leaves, the main lead shoots emerging spikily from the short lateral branches at their base, giving a delicate filigree appearance. (12 in./300 mm.)

petiolare (*H. petiolatum*) cannot be relied on for hardiness, although it will sometimes come through a mild winter.

A few plants overwintered in a frost-free greenhouse provide plenty of young plants to set out after the May frosts. Ideal in urns and tubs it grows fast, throwing out long curving branches (themselves and the pretty round leaves whitened with dense felt), so that the containers can be almost hidden by the end of the season. Attractive, too, if allowed to sprawl several feet across paving, breaking the hard edge. (9 in./ 230 mm.)

petiolare 'Yellow Form'. Lemon-gold leaves, rather delicate, prefers part shade. (6 × 24 in./150 × 600 mm.)

– **'Microphyllum'** has much smaller, more silvery leaves. Useful in small containers, although its spread is almost as vigorous. (6 × 24 in./150 × 600 mm.)

– **'Variegatum'.** Leaves in two shades of grey, not quite so vigorous. (9 in./230 mm.)

plicatum makes a large (3 × 4 ft/1 × 1 m+), beautifully rounded bush in my gravelly soil. With its narrow downy leaves it makes one of the whitest of bushes among my greys. Some people do not care for the terminal spikes of small bright yellow flowers, but I have a small bush set half way down a shallow flight of steps. Looking down onto it, it is the lightest, gayest thing around in the dull dead days of July. Cut well back after flowering it refurnishes itself with new white shoots before winter.

I must admit that many years I do not prune my greys as regularly as I suggest. With most of them no harm is done, provided there is plenty of room for them to spread. And if I have left it rather too long, so that they have become leggy and straggly, most of them can be cut hard back in spring, practically to the base, and will become a new bush of fresh foliage within a couple of months. If they are beyond that most of them can be easily struck out of doors in a sheltered border, the cuttings put in in early September.

'Schwefellicht' ('Sulphur Light') is a recently introduced hybrid. Not a woody shrub, it makes low mounds of soft narrow leaves, white with wool, useful as ground cover on the edge of a very well-drained border. Flower stems about 12 in./300 mm in late summer carry clustered heads of bright citron-yellow everlasting flowers. (12 in./300 mm.)

sibthorpii (*H. virgineum*) is a rock-wall plant from Mount Athos, Greece. Lovely if you can grow it, it makes neat mounds of very white rounded leaves. Beige-pink buds open to show straw-coloured everlasting yellow daisies which dry perfectly if hung upside down. This plant hates winter wet so, if not covered, at least it must be grown on the grittiest of soil, preferably on a slope. (6 in./150 mm.)

splendidum is more familiar to me as *H. alveolatum*, also *H. trilineatum*. With, or without, three names it is perhaps the most distinguished-looking of the helichrysums I grow. It has short, broad, ribbed leaves, slightly twisted, very white with wool on both sides, arranging themselves in a terminal rosette on the tips of the many upturned branches of a stiff woody bush. After several years it can look rather leggy, but cutting back into the old wood in spring rejuvenates the bush, and making new breaks it recovers itself with bright new foliage. (2 × 2 ft/600 × 600 mm.)

stoechas 'White Barn'. Mrs Underwood spotted this plant in my garden many years ago. Thanks entirely to an unforced marriage among my helichrysums this has proved to be a plant worth growing. Much larger in every way than *H. plicatum*, it has leaves almost as large, white and woolly as *Lavandula lanata*. It has very pale sulphur-yellow flowers, beautiful in silky bud. (2 × 2 ft/600 × 600 mm.)

HELLEBORUS are members of the Christmas Rose family. All of them really require a more retentive soil than comes under the heading of this book. However, some can be grown in dry gardens, especially if plenty of humus is incorporated into the soil, and the site is north- or east-facing, giving the maximum relief from scorching sunlight. Mulching with well-rotted muck is essential if the soil is poor and light.

argutifolius (*H. corsicus* or *H. lividus corsicus*) is found in Corsica, Sardinia and the Balearic Islands. Makes a dome (2 × 3 ft/1 × 1 m) of stout stems bearing handsome claw-like foliage of cool jade green. Starting at Christmas the apple-green flowers begin to open, and by April each stem carries a huge bouquet of a green so pale as to be luminous. Does not do so well in deep shade under trees; prefers half shade. Will grow in full sun in good soil.

foetidus is a British native. I seem to have found this plant wherever I have stopped in France, but possibly more commonly in southern Europe. It makes neater, smaller clumps of dark holly-green divided fan-shaped leaves, from which fall clusters of palest green bells, thimble sized, edged with maroon. Looks best among shrubs, with *Iris foetidissima* and *Vinca minor* 'La Grave' ('Bowles' Variety'). (18 in./ 460 mm.)

niger, the Christmas Rose, pure white and lovely, a single flower to each stem, does not thrive in poor gravelly soils. On heavier, tackier soils with added humus it needs time to settle down. (12 × 18 in./300 × 460 mm.)

orientalis hybrids. Under this vague title I grow some of the loveliest hellebores from seed. It is next to impossible to throw any away as being inferior. All are lovely, some outstanding. All shades, from creamy-white, greenish-white, some spotted and speckled, apple-blossom pink to deepest plum-purple, on branching stems. Masses of humus and plenty of patience are rewarded by the sight of these lovely plants gradually making bigger and bigger clumps, massed with buds. I have lost these buds once to mice – I could not think why in February. They were not half-way to flowering. In very wet and humid periods in late winter they are attacked by a fungus, best treated by spraying with Captan or Bordeaux mixture.

HERMODACTYLUS tuberosus (*Iris tuberosus*) is common on rocky slopes and hillsides in Greece, Italy, Dalmatia, Albania, the south of France and north Africa. Best suited in a warm sunny spot, in light and chalky soils. The delicate flowers are about 2 in./50 mm across, translucent green in colour, with an almost black velvety patch on each fall. They are sweetly scented. The long thin leaves go on growing after the flower is finished. The flower stem is 6–12 in./150–300 mm high.

HESPERIS matronalis, Sweet Rocket or Dame's Violet, is a steppe or meadow plant found from southern Europe into Siberia, usually on the edges where the bushland starts. It will grow almost anywhere, putting up with poor conditions, happy in limy soil which it prefers. I find it useful in gaps in shrubberies, the kind of place that suits *Lunaria* (Honesty). It makes a tall (4 ft/1.2 m) healthy-looking green plant with branching stems carrying sweet-scented flowers for weeks in summer, best enjoyed on that last walk round at dusk. Grown from seed the colours will range from white to deep lilac.

HIERACEUM. These plants, the Hawkweeds, have dandelion-like flowers, and most are able to stand very hot spots.

villosum is not at all troublesome. The very soft silvery-grey woolly foliage in a neat clump has handsome, large, cool yellow 'dandelion' flowers. (9 in./230 mm.)

waldsteinii makes large rosettes of cabbage-shaped leaves, beautifully felted white in poor gravel soils. Wiry branching stems carry small yellow flowers, followed by pretty 'clock' seed heads. I've never had too many seedlings, for the seeds are not always viable. (18 × 9 in./460 × 230 mm.)

HOSTA, Funkia or Plantain Lily. Probably the most popular 'foliage' plant grown in gardens today. There are more than forty different species in Japan, with a few more to be found in Korea and China. This does not include the innumerable garden clones and hybrids that have come to us from Japan. One has to remember that Japan is a long drawn-out chain of islands, much of it with far higher rainfall and moister atmosphere than the drier parts of Great Britain.

Most hostas are woodland plants, and while some will stand full sun, providing there is ample moisture, all of them make far larger, more perfect leaves in partial shade, although probably fewer flowers. In the dry shady garden, that is, under north or east walls, or in the shade of trees and shrubs (not *too* infested with loofah-like roots), it will be necessary to make large holes and fill them up with as much moisture-holding material as is available. Afterwards a good mulch will help considerably, preferably of farmyard manure, applied every other year if you are determined to have the best results.

Slugs and snails love hostas as much as we do, so apply a poisoned bait just as the leaves emerge, and later under the leaves as they have developed where the rain cannot wash it away. Dispensers of bait are obtainable for easy application. We use a product called Draza G., containing 4 per cent methiocarb. I will list only a few of the most vigorous forms. If you already have them I recommend you to read *Perennial Garden Plants* by G. S. Thomas, who devotes seven pages to them for your delight.

fortunei albopicta, needing partial shade, shelter from harsh winds and time to settle down, will become one of the most spectacular plants in the spring garden. Large heart-shaped and pointed leaves unfold to show a bright butter-yellow centre with a margin irregularly slashed in two shades of green. Throughout May the leaves hold this brightness but by midsummer, when the leaves have matured, the central zone has faded to pale green, the leaf remaining faintly two toned. It retreats into the background of green shades, but no other hosta has such heart-quickening beauty at its best. (2¼ ft/760 mm.)

'Honeybells' is a hybrid from *H. plantaginea* with stronger pale green foliage. The palest lilac flowers are also scented. I find this plant more robust than *H. plantaginea* and have planted it among shrubs. (3 ft/900 mm.)

lancifolia is by no means spectacular, but could be more widely appreciated for its form. We have plenty of large round leaves, and tall blade-like leaves. This plant is in between. The shining dark green leaves are narrow and pointed on long stems, and make up quickly into bold clumps which can be divided to spread around to make ground cover (as can all forms). One of the best to flower, the deep lilac trumpet flowers on tall graceful stems are a pleasure for weeks in the autumn, surrounded perhaps by colchicums. (2 ft/600 mm.)

plantaginea was introduced to Japanese gardens from China, where it has long been cultivated. Our season is barely long enough for it, and often the flower buds are showing in late autumn, only to be nipped by frost before they have opened. Under a west wall (or in a warm sheltered shrubbery) this plant will produce a handsome mound of glossy light green leaves which remain in pristine condition until they die down. If favourably sited there will be time for the astonishingly large pure white lily-like flowers that will open in October, delicately scented. This would be a lovely plant for a tub in a conservatory, or on a terrace where watering would not be neglected. The French often use hostas in tubs (even in cut-down oil drums!). For roof gardens, or very small patio gardens any of the hostas provide a 'bosky' atmosphere.

sieboldiana. Given time and good living this hosta can produce some of the largest, most handsome leaves. They can be 12 in./300 mm wide and almost 2 ft/600 mm long, a beautiful bluish-green with wax-like bloom, deeply ribbed and slightly quilted. The flowers are palest lilac, too crowded on a short stalk for elegance, but the seed pods split open in late autumn to make a very effective spike of 'wooden' flowers. Finally, these huge leaves become glowing mounds of honey-gold as they prepare for the coming winter, when they disappear completely.

– var. **elegans** is a very fine selected form of this species. The great leaves are deeper blue, the veining and quilting more pronounced. It is better than *H. sieboldiana* itself, but would not be so in poor soil. So, if you have no hostas, I would start with *H. sieboldiana*. (3 ft/900 mm.)

undulata var. albomarginata (*H. 'Thomas Hogg'*). I have come to realize that I have been growing this useful vigorous plant as *H. crispula*. There is a similarity, but *H. crispula* is larger, with more wavy edges to the leaf, the centre a deeper green, the white outer margin broader. *H. undulata* var. *albomarginata* does well in the shade and drip of trees, and continues to send up its white-edged leaves until the end of the growing season. It has tall stems of lilac trumpet-shaped flowers. (2 ft/600 mm.)

ventricosa is another good green form. Rounded, rich green leaves, ribbed and shining, make handsome clumps. The flowers, produced in late summer are the finest of any hosta I know, being large and bell shaped, a deep bluish-purple, darkly veined. There is a superb variegated form, not at its best in the very dry garden. (3 ft/1 m.)

HUMULUS lupulus, the Common Hop, is found wild throughout the temperate world. It will grow in any garden soil, but is more vigorous in deep loam.

– **'Aureus'**, the Golden Hop, can be accommodated in dry shade provided it is given a good start. Too dense shade would not produce the best colour, while total exposure all day could result in scorching. Rampant when satisfied, its

10 ft/3 m trails produced annually are garlanded with leaves of pure gold.

HYPERICUM androsaemum, Tutsan. Easy in dry shade, useful between main shrub planting. Its young leaves are tinged reddish bronze while the fluffy yellow flowers set in pale green collars turn into brick-red berries which finally turn black. All these colours and stages can be found together on one bush. (2½ ft/760 mm.)

calycinum, Rose of Sharon, grows with *Euphorbia amygdaloides robbiae* in the oak woods of the Balkans. Ignored most of the year it can be a picture when covered in large gold flowers. Useful low evergreen ground cover in rough places, thrives in dry shade. But it is invasive, so should be checked if space is limited.

'Hidcote' will grow in dryish shade, but provide plenty of humus for best results. Makes a compact, rounded shrub about 4 ft/1.2m high, more widely spreading. Can be controlled by pruning every other year, which results in larger blossoms; golden-yellow saucers are produced from late summer to October.

× inodorum 'Elstead' is a hybrid with *H. androsaemum* as one of its parents. Taller, over 3 ft/1 m in reasonable soil, it is most handsome in autumn with its pointed cherry-pink berries and flame-coloured foliage.

IBERIS sempervirens, Candytuft. Wild on rocks and stony places in southern Europe, this familiar plant makes wide-spreading cushions 3–4 ft/1 m+ across, and about 12 in./300 mm high. Dazzling white heads of flower crowd over dark evergreen leaves, invaluable among helianthemums and greys.

INCARVILLEA delavayi found by the Abbé Delavay in western China, makes an enormous root like a long red radish, which allows it to produce a clump of dark green divided leaves above which stand stout stems carrying several large tubular-shaped flowers with flaring frilly petals of deep rosy-pink. It likes a sunny place in well-drained soil, not devoid of nourishment. The seed pods are handsome too, like great carved beaks. (2 ft/600 mm.) There are others, lighter coloured, shorter stemmed.

IRIS. Fortunately many thrive in dry conditions, both in sun and shade. The well-known Germanica hybrids or June-flowering bearded iris are legion, preferring well-drained soil in sun without too much nitrogenous manure.

One group of iris very suitable for dry sunny soil are called the Juno irises. They differ from other iris in having tuberous roots which send up in early spring a stout stem carrying broad pointed glossy leaves, clasping the stem in pairs. At the upper end, each leaf axil carries several flower buds. These curiously beautiful plants come from the mountain steppes of the West Tien Shan ranges of Russian Turkestan. I grow the following Juno irises, all under south-west walls where they flower well and seed: *I. bucharica* has white and yellow flowers; *I. magnifica* pale lilac and yellow, sometimes white; *I. aucheri* (*I. sindjarensis*) from Mesopotamia has icy lilac-blue flowers.

A group of iris which thrives in dry shade includes *I. douglasiana*, found in shades of blue and white, with medium-sized flowers, beautifully veined, on slender stalks, with evergreen grassy foliage. This iris is related to several more lovely iris which have been found along the Pacific coastline of California, including *Iris tenax* which makes a smaller plant, with dainty flowers in rosy-purplish shades, and *Iris innominata* from Oregon, with small bright yellow flowers and very grassy foliage. These, with yet more, have hybridized so that for myself I am unable to honestly make great distinction between them. They are collectively known as the Californian Pacific Coast hybrids. All make evergreen clumps of dark narrow leaves, many with attractive rosy leaf bases. The flowers, several on a stem, are endless blends and combinations of white, cream, yellow, bronze, rose, lilac and purple, frilled and veined or smooth and silky. The seed heads are attractive too, dark brown outside, pale beige inside, splitting wide open like wooden flowers on curving twisted stems. These iris do not like lime, but all will grow in part shade, and are useful on the edges of shrubberies.

filifolia from southern Spain and north-west Africa has the narrowest rush-like leaves emerging from mottled leaf sheaths; the large fat buds open to show very closely rolled petals of deepest crimson-purple, with a touch of gold. (12 in./300 mm.)

foetidissima var. citrina, known incorrectly to me and many as 'Chinese form', is one of my favourite plants. It is vastly superior to our native Gladwin iris which still grows in the west country, with much smaller flowers of dingy blue. The flowers of *I. f.* var. *citrina*, not large, are yellow-ochre in colour with fine brown veining. However they are not the main charm. It is the great sheaves of shining evergreen leaves, so welcome all winter in bare shrubberies with ivies and bergenias for company, that create such a lively picture, with enormous green seed pods in October and November bursting open to show packed orange seed. It is worth pulling out dead or damaged leaves in spring to make way for the new fresh leaves, and occasionally to set out young seedlings to provide vigorous fresh clumps. (2½ ft/760 mm.)

– **'Variegata'.** The variegated form, strongly striped in ivory and greyish-green, deserves a well-prepared site in partial shade, the only variegated iris to overwinter well. (18 in./ 460 mm.)

graminea from central and southern Europe makes dense clumps of dark green narrow leaves among which you find the short-stemmed purplish-violet flowers. Pick one on a warm day, shut your eyes and think of greengages as you smell the flower. You can almost taste it, the perfume is so strong of old-fashioned plums. (15 in./380 mm.)

japonica 'Ledger's Variety', makes short fans of broad ever-green leaves emerging from the ground on little trunks. The flowers, poised above them on thin branching stems, are orchid-like, being small, flat and frilled, white in colour with touches of blue and orange. They need a hot sunny position in well-drained soil to provide plenty of flower. (18 in./460 mm.)

– 'Variegata', leaves boldly striped with white which also come through mild winters. I grow this on the warm side of shrubberies. (12 in./300 mm.)

pallida is a very old, cultivated bearded iris, valued chiefly for its handsome fans of grey-blue leaves, lasting well throughout the summer. (2½ ft/760 mm.)

pallida 'Variegata' makes strong fans of beautiful variegated leaves which create a dramatic accent among low plants. There are two forms, one striped with ivory, the other with gold. (18 in./460 mm.)

pumila and I. lutescens (*I. chamaeiris*) hybrids. There are many named colour forms of these late spring-flowering pygmy irises. Most have comparatively large flowers on very short stems (4 in./100 mm), attractive on the rock garden, or edge of the border. They can be found with blue, white, yellow, and purple flowers. One of the best is *Iris* 'Green Spot', whose white-green veined flowers hold out their falls proudly to show a bluish-green 'bruised' spot. (6–8 in./150–200 mm.)

All the *Iris pumila* hybrids like a chalky soil and full sun; they are garigue plants, found in dry stony places from Spain to Dalmatia.

reticulata is from the Caucasus, Armenia and Iran. It cheers up February with its small scented violet-purple flowers, followed by long stiff grassy leaves. There are now several colour forms, shades of blue and reddish-purple. Another bulbous iris, earlier still, is *Iris histriodes* 'Major' whose fat white candle-like buds appear in early January, opening large blue flowers held almost at ground level. (6 in./150 mm.)

tectorum is called the 'Roof Iris' because that is where it is grown in China. A warm dry site under a wall will suit it. It makes fans of broad soft green leaves, has lilac flowers with prettily crimped falls. There is also a white form. (12 × 12 in./300 × 300 mm.)

tingitana var. fontanesii (*I. fontanesii*) from north Morocco and southern Spain has outstanding foliage, long arching ribbon-like leaves gleaming like aluminium, with large bold flowers in shades of rich blue. (18 in./460 mm.)

unguicularis (*I. stylosa*) is found in rocky stony places in Algeria, in olive groves and bushy places. Wedged under the driest and hottest of walls it puts up with complete neglect, but although it must be baked it does appreciate a little feed of some organic manure occasionally, and the removal of the oldest worn-out parts. The most free-flowering form in my garden is 'Walter Butt', which has large flowers of palest icy blue, primrose scented. I also have a white form with not such broad falls, and 'Mary Barnard' which has large purple flowers with darker veins. All forms have silky delicate petals, and are best picked in bud to watch their fragile loveliness unfold without damage. There is a form of species from Greece and Crete with darker, narrower leaves, and dark purple flowers called *Iris cretica*. (15 in./380 mm.)

KNIPHOFIA come from South Africa. The old-fashioned Red Hot Poker with its great clumps of swirling ragged leaves and coarse flowers of red and yellow was not a favourite plant of mine. In recent years several botanic gardens and nurseries have hybridized different species with tempting results. It is now possible to find pokers in many shades, from creamy white, all shades of yellow, to brilliant reds and oranges, self coloured and two toned, and in all sizes to suit, from 2 ft/600 mm to over 6 ft/2 m. All need full sunlight and good drainage, but the very large forms especially will not do their best on soil that easily dries out.

galpinii is a species from the Transvaal, with very grassy foliage and slender (3 ft/1 m) stems carrying brilliant orange flowers. Many of the recent hybrids with narrow flower heads and dainty foliage have this blood.

northiae was named after a superb Victorian flower artist called Miss North. (For too long I walked past the red brick building that houses her amazing collection of paintings in Kew Gardens.) I grow her plant on the south side of a greenhouse in poorest gravel where it has made several trunks, each holding a great rosette of grey-green leaves, 6 in./150 mm wide curving ribbons that swirl to the ground in curling dying tips. The short-headed flowers are not remarkable, being a dull greenish-red, but the effect of the great mound of foliage in this hot spot is almost tropical. Could be tender in cold districts, but straw or bracken might be enough to protect it.

thomsonii var. snowdenii, delicate looking as a *Lachenalia*, this lovely poker is not very hardy. Autumn flowering, it has tall stems (3 ft/1 m) carrying widely spaced down-curved tubular flowers in soft shades of coral and red. It is growing here in hottest gravel.

There are splendid hybrids, many produced by Alan Bloom of Bressingham and Eric Smith under the name Buckshaw hybrids, and more again from the Slieve Donard Nursery. I too have had surprising results from seed sown from mixed plantings.

'Green Jade' appeared here about ten years ago from a random sowing. It makes a medium to large plant (4 ft/ 1.2 m), the flower head a delicate jade green. More recently a green has appeared among my seedlings which I have called 'Chartreuse'. It has a larger stronger head than 'Green Jade' but a more yellowish tone.

'**Little Maid**' we named because it looks like a miniature version of 'Maid of Orleans'. It is short and dainty, suitable for the edge of a border, with neat short foliage, above which stand 2 ft/600 mm stems with a very slender flower head extending halfway down the stem. Green in bud, the flowers open ivory white. It makes a display for weeks in the autumn and is lovely picked.

'**Maid of Orleans**', raised by Amos Perry, is medium to large, with creamy-white flowers from bronze buds. There are hybrids available which have the stature of this plant with flowers flushed with pink and coral. ($3\frac{1}{2}$–4 ft/1–1.2 m.)

'**Prince Igor**'. I found this plant many years ago, and could not honestly vouch for the name. Superb for the large garden in isolation, or as a background plant. Huge flaming torches of brilliant orange-red stand up to 8 ft/2.4 m in good soil. Looks magnificent near water, in association with Pampas Grass, or *Phormium*, but must be planted well up, so as not to be waterlogged.

For gardens with less room the smaller, free-flowering hybrids are preferable. They are available, standing no more than $2\frac{1}{2}$–3 ft/1 m with slender, taper-like torches, lovely to pick in delicate shades of yellow, burnt orange, coral reds; some of the prettiest are ivory flushed with coral.

LAMIUM, Dead Nettle, a shade-loving plant from temperate Europe and Asia, found in open woods and hedges. Will grow in light or heavy soil, standing considerable drought in shade provided it has ample humus.

galeobdolon. The Yellow Archangel is also found wild in Great Britain. In gardens we grow the handsome variegated form. (1 ft/300 mm.)

– '**Florentinum**' (*L. g.* 'Variegatum'), whose dark green leaves, heavily frosted with silver, are very beautiful in winter also. But it is very invasive, needing to be carefully checked if space is limited. In wild gardening it will control grass. (1 ft/300 mm.)

maculatum. The type has mauve-pink flowers freely produced in early summer over carpets of dark green leaves with central silver stripe. Although spreading effectively to make good ground cover close under shrubs, it is not a strangler. There are two other colour forms, 'Roseum' with soft pink flowers, and 'Album', pure white. *Lamium maculatum* 'Aureum' will not thrive in poor dry conditions. (6 in./150 mm.)

LATHYRUS latifolius. The Perennial Pea, familiar to us in cottage gardens grown over a fence, smothered in mid-summer with clustered heads of small vivid magenta-pink flowers. (Climber, up to 5 ft/1.5 m.)

– 'White Pearl' is less commonly seen, but could well be more widely used as a choice climber on a dry sunny fence or sprawled over a bush or on a bank. It has sprays of beautifully shaped white flowers, not scented. (Climber.)

LAVANDULA lanata grows with rosemary, *Genista cinerea* and *Salvia lavandulifolia* in south Spain. It has the whitest woolliest foliage of any lavender with very dark blue flowers in midsummer. Needs a warm sheltered spot, in well-drained soil. (18 in./460 mm.)

angustifolia (*L. spica*), the Old English Lavender, probably a hybrid between two species native to the south-west Mediterranean. There are today many forms, well known, such as *Lavandula* 'Hidcote', 'Munstead', 'Twickel Purple'. Some make large robust bushes, with long flower spikes, others make dwarf plants more suited for edgings, with deeper velvety-blue flowers.

stoechas is hardier. It grows throughout the Mediterranean region in the garigue in open stony places. It makes a stiff spiky little bush about 18 in./460 mm high, with curious little knobbly flower heads bearing two kinds of flowers. The fertile flowers are small, very dark purplish-blue arranged in vertical rows. Above them, to entice pollinating insects, is a flag or pennant of large wavy petals of a lighter shade of purple.

LEPTINELLA squalida (*Cotula squalida*) is an ugly name for a pretty little ramper, useful in paving cracks, or in dry difficult places where little else will grow; to be avoided among choice rock plants. Masses of tiny fernlike leaves press themselves into flat mats of green and bronze. It seems to thrive from dust to damp. (2 in./50 mm.)

LEUZEA centauroides (*Centaurea pulchra* 'Major') needs to settle down to become the stately showpiece of a group. Then it makes an imposing clump of dark grey jagged leaves lit with white undersides for contrast. The stiff 3–4 ft/1 m+ flower stems carry large buds of silver transparent scales. Large florets would detract from such detailed design; the opening buds explode into cyclamen pink fluff, in June and July. (3 ft/1 m.)

LIATRIS. Blazing Star, Kansas Feather – these colourful names describe very attractive and unusual plants from the prairies of the midwest USA. They need full sun and well-drained soil, but like many meadow and steppe plants they need plenty of humus. Making a very effective accent in the late summer border they send up several stiff stems carrying narrow dark green leaves right up the stem to the flowers which are a spire of close-set fluffy heads, each made up of a cluster of thread-like petals and stamens. The colour is bright magenta pink, sometimes white. Unusually for flower heads, they open from the top downwards.

pycnostachya. Kansas Gay Feather is the tallest, with mauve-pink flower heads. (4 ft/1.2 m.)

scariosa also is a taller form. Both these come from the deep soil prairie and need more substance. I had the lovely white form *L. s.* 'Snowflake', with its fluffy bobble heads more widely spaced, but fear I have lost it in too dry conditions. (3 ft/1 m.)

spicata (*L. callilepis* of gardens). Very striking with dark buds and brilliant magenta-pink flowers. Also white. This plant is found on poor dry ridges and will stand all but the deadliest drought. It is shorter (2 ft/600 mm.)

LIBERTIA. Other plants valued for their striking form, long after the flowers have gone. Explosive clumps of holly-green fans of stiff narrow leaves are a feature all year against a south or west wall in well-drained soil, unless you live in the warmer west country.

formosa from Chile. Holds well above the leaves tall slender spires of small three-petalled flowers, followed by brown bobbly seed heads, very attractive picked or growing. ($2\frac{1}{2}$ ft/ 760 mm.)

grandiflora, from New Zealand, has fewer flowers to a spike but larger. ($2\frac{1}{4}$ ft/760 mm.)

ixioides, also from New Zealand, is similar, but forms smaller clumps. Both leaves and seed pods are orange tinted in late autumn and winter. (2 ft/600 mm.)

LIMONIUM, Statice or Sea Lavender.

bellidifolium is a little charmer for the raised bed or rock garden. Neat round rosettes of round evergreen leaves send up very straight stems (9 in./230 mm), stoutly branched, carrying lavender flowers.

platyphyllum (*L. latifolium*) tolerates full sun in well-drained soil. Makes large rosettes of long, wavy, dark green leathery leaves. In July and August large wiry branching heads are covered with tiny lavender-coloured flowers. (12 × 18 in./

300 × 460 mm.) 'Violetta' is an improved form with larger flowers.

LINARIA purpurea. A small-flowered perennial toadflax found in dry stony places in southern Europe and Italy. Makes a tall columnar plant (3–4 ft/1–1.2 m), its branching stems crowded with long spires of tiny purple antirrhinum-like flowers for weeks in summer. Seeds freely.

– **'Canon Went'** is the charming pale pink form. (2 ft/ 600 mm.)

dalmatica from south-eastern Europe, the Caucasus and Armenia, found with *Salvia verbascifolia* and *Nepeta racemosa* (*N. mussinii*). Close-set oval pointed leaves waxed blue-green on curvaceous stems are topped with branching spires of bright yellow and orange snapdragon flowers. (3 ft/1 m.)

trionithophora comes from Spain and Portugal. Found growing with *Erica* spp., *Cytisus multiflorus* (*C. albus*) and *Genista hispanica*. It must have a sunny site, and well-drained soil; probably only hardy in the southern counties. Wide-branching stems with scanty grey leaves carry extraordinary 'flights of birds', the buds looking exactly like little budgerigars just before they open into sizeable purple flowers with yellow tongues. Sometimes pale pink flowers. Seeds freely. (3 ft/1 m.)

LINUM perenne, Flax, related to the provider of linen and linseed oil, *Linum usitatissimum*, found in dry hills and steppes in central Europe and east Asia. Although not long lived it seeds freely. It needs well-drained soil in full sun. A pretty plant when its dozens of fine stems radiating from a central point carry airy sprays of silky sky-blue flowers in long succession. (15 in./380 mm.)

narbonense, found in Spain to Italy and Algeria on dry hills, is a good perennial in warm sheltered conditions. Running mildly it has darker leaves and lovely large flowers of deeper blue. (18 in./460 mm.)

LIRIOPE muscari. A shade-loving plant found in China and Japan. In gardens will grow in well-drained soil in sun or shade, standing dry shade well. They appreciate a well-prepared site, take a little time to settle down, but when established make low robust clumps of evergreen strap-shaped leaves (about 15 in./380 mm). Flowers appear in September/October, small violet-purple barely opened bells, reminders of the spring *Muscari*, are thickly clustered along half the length of the 12 in./300 mm bright purple stems.

LONICERA, Honeysuckle. There are both climbing and bush forms adapted to stand considerable drought in shade or half-shade, provided there is adequate humus.

Climbers

There are many species and varieties, some evergreen. Not all will tolerate really poor conditions. They are prone to aphis attack, less damaged in shade. If the aphis are noticed in time, usually early spring, but possibly any time, they can be dealt with before the young shoots are ruined.

LONICERA × americana is a magnificent scented hybrid, very vigorous, flowering abundantly, in late June–July. The large trumpet flowers are creamy-white with reddish-purple outside. Splendid over large stumps or walls, will stand sun provided not too dry.

× brownii 'Fuchsoides' seems to like to be on a warm south or west wall where its clusters of ceiling-wax red flowers may contrast with *Calceolaria integrifolia*. Not scented.

japonica is a rampant evergreen or semi-evergreen. Useful as a screen over north- or east-facing fence, wall or unsightly object.

japonica 'Aureoreticulata' has smaller leaves, brightly netted with gold veins. Has odd habit of producing oak-shaped leaves early in season on old stems, but the new trailing stems abundantly produced (if pruned every few years) have the usual oval leaves. Small cream flowers along the stems are not conspicuous, but sweetly scented.

– 'Halliana' is a good form of Lonicera japonica with rich green shining leaves, with small sweetly scented cream flowers all along the stems, followed by black berries.

periclymenum, our own native Woodbine, also found throughout Europe and north and central Morocco. Often seen trailing its way up anything available in open woods. There are two excellent forms found in gardens.

– 'Belgica', early Dutch honeysuckle, flowers in May and June but little thereafter. Most sweetly scented in the evening, rich pink and cream flowers.

– 'Serotina', late Dutch honeysuckle, starts flowering as Lonicera 'Belgica' finishes, and continues on and off until the autumn, when often there are dark red currant-like berries and flowers at the same time. I like its young purple stems, and purple-tinted unfolding leaves.

Shrubs

Of the shrubby kinds of Lonicera I grow the following in soil enriched with humus.

nitida 'Baggesen's Gold'. Well grown this can be enchanting. In winter the leaves are pale green, but new growth in spring, bronze tipped, opens into cascading sprays of tiny leaves minted gold. Best against a dark background (good among heathers) where it is not in full sun all day, which can produce scorch, shown by whitening of the leaves. Careful pruning when established will encourage long arching sprays, useful for cutting, delicate in the garden. (3 × 3 ft/1 × 1 m.)

pileata makes useful evergreen ground cover, being a smallish shrub with predominantly horizontal branches, valuable under trees, and among shrubs, or on awkward corners and edges in full sun. Never very eye-catching, but pretty in spring when its new pale leaves make contrast with the dark overwintered leaves. Berries are violet-blue when they choose to appear. (9 × 24 in./230 × 600 mm.)

× **purpusii** (*L. fragrantissima* × *L. standishii*) is a welcome winter-flowering shrub. A medium sized bush for a not too conspicuous place, it carries among its overwintered leaves creamy-white flowers, powerfully scented. (4 × 4 ft/1.2 × 1.2 m.)

LOTUS hirsuta (*Dorycnium hirsutum*), another plant of the garigue, is a small sub-shrub (about $2\frac{1}{2}$ ft/760 mm) covered with soft hairy leaves which set off terminal clusters of pink-washed white pea flowers. In autumn these become star-shaped clusters of reddish beans, finally chocolate.

LUNARIA annua, the Common Honesty, is found wild in southern Europe in hedges, woods and waste places. In the garden it looks handsome with shady backgrounds, where its vivid purple flowers, sometimes white, look well with all the vivid yellow-greens of late spring. (3 ft/1 m.)

– **variegata** comes true from seed, making a large rosette faintly edged with white the first season. But the second year every leaf is broadly margined white, the small leaves ascending the flower stem become whiter still until some have little green at all. A few, well placed, can be very dramatic in dark shady places. ($2\frac{1}{2}$ ft/760 mm.)

rediviva is a perennial Honesty, with lavender-coloured flowers and elliptical papery seed pods. (2 ft/600 mm.)

LUPINUS arboreus grows wild on the sand dunes of the Californian coast. It quickly makes a large sprawling shrub, useful in new gardens, superb dotted about sunburnt rough land. Not long lived it needs light soil, full sun, and seeds providentially. It has dainty-fingered foliage, covered in midsummer with short spikes of clear yellow, sometimes white flowers, sometimes a dingy yellow-blue which need to be hastily removed.

LYCHNIS coronaria is found in rocky stony places in southern Europe and western Asia, making woolly rosettes of grey-green leaves from which rise tall branching stems, also white and woolly. These are topped with many round-faced campion flowers of velvety plum-red, wonderful against the almost white foliage of midsummer. There is a white form with more crinkly leaves, and another white with a pink eye. (3 ft/1 m.)

flos jovis, much smaller, is endemic in the central Alps, on granite and schist rocks and screes. From neat furry mouse-eared tuffets of leaves come short branching stems covered with rose-pink campions. (10 in./250 mm.)

viscaria, the Sticky Campion, found throughout Europe, via Siberia to Japan, in dry fields and clearings, but will not tolerate quite such arid conditions as the above. It makes low grassy clumps of dark green leaves, similar but a little broader than *Armeria*. Makes useful edging or ground cover. In May and June 10 in./250 mm stems hold clustered heads of vivid frilly pink flowers. The inter-nodes are sticky so presumably gnat's blood is part of their diet. There is a double pink and a lovely white form with pale green stems and calyces which enhance the cool flowers.

MARRUBIUM cylleneum. One of the loveliest foliage plants for hot dry positions in well-drained soil. Sometimes confused with *Ballota*; its flower formation is similar but not so handsome as the velvety-green bobbles on *Ballota*. The foliage is very different, the leaves are soft sage green with a fine silky pile, like old velvet. The terminal rosettes are exquisite in foliage arrangements, or against the dry soil. It makes a low mound (about 18 in./460 mm.)

MELISSA officinalis, the Lemon Balm, is wild in the eastern Mediterranean and south-west Asia, in vineyards and hedges in dry shade. It makes creeping clumps of dark green crinkled foliage; tolerant of the dustiest soil. (12 in./300 mm.)

– '**Aurea**' is much better in half shade where its brassy yellow-edged leaves make a glowing patch until they start to flower, when they become tired and drab, best cut down to let something else take your eyes. The crushed leaves smell strongly of lemon. (12 in./300 mm.)

– '**All Gold**'. This form I have recently acquired and am delighted with it. Its totally gold leaves have remained in fine condition all summer until October. Partial shade prevents leaf scorch on this delicately lovely foliage plant. (12 in./ 300 mm.)

NECTAROSCORDUM siculum (*Allium siculum*) is possibly the most unusual and handsome of these plants. Vile scented (but only noticeable when damaged), it sends up tall, thick stems topped with flowers encased in papery envelopes like pointed candle snuffers. These split, and out falls a dangling head of large open bells, heavily suffused maroon-purple and a cream and green base. This form comes from the south of Corsica and Sicily. (3 ft/1 m.)

siculum subsp. bulgaricum (*Allium bulgaricum*; *A. siculum dioscorides*) is found in the Crimea, Turkey and Cyprus, and has cream waxen bells striped green and faintly purple. In both, as they are fertilized, each individual flower stem turns upwards and the sepals dry to form straw-coloured little turrets, like fairy-tale castles on top of 3 ft/1 m stems.

NEPETA racemosa (*N. mussinii*) is a parent of the garden forms, and is found in the Caucasus and Persia.

× faassenii, catmint, much valued as edgings in dry sunny gardens. Its perfect symmetry is often ruined by cats, although some can be deterred by prickly shoots such as gorse or rose being tucked among the mounds of soft woolly grey leaves. Flower spikes of pale lavender. (18 in./460 mm.)

gigantea 'Six Hills Giant' of gardens is larger and hardier in colder damper areas. (3 × 3 ft/900 × 900 mm.)

sibirica (*Dracocephalum sibiricum*, *Nepeta macrantha*), a giant catmint from the Far East, makes underground runners which send up crowded stems carrying dark grey leaves with large handsome blue-lipped flowers. A fine sight for weeks in midsummer, it is very useful for filling in a well-drained sunny border. (3 ft/1 m.)

NERINE. Bulbous plants from South Africa, they do well in the southern counties in well-drained enriched soil. In colder areas with heavy soil, or if the possibility of severe ground frost is likely (that is, it will penetrate 6 in./150 mm or more), winter protection in the form of cover with peat, ashes, straw or the autumn debris, would be advisable. Under south or west walls they rarely suffer, and if suited increase abundantly, occasionally needing to be dug up, divided, and the best replaced in reconditioned soil, that is, having added well-rotted compost.

bowdenii, one of the joys of autumn with perhaps the Purple-leafed Vine (*Vitis vinifera* 'Purpurea') clustered with black grapes behind them. Each strong stem carries a head of several open trumpet-shaped rosy-pink flowers, frilled and glistening with microscopic silvery dust. Other shades of pink and red are being introduced. There is also a white form. (2 ft/600 mm.)

undulata. The long strap-shaped leaves remain throughout the winter, unlike *N. bowdenii*. Flowers later and more prolifically, seen individually less showy, but a narrow border under a west wall crowded with over a hundred dainty heads, each flower pale pink with the petals crimped along the edges, brings 'orchid-like' again to my mind, as the dark evenings draw winter into the garden. (18 in./460 mm.)

NIPPONANTHEMUM nipponicum (*Chrysanthemum nipponicum*) is another late flowering daisy with dark green leaves, ideally suited for a warm site under a wall to encourage its brilliant white flowers in November. (2 ft/600 mm.)

OENOTHERA, Evening Primrose, a vast genus from North America. *O. biennis* is very familiar, sometimes seeded along railway cuttings; it is showy with its tall stems of pale lemon-yellow flowers, but too prolific and a biennial. Needing full sun, and thriving in well-drained soil, the following are just two of the many perennials.

fruticosa (*O. tetragona*). There are may forms included in this group.

– subsp. glauca (*O. t. fraseri* 'Glauca') makes neat rosettes of dark green leaves, burnished red in winter. In midsummer there are bright branches of light yellow flowers with red buds. The whole plant seems to be suffused with red and orange in autumn. (2 ft/600 mm.)

macrocarpa (*O. missouriensis*). One of the finest edge-of-the-border plants, it makes sprawling lax crimson stems well covered with dark green leaves, white ribbed, carrying heads of long pointed buds, opening over weeks into enormous flat open funnels of bright yellow. (6 in./150 mm × $2\frac{1}{2}$ ft/ 760 mm.)

ONOPORDON acanthium, a gigantic thistle from southern Europe and Asia, found on waste land and stony places. Takes two years to become possibly the most dramatic feature plant in the garden in the poorest and hottest situations. The first year it makes a large rosette of huge spiny leaves copiously felted with white down. Next season the sturdy flowering stem creates a branching pyramid carved in stiff white felt, pointed with prickles and topped with pale lilac thistle flowers. Unfortunately it is a biennial, but seeds freely. (6–8 ft/2–2.5 m.)

ONOSMA. A race of mountain plants capable of standing very hot conditions, but must be well drained, particularly in winter, as their hairy leaves are rotted by cold winter wet. Ideal between rocks, on a raised bed (if enough room) or hanging over a wall.

alborosea I have seen in a west country garden hanging over a rocky bank like a great grey shawl, composed of stiff rosettes of velvety grey leaves. In early summer each rosette carries short stems of drooping white buds which open into pink flushed bells. It comes from Asia Minor. (4 in./100 mm × 2 ft+/600 mm+.)

echioides, Golden Drop, is found in Europe from Spain to Greece. It makes dense clumps of narrow darker grey-green bristly leaves, above which the stems, sometimes branching, carry curving heads of waxy lemon-yellow drops. (12 in./ 300 mm.)

ORIGANUM. Our own common Marjoram, *O. vulgare,* is also found growing wild along the roadsides in France, throughout Europe and Russian Asia, in hilly bushy pastures usually on limestone. Attractive in July with its short airy spires of pinky-mauve flowers it is valued for its deliciously aromatic foliage, the secret of many tasty soups and dishes.

– 'Aureum' makes attractive ground-covering carpets of bright golden leaves before sending up indifferent flower stems. Cut back immediately it will refurnish itself with bright foliage for the rest of the season. Will stand dry soil, but the shade from surrounding plants will help protect the foliage from ugly brown scorch marks. Cooks as well as pot marjoram. (6 in./150 mm.)

× hybridum from the Levant makes a low plant of neat woolly dark grey leaves. In late summer there are airy stems crowded with little pink, mauve and green hops – charming. (10 in./250 mm.)

rotundifolium from Turkey is outstanding. Lax short stems are set with round smooth blue-green leaves. The flowers are minute and hidden between clusters of large palest green bracts that tip every stem. (8 in./200 mm.)

ORNITHOGALUM, Star of Bethlehem. There are many, some to be avoided as invasive weeds.

nutans, native in Britain and Europe, is a bulb for the wild garden. Spreading rapidly with grassy leaves it can be a nuisance in a border, but where it can be naturalized, among shrubs or edges of woodland, its flowers, rather like wide open hyacinths in glistening silvery-grey and green, are quite ethereal; perhaps with grape hyacinths and palest primroses. (8 in./200 mm.)

pyrenaicum, found throughout south-western Europe, in dry stony places, it makes clumps of large bulbs, which send up very straight stems topped with slender, spires of greenish starry flowers. By midsummer the leaves have almost disappeared, their duty done. The seed pods are neat and attractive.

OSTEOSPERMUM (*Dimorphotheca*) are South African daisies. They thrive on light sandy soils, in warm situations. Most of them must be considered tender. Two have survived here for many years.

jucundum (*D. barberae* of gardens) is generally considered to be hardy. It has large magenta-pink daisies over clumps of narrow green leaves which have a pleasant pungent smell when touched. It flowers mid and late summer. (About 12 in./300 mm.)

– var. compactum is more dwarf. I have only just obtained one, and will put it on my new raised bed.

'Prostratum' (*D. ecklonis 'Prostrata'*), also known as Wisley hybrid, makes a low sprawling plant covering itself all the summer months with mauve washed buds opening to dazzling white daisies with navy-blue centres. (9 in./230 mm.)

'Blue Eye'. This, my favourite, is *not* hardy. It makes large bushy plants, and if a mild winter allows its survival under a south wall it will scarcely be out of flower all summer, but it is in late summer and autumn, when it can be a mound 3 ft × 3 ft/900 × 900 mm smothered in large rose-pink daisies on tall stems that it looks so entrancing among the greys; worth keeping a few young plants overwintered in the greenhouse.

OTHONNA cheirifolia (*Othonnopsis*) from South Africa is a distinctive foliage plant for the dry sunny border. It makes low sprawly clumps of blue-grey paddle-shaped leaves, waxen in texture, covered in late spring with fresh yellow daisies. Needs a warm site in well-drained soil, with a little winter protection in cold wet districts. (10 in./250 mm.)

PACHYPHRAGMA macrophylla is found wild with *Brunnera macrophylla* and *Symphytum ibericum* (*S. grandiflorum*). An established carpet of these round shining green leaves overlapping is a very pleasant sight all summer. Veins and stems become purple tinted in winter, disintegrating in spring as multitudes of white starry flowers appear early in March like snow patches under the bare-twigged shrubs. (12 in./300 mm.)

PACHYSANDRA terminalis, from Japan, is invaluable for making close evergreen ground cover in shade. Underground runners send up glossy green rosettes of slightly toothed leaves. Greenish-white flowers appear on short spikes in early spring. There is a variegated form with creamy-yellow leaf margins. Not happy in shallow chalk soil. (12 in./ 300 mm.)

PAPAVER, Poppies, thrive in hot sunny situations, in well-drained, but not too impoverished soil. All have a milky-white sap. To prepare them for flower arranging it is best to pick them with the bud splitting. Stand the freshly cut ends in an inch of hot water for a short while, then add cold water and leave till needed.

orientale. The large Oriental Poppies make indestructible perennials, for every piece of root left in the ground will produce a stout plant. With their huge frilled silk-textured flowers in brilliant colours they need careful placing. They look well in the 'Mediterranean' garden among the greys and silvers, or isolated, in groups, in open spaces in short grass where perhaps crocus bloomed in spring, with cypress or junipers as background. Mr Amos Perry took *P. orientale* together with *P. o. bracteatum* which has small leaves beneath the flower bud, and produced named hybrids ranging from deep mahogany reds through salmon pink to white. Another great plantsman, Sir Cedric Morris, produced the following, which we call:

– **'Cedric's Pink'.** Although it has the rather lax stem that have many of these gorgeous flowers, it must be forgiven for the seductive flower, reminiscent of Toulouse Lautrec's ladies. Huge frilled silky petals of ashen-rose open slowly to reveal a central velvety knob of purple velvet surrounded by large purple-black blotches. The plumes of Bronze Fennel nearby suggest feather boas. (3 ft/1 m.)

rupifragum is found among rocks and screes in southern Spain. Multiple rosettes of blue-grey leaves, coarsely toothed, form evergreen clumps which carry, on slender stems, semi-double, sometimes single, flowers with tissue paper petals of soft orange, in flower throughout the summer. (18 in./460 mm.)

spicatum (*P. heldreichii*), from Asia Minor, is territorially much less demanding. Attractive rosettes of pale green hairy leaves send up straight stems carrying branched heads of fat round buds, opening to crumpled petals of soft apricot. (2 ft/600 mm.)

PARONYCHIA. Thyme-like plants making flat carpets for edgings or paving in hot sunny positions.

capitata, mats of downy-grey leaves and heads of transparent tissue paper bracts. (1 in./25 mm.)

kapela (*P. serpyllifolia*), shorter still, useful paving plants.

PENSTEMON. A genus from north-west America needing well-drained soil and a warm situation. There are many large-flowered, large-leafed hybrids but not all are reliably hardy. Some will often survive in warm sites, sheltered from cold and drying spring winds, with a few cuttings for safety tucked away in a cold frame.

'Andenken an Friedrich Hahn' (*P.* 'Garnet'), in the shelter of a wall, makes a large plant (3 ft/1 m) producing handsome racemes of rich garnet-red flowers for months until autumn frosts.

barbatus (*Chelone barbata*). From very flat spreading clumps of green leaves spring surprisingly tall, slender stems which hold a branching spire of long, narrow scarlet tubular flowers with pale hairy throats. (3 ft/1 m.)

campanulatus, from Mexico and Guatemala, has narrow leaves and smaller flowers. Hybridized possibly with *P. hartwegii* (large and scarlet flowered) it has produced many of the florist's varieties. There are also several fairly hardy named varieties, with narrow leaves. Among these are:

'Evelyn' makes a compact bush of the narrowest leaves producing quantities of pretty rose-pink flowers. 'Apple Blossom' has slightly larger and paler flowers. Both about 18 in./460 mm.

fruticosa var. scouleri (*P. scouleri*), somewhat taller than the last two, makes a loose cushion plant (about 12–15 in./ 300–80 mm), covered with large handsome trusses of lilac flowers in early summer, very lovely. There is a beautiful white form, *P. f.* var. *s. f. albus*.

gloxinioides (of gardens) is a race of mainly tender bedding plants. There are several named forms. Among them is believed to be the hybrid × 'Sour Grapes', the hardiest Penstemon I grow. In poor gravelly soil (with compost) it stands drought unbelievably well, making generous clumps of rich dark green foliage with a constant succession of flowers, the size of grapes, opal coloured, soft green, amethyst and blue, all found in the same flower. (2½ ft/760 mm.)

hartwegii, from Mexico has been the parent of many garden hybrids. It has brilliant scarlet flowers with rich green leaves. (2½ ft/760 mm.)

isophyllus will make a woody-stemmed plant against a wall from which it throws up long stems of scarlet flowers, paler inside.

Apart from these herbaceous penstemons there are others which make low evergreen bushes or carpets, suitable for the rock garden or as edging. These include:

davidsonii var. menziesii (*P. menziesii*), a low growing evergreen from north-west America, north of the central Sierras in California. Prostrate woody stems are well covered with small dark green leaves, tinted purple in winter. In spring the plant is lost beneath the large violet-blue tubular flowers which smother it. A good edging plant among helianthemums and mountain phlox. (6 in./150 mm.)

newberryi (*P. roezlii*) is a granite rock plant from the Sierra mountains of central California. It forms a small dome-shaped shrub of round grey-green leaves covered with rosy-pink flowers in midsummer. Not so sprawling as *P. davidsonii* var. *menziesii.* (10 in./250 mm.)

PEROVSKIA, Russian Sage, is related to salvias, and found in eastern Asia from Afghanistan to Tibet. A most welcome addition to the dry sunny garden in autumn. Treated like fuchsias, and cut down to the ground every spring, it will be encouraged to make strong new shoots. There are two species:

abrotanoides has been bred with *P. atriplicifolia* to produce hybrids which have more branching flower spikes. These are 'Blue Spire' (Notcutt) and 'Blue Haze' (Bloom).

atriplicifolia makes a very beautiful plant. Each year it shoots up many slender white stems clothed with small grey-toothed leaves, aromatic when crushed. The long narrow panicles of lavender-blue flowers are a delight in late summer and autumn. It needs full sun, good drainage, and just a little help if your soil is nothing but stones. (4 ft/1.2 m.)

PHLOMIS fruticosa, the Jerusalem Sage, is a garigue shrub, found in southern Europe in dry rocky places from France to Palestine. In gardens it makes a handsome companion for cistus with its greyish-white woolly leaves on gnarled woody bushes. The new young shoots are also felted white. The flowers are bright yellow, hooded and lipped, in whorls at the top of the stems. (4 ft/1.2 m.)

russeliana (*P. samia* and *P. viscosa* of gardens), from north Africa, makes large weed-smothering clumps of soft crinkled heart-shaped leaves. The stiff branching flower stems carry several whorls of butter-yellow hooded flowers which are held in a cluster of green tubes tight against the stem. This remains when the flowers fall, becoming dark brown by autumn, an interesting shape for the dried arrangement. (3 ft/1 m.)

PHLOX. The dwarf mountain *Phlox* take over in the garden from *Aubrieta* with their carpets of fine-cut leaves, studded with jewel-like flowers in many shades of pink, blue and white. They flourish in full sun and well-drained soil, but do even better if a little peat or compost is added in which to tuck their rooting stems. They are all evergreen, but for cold exposed gardens, forms of *Phlox douglasii* will be more hard wearing than *Phlox subulata*.

A peep into Farrer's *The English Rock Garden* and one is dumbfounded by one's ignorance about these lovely alpine plants. Here are a few, of the few, I know:

douglasii grows on gravelly soils in the Rocky Mountains from Montana to Utah. The foliage is much narrower, the plants make close dense mats with round-petalled flowers pressed close. There are numerous cultivars, in blue, pink and white, some dark-eyed. These include 'Boothman's Variety', clear mauve with violet eye, 'May Snow', looking like a snowdrift over bright green leaves, and 'Rosea', soft lilac-pink flowers. (3 in./76 mm.)

× procumbens (*P. amoena* of gardens) (*stolonifera* × *subulata*) makes fairly tight little mounds of narrow leathery leaves, sending up clustered heads of pinky-lilac blossoms, on 6 in./150 mm stems.

– 'Variegata' is splendid, growing strongly for a variegated plant, it excels itself by managing to produce heads of silky-pink flowers which actually add something to the already colourful foliage. (6 in./150 mm.)

subulata is distributed through sandy rocky soils in the eastern USA from New York to Florida. It makes longer stems than *P. douglasii*, with slightly longer leaves and is capable of covering yards of dry soil with an evergreen carpet if need be. The flowers are slightly larger without the round-eyed look, having notched margins to the petals. Few flowers produce such impact, spilling down a noble rock garden, enviable on the edge of the smallest border. Well-known forms include the old fashioned pearly-blue 'G. F. Wilson', and the vivid magenta-pink 'Temiskaming'.

PHUOPSIS stylosa (*Crucianella stylosa*) is found on dunes along the borders of the Caspian Sea and Iran. It makes quick ground cover on well-drained sunny borders. From stringy yellow roots, smelling like *Fritillaria imperialis*, it produces lax stems covered with whorls of narrow light green leaves. These are topped in midsummer with rounded heads of tiny rose-pink flowers, looking like pink pincushions, stuck with pink pins. (10 in./250 mm.)

PHYGELIUS, Cape Figwort, comes from South Africa, and will thrive under south or west walls if the soil is enriched. It tends to run out from a woody stock, sending up long shoots terminating in a large open head of scarlet tubular flowers with yellow throats and protruding stamens. Can also be grown in sheltered borders, cut down in the spring to encourage strong shoots. There are two kinds:

aequalis has close heads of soft coral-red flowers with yellow throat and mahogany lip. (Up to 3 ft/1 m.)

capensis, sometimes seen looking into bedroom windows if trained up a wall. Has bright red flowers in a more open airy head. Can be trained up to about 6 ft/2 m on a warm wall, but more usually seen at about 3 ft/1 m.

PILOSELLA aurantiaca (*Hieraceum aurantiacum*) or 'Grim the Collier' as Mrs Fish called it. She had another name too, not surprisingly, because it can be a real pest in the wrong place! It makes very flat dark green rosettes which send up buds and stems liberally decked with black hairs. The flowers are burnt orange on 12 in./300 mm stems. It increases enthusiastically although, being shallow rooted, it is not difficult to eradicate. I have a better form, with more brilliant flowers, more red than orange, on shorter stems, which I would not like to lose. At the moment it is very successful in helping *Viola labradorica* to keep part of a dry bank free of weeds. An extraordinary mixture, but it works.

PLANTAGO, Plantain. Usually to be weeded out of the lawn. There are two decorative forms; both will tolerate sun, but do better on heavy soil, suffering from mildew if too dry at the root.

major 'Rosularis'. Instead of the usual thin rat-tail inflorescence this plantain has intriguing pyramidal deep-green rosettes, reminiscent of a green zinnia. Does not mind a little shade. (9 in./230 mm.)

– 'Rubrifolia' makes very broad-ribbed leaves, a handsome shade of purplish brown or maroon, good among greys. (12 in./300 mm.)

POLYGONATUM, Solomon's Seal. There are several species and hybrids, growing almost anywhere provided it is not hot and dry. But they look better and do better in shade or part shade. In dry shade they will thrive if the soil is enriched with humus, and time is allowed for the rhizomes to spread and send up a forest of curving stems, hung with shining dark green leaves.

falcatum. Is usually seen in its variegated form. Compared with the commonly grown Solomon's Seal, it has shorter red-tinted stems with more rounded, less pointed leaves, narrowly edged with white. ($2\frac{1}{2}$ ft/760 mm.)

× hybridum (*P. multiflorum* of gardens), the common Solomon's Seal. There are varying forms, some larger, some which set bloomy greenish-black berries long after the little pendant green and white bells of spring have been forgotten. With *Hosta sieboldiana* they die away in a blaze of golden glory as the autumn frosts touch them. (3 ft/1 m.)

multiflorum is our British native (also in Europe and Asia). Not as good as *P. × hybridum*, but may it be preserved in its natural home somewhere! (3 ft/1 m.)

POTENTILLA, Cinquefoil. A very large family, including herbaceous, alpine, and shrubby types. The mountain potentillas will stand drought reasonably well, also the shrubby varieties. The larger leafed herbaceous types from the sub-alpine meadows can be grown with low rainfall, especially on heavier soils, but in dry conditions all welcome the addition of humus.

atrosanguinea from the Himalayas has large rich green leaves, and branched stems of velvety blood-red flowers.
   Many hybrids have been made including 'Gibson's Scarlet' and 'Flamenco', and several double forms. I would not call these good drought resisters in East Anglia, but plenty of humus sees them through most seasons.

– var. argyrophylla (*P. argyrophylla*) from Kashmir and Nepal makes neat clumps of silvered strawberry-like leaves with long sprays of yellow flowers, each orange-centred. (18 in./460 mm.)

The shrubby potentillas probably decorate the garden longer than any other shrub, their small single rose-like flowers mostly white or yellow providing colour when other plants are resting. They start flowering in early summer, continuing until autumn frosts. They make rounded twiggy bushes with pretty divided leaves, usually green, sometimes silvered. Will suffer in severe droughts.

fruticosa, found throughout the Northern Hemisphere, including Britain, but has big gaps in its distribution. Grows in bushy, stony or rocky places, usually in the Alpine zone, except in the far north. There are many lovely named varieties, including:

– var. arbuscula (*P. arbuscula*) differs in having rust-coloured shaggy branches. It makes a small, somewhat horizontal bush, rarely more than 2 ft/600 mm, suitable for the edge. Its large soft yellow flowers continue to please throughout the season.

189

– 'Elizabeth' (*P. arbuscula* × *P. fruticosa mandschurica*). A splendid hybrid from Hillier, forming a large dome-shaped bush (3 ft/1 m) with canary-yellow flowers.

– 'Manchu' (*P.* 'Mandschurica'), low, slow growing, white flowers on greyish foliage. (2 ft/600 mm.)

– 'Primrose Beauty', arching branches, grey-green leaves, primrose flowers with deep yellow centres. (2½ ft/760 mm.)

– 'Red Ace' is the new red-flowered form, petals bright red with yellow undersides. Tends to fade in high temperatures and drought conditions although it does prefer sun – so, not for the really dry garden. (2 ft/600 mm.)

– 'Sunset', a small shrub with flowers varying according to heat, from yellow to brick red. Looks best in autumn when sun loses power to bleach the colour. (18–24 in./450–600 mm.)

– 'Tangerine' is more spreading, with delicate coppery-yellow flowers, best in part shade. (18 in./450 mm.)

– 'Vilmoriniana', creamy-white with silvery leaves. Grows up to 4 ft/1.2 m.

PTEROCEPHALUS perennis (*P. parnassi*). This awkward name belongs to a charming little dwarf scabious from Greece. Excellent edging or ground cover in well-drained sunny soil, its soft spreading carpets of grey foliage are studded with stemless pale pink pincushions. (5 in./130 mm.)

PULMONARIA – the common name Lungwort refers to the irregular spotting on the leaves of some of these plants which reminded the old herbalists of a lung. They are very useful plants in shade, either under north walls, or under trees and shrubs. They wilt easily, especially if touched by sunlight, but are no trouble in shade with enough humus. The large handsome rosettes of leaves (of all but one) make that dominant feature among small-leafed plants that is vital to good design. The foliage is least remarkable in spring when the plants send up dozens of flowering stems carrying small rather twisted leaves, while the old rosette leaves become engulfed and disappear. When the flowers are finished and cut down new large basal leaves appear which remain handsome throughout the year. Most of the pulmonarias have bristly leaves rasping to the touch.

angustifolia is found wild in woods throughout central and southern Europe extending to Sweden and Russia. Very rarely found in Britain. There are several forms or subspecies, one called *Pulmonaria a.* subsp. *azurea* makes neat close clumps of small dark green leaves, unspotted, which disappear in winter. In very early spring short sprays of rich blue flowers create a carpet of colour in the winter-bare garden. There are several named cultivars, 'Mawsons Variety' and 'Munstead Variety', both very similar. (9 × 18 in./230 × 460 mm.)

longifolia is also sometimes believed to be a sub-species of *P. angustifolia*. It makes very striking rosettes, its dark leaves being very long, narrow, and pointed with conspicuous white blotches. The flowers are rich blue. (12 × 18 in./300 × 460 mm.)

I have two more pulmonarias similar to *P. longifolia*, probably forms of the same, both distinct. One was collected in Portugal by Sir Cedric Morris, and has larger basal leaves, the spotting less marked. The flowers on tall stems are a fascinating mournful purple. The other form has similar foliage, but flowers of a good dark blue.

officinalis from central Europe grows wild in open woods, preferring a calcareous soil. It is known by several local names, 'Spotted Dog', 'Lungwort', 'Soldiers and Sailors' and 'Jerusalem Cowslip'. Less handsome than *P. saccharata*, but its small heart-shaped leaves are daintily spotted, and the clusters of bright pink flowers fading to blue are not without charm. (10 × 18 in./250 × 460 mm.)

rubra is found in south-east Europe, the Balkan peninsula and in the spruce forests of the Carpathians with *Dryopteris filix-mas*, *Lamium galeobdolon* (*Galeobdolon lutea*) and *Polygonatum verticillatum*. It makes totally weed-smothering clumps of very large pale apple-green leaves, unspotted. The flowers, which can appear by Christmas and continue well into April, are bright coral red, without a hint of blue. (12 × 24 in./300 × 600 mm.)

saccharata – there is some doubt about the origin of this plant, but it has been reported from open woods along the north coast of Spain. I have seen something very like the garden form of it on the French side of the Pyrenees while travelling east of Bilbao, in scrubby bushy places. The best selected garden forms have large bristly dark green leaves handsomely blotched with white. A form almost completely 'silvered' with spots is called *P. saccharata* 'Argentea'. The flowers are larger, more intensely coloured than those of *P. officinalis* with conspicuous dark calyces.

I have an excellent white-flowered form of *P. saccharata* given me by Miss E. Strangman with much larger flowers than the white *P. officinalis*. (12 × 24 in./300 × 600 mm.)

PULSATILLA vulgaris (*Anemone pulsatilla*), the lovely Pasque Flower, found in Britain on chalk, and throughout Europe in dry sunny meadows and slopes, both on chalk and sand. From ferny green leaves in early spring emerge silk-cocooned buds, opening to soft purple flowers, each filled with golden stamens, followed by copper-brown heads of feathered seed. There are others in shades of mahogany-red and a lovely white form. (10 in./250 mm.)

RAOULIA, related to *Helichrysum*, from New Zealand and Australia. For very well-drained gritty soils with low rainfall; they dislike winter wet.

australis, from Canterbury Plain, New Zealand. Found on dry river gravels with *Muehlenbeckia axillaris*, it makes close mats of tiny silvered rosettes, creeping like quicksilver among rocks and stones. Flowers like pale yellow dust. ($\frac{1}{4}$ × 12 in./ 6 × 300 mm.)

– Lutescens Group (*R. lutescens*), leaves so small the plant hugs the ground like a grey-green mould. (Less than $\frac{1}{4}$ × 12 in./6 × 300 mm.)

hookeri, similar, but fractionally larger and better – less likely to survive wet winters. ($\frac{1}{2}$ × 12 in./12 × 300 mm.)

tenuicaulis, easy and rampant. Flows like water over and around rocks, a flat living carpet of light green. ($\frac{1}{4}$ × 12 in./ 6 × 300 mm.)

RHODANTHEMUM hosmariense (*Chrysanthemum hosmariense*) is one of those seemingly modest plants that grow on you. It makes a compact cushion about 10 in./250 mm high and across, of firm, narrow-cut grey leaves. By autumn it is packed with buds of soft grey-green overlapping scales outlined with velvety black. The firm white daisy flowers continue to open and expand during any mild spell in winter, spring produces a wealth of blossoms, while the odd bloom appears throughout the summer. I find it prefers a sheltered site, perhaps with *Iris unguicularis*. (Origin – Morocco.)

RHODIOLA heterodonta (*S. heterodontum*), similar growth from woody base stock as *S. rosea*. (9 in./230 mm.) Grey stems carry waxy leaves almost iridescent with lilac, amethyst and blue on grey; bronze-red flower buds and fluffy flowers make a fine contrast.

rosea (*Sedum rosea*), Rose Root, Midsummer Men. Alpine and colder regions of Northern Hemisphere to Arctic, with *Potentilla fruticosa*, in rocky and even wet places in tundra (perhaps because of permafrost?). In Great Britain it grows anywhere, ideal among small alpines where its form and colour make a focal point. The whole development of this plant throughout the spring is a joy to watch. From a woody root stock tight pinkish-bronze buds slowly elongate into radiating stems of waxed blue-grey leaves. Finally, they are topped by sharp lime-green starry flowers, bursting with anthers in early summer. (9–12 in./230–300 mm.)

RUBUS. The following 'brambles' make useful cover in dry shade:

idaeus 'Aureus', the golden-leafed form of the wild raspberry, only about 18 in./460 mm, its rich gold leaves light up a dull corner in spring, remaining lemon yellow for the rest of the season.

pentalobus (*R. fockeanus*). Creeping stems pressed flat to the ground, closely covered with small round scalloped leaves, crêpe-textured and evergreen, they become bronze tinted in autumn. An edging plant.

tricolor, handsome evergreen ground cover under trees and shrubs where something rampant can be tolerated. Prostrate stems covered with soft reddish bristles carry polished green leaves which have a broad bronze margin in winter. Make 6 ft/2 m growth in a season. Long trails useful for flower arranging.

RUTA graveolens, the Rue, native of the European Mediterranean and Turkey, found in dry stony places; prefers chalk but does very well in sandy soils. The species flowers better, but its foliage is poorer than the following:

– **'Jackman's Blue',** makes loose mounds of blue waxen filigree foliage. Needs to be cut back occasionally in spring to keep tidy and encourage good leaf. Some people are allergic to it, so wear gloves when pruning. (18 in./460 mm.)

– 'Variegata'. Very effective in early summer, the new young growth is more cream than green, gradually becoming green as it matures. Needs to be kept well pruned. (18 in./ 460 mm.)

SALVIA, Sage. The aromatic drought-resisting species from the Mediterranean regions are invaluable in the dry sunny garden.

argentea, possibly a short-lived perennial in cold heavy soil, it has survived flowering and seeding in my garden in dry gravel for many years. Forming a basal clump the amazing young leaves are so heavily shrouded in white wool, especially the backs, they could be used as a powder puff. As the branching flower spike of white hooded flowers develops this protection fades away. When cut down new young leaves make a feature in autumn. Does well on dry walls. (3 ft/1 m.)

candelabrum, a plant from southern Spain, hardy only in the warmest counties and corners. I have grown it under a west wall for many years. It makes a loose bunch of woody stems clothed with large handsome dark sage-green leaves, velvet textured beneath, crêped and veined above, also aromatic. Branched flower spikes carry widely spaced large violet-purple and white flowers in midsummer. Stands 2½ ft/760 mm in flower.

nemorosa, more familiar as S. 'Superba', well named. From basal clumps of crinkled green leaves it sends up many stiff stems topped with close-set spikes of violet-blue flowers enclosed in reddish-purple bracts, still vivid when the flowers fade. If dead headed will make a second flowering. (2½ ft/ 760 mm.)

officinalis 'Icterina', Golden Sage, a variegated form of cooking sage. The young foliage is beautifully marbled primrose, gold and sage green. Remains all winter. Best in a warm, well-drained site. (18 in./460 mm.)

pratensis Haematodes Group (*S. haematodes*), from Greece. Very flat rosettes of crinkled grey-green leaves veined purple send up numerous 4 ft/1.2 m stems crowded with lilac-blue flowers. A haze of soft colour above the greys.

– **'Purpurascens'**, Purple Sage. Again the young foliage is a delight, soft greyish-purple velvet with spikes of purple-blue flowers. Occasional shoots variegated pink, cream and purple. Will form lax bush 4 ft/1.2 m across, but can be controlled by pruning in spring.

– **'Tricolor'**. No need for flowers among this mound of velvety foliage vividly splashed white, cyclamen and purple. (2 ft/600 mm.)

SANTOLINA chamaecyparissus, a small garigue shrub from southern Europe, in stony places, preferring chalk. In the garden it provides invaluable middle ground, or ground cover. Soft bushy mounds become almost white in hot dry soils; the finely cut, heavily felted, aromatic leaves are crowded onto short shoots. In late summer they are covered with bright yellow button flower heads. (18 in./460 mm.)

pinnata subsp. neapolitana (*S. neapolitana*) from southern Italy, Spain and Portugal, is never quite so white. It presents a less dense appearance, more feathery with longer leaves more grey than white. The pale yellow flowers look perfect with the foliage, but smell vile, so best not too close to the sitting area. ($1\frac{1}{2}$ × 1 ft/460 × 300 mm.)

rosmarinifolia subsp. rosmarinifolia (*S. virens*), small moss-green cypress-like leaves cover this compact round bush, providing welcome variety among the greys. Bright yellow button flowers. ($1\frac{1}{2}$–2 ft/460–600 mm.)

SAPONARIA, Soapwort, Bouncing Bet. The juice of leaves of *S. officinalis* forms a lather in water which will dissolve grease, like soap.

ocymoides is a sun-loving plant found in central and southern Europe in stony places and on limestone rocks. It quickly makes a large sprawling carpet of evergreen leaves which is obliterated in early summer by close-packed bright pink campion-like flowers. Ideal cascading over a dry wall. (3 in./80 mm.)

SEDUM, Latin: *sedeo,* to sit, referring to the way these plants can find a living perched on rocks. Hence many, but not all, are adapted by their fleshy moisture-holding leaves to survive drought and starved conditions. A large genus of about 300 species; here are a few of them:

acre, Wall-pepper, commonly seen on walls and roofs. Very widely distributed – Britain to Persia, Norway to Morocco. There is a form called 'Aureum'; the young tip growths are bright butter yellow. (3 × 12 in./80 × 300 mm.)

album. Europe, Asia, on walls and rocks, succulent clusters of rich green leaves, topped with a froth of white flowers. Splendid confined to a wall top, menace in the garden, for every dropped leaf makes a new plant. (4 in./100 mm.)

– subsp. teretifolium 'Murale', not troublesome, very lovely with its mahogany bead-like leaves followed by a pale pink cloud of tiny starry flowers. (4 in./100 mm.)

anacampseros. Southern Europe, Alps and Pyrenees on silicious rocks. A strong ground coverer with whorls of closely packed blue-grey leaves. The ball-like flower heads are grey-blue in bud, opening to pinkish-brown. (6 in./150 mm.)

kamtschaticum, Japan to Kamchatka and eastern Siberia, common on rocks in mountains. (3 in./76 mm.)

– var. floriferum 'Weihenstephaner Gold' (*S. floriferum* 'Weihenstephaner Gold'), super plant, super ground cover. Trailing red stems carry coarsely toothed red-tinged leaves, every tip rosette carrying a large cluster of bright yellow flowers. (6 in./150 mm × 18 in./460 mm.)

– **'Variegatum'** makes a colourful feature on raised beds or rock garden. Fleshy rosettes of green and white leaves flushed with pink. Clusters of pink buds open to orange and yellow stars. (3 in./76 mm.)

lydium, western Asia Minor, damp places, lower alps. In Great Britain it grows anywhere, making 1 in./250 mm carpets of emerald green, which become tinted bright red in dry conditions. Dense heads, pale pink flowers.

middendorffianum. Eastern Siberia and Manchuria. Most attractive low ground cover. Neat flat leaves form small greenish-bronze rosettes, while the heads of little yellow starry flowers have a reddish tinge. (3 in./80 mm.)

pluricaule. Sakhalin and eastern Siberia. Makes very close round cushions of fleshy grey-green leaves smothered in October with bright mauve-pink flowers. (2 in./50 mm.)

populifolium. Siberia. Should be more widely known. It forms a dwarf woody shrub, with flat, toothed, slightly succulent leaves, smothered in late summer with heads of fluffy greenish-pink flowers. (12 in./300 mm+.)

'Ruby Glow'. One of the larger sedums, good for the edge of the sunny border. Forms a large rosette of lax purple stems, about 10 in./250 mm long, with purple-grey succulent foliage topped with clusters of wine-red starry flowers, in early autumn.

sediforme (*S. altissimum*) is found in rocky places around the Mediterranean, preferring chalk and clay. Long writhing shoots circled with succulent pointed leaves of vivid grey-blue from which rise tallish stems carrying flat heads of fluffy lime-green flowers. (12 in./300 mm.)

spathulifolium. Mid California to Vancouver, on rocks. Forms close clumps of fleshy purple-grey rosettes, plum-red in winter. Yellow flowers in summer. (2 in./50 mm.)

– 'Cape Blanco' (*S. s.* 'Cappablanca'). The same growth, but rosettes heavily coated with beautiful white waxy bloom. (2 in./50 mm.)

spectabile, from northern China. Makes a tall handsome herbaceous plant, with its fleshy pale green leaves providing colour, texture and form throughout the growing season. Produces a very large flat head of cyclamen-pink starry flowers in autumn, always decorated with butterflies. There are various clones. Some are a washed-out pink, others are brighter and deeper tones of mauve-pink.

'Herbstfreude' (*S.* 'Autumn Joy'). Possibly a hybrid between *S. spectabile* and *S. telephium*. This is one of the very best autumn plants. Similar in habit to *S. spectabile*, its stout stems carry heads 6 in./150 mm across, of densely packed starry flowers ranging in colour, as the flower matures, from deep salmon pink to a rich coppery red. No hint of mauve. Finally the rich brown seed head remains an interesting feature all winter. (2 ft/600 mm.)

telephium, Britain, Europe, Siberia to Japan, in woods, hedges and rocky places. Rather a floppy plant, not generally considered to be a good garden plant, although there is an interesting form selected by Gertrude Jekyll called 'Munstead Red'. (15 in./380 mm.)

– **maximum** (*S. maximum*). Europe, Siberia, rocky places, dry pastures and steppe. Has large grey-green fleshy leaves touched with bronze. In late autumn tall heads of pale green stars, flushed with bronze make unusual colour for the time of the year. (18 in./460 mm.)

– – **'Atropurpureum'** (*S. m. atropurpureum*). From spring to autumn a dramatic feature plant. Thick fleshy leaves of bloomy purple-brown make a dark accent. In late summer the flat heads of small starry flowers combine rosy-pink and brown, while the chocolate brown seed heads continue to add interest. (2 ft/600 mm.)

telephium 'Variegatum'. 12 in./300 mm stems clothed in pale succulent leaves strongly variegated with cream and gold make a noticeable plant. Large heads of green-tinted pink flowers. Inclined to revert; non-variegated shoots must be removed.

'Vera Jameson'. A hybrid discovered by Joe Elliott, probably a cross between *Sedum telephium* subsp. *maximum* 'Atropurpureum' and *S*. 'Ruby Glow'. Deep bronze-purple leaves on lax stems, shorter than *S*. 'Ruby Glow'. Lovely near silvergreys like *Tanacetum densum*, or *Artemisia schmidtiana*. Flat heads of dusky-pink flowers in autumn are a bonus. (8 in./200 mm.)

SEMPERVIVUM are related to *Sedum*, and like them have the capacity to thrive with very little moisture. They are mountain plants found on rocks and in crevices exposed to the hottest sunshine throughout southern and central Europe, Asia and Africa. There are about fifty species, and countless variations and hybrids. They range in size individually from that of a pea to something that will cover a teaplate 6–7 in./150–80 mm across. All make perfect rosettes of wedge-shaped fleshy leaves, sometimes marble-smooth, sometimes hairy, even meshed with a spider web of fine silky threads. They make ever-increasing clumps of tightly packed rosettes, with a bewildering variation and subtlety of colour; translucent mahogany reds, apple green with crimson tips, crimson based with pale green tips, bloomy purple, jade green with chocolate tips – one can easily become addicted to sempervivums.

The largest species do need plenty of humus mixed with a well-drained soil to stand the worst droughts, but the smaller species, especially those coated in moisture-conserving veils of hair, will put up with the driest conditions, looking perhaps best of all in sinks or low bowls.

SENECIO. The following species of *Senecio* make beautiful garden plants in reasonably warm gardens with well-drained soil.

cineraria (*Cineraria maritima*). Sea Ragwort, from rocks and sandy places in the western Mediterranean. There are several forms of this plant, the hardiest being *S. c.* 'White Diamond'. So many greys and silvers are 'filigree'. Too much of them and the adjective could be 'fussy'. This plant is invaluable for providing relief in form with its bold rosettes of jagged cut leaves whitening as the dry days lengthen. Can make a mound as large as a lavender bush. (18 in.+/460 mm+.)

viravira (*S. leucostachys*) comes from Patagonia. It inhabits gravel semi-desert, with cold but dry frosty winters. In Britain it is inclined to be tender because it gets too much rain! I grow it under the eaves of a west wall where it must be dust dry. With its roots tucked under paving it shoots up through a *Fuchsia* (how does that survive the heat?) reaching 5 or 6 ft/2 m by the end of the summer. Its fine-cut leaves make a pattern of white lace among the red and purple *Fuchsia* bells. It cannot, it seems, be too baked or too starved. The flowers are little clusters of palest cream, groundsel-like.

SERIPHIDIUM maritimum (*Artemisia maritima*) grows along the Mediterranean and Atlantic coasts, where shingle and sand edge the salt marshes. (12 in./300 mm.)

SILENE uniflora (*S. maritima*). Sea Campion, found on sand dunes, beaches and rocks on the European Atlantic coast. Also on stabilized dunes in Great Britain. A form we grow in gardens is:

– 'Robin Whitebreast' (*S. maritima* 'Plena'), creamy-white double flowers looking uncommonly like Mrs Sinkin's Pinks tumble from spreading prostrate mats of waxy grey foliage.

Ideal on a raised bed or wall where its flowers can flop to advantage.

SISYRINCHIUM angustifolium. Blue-eyed Grass. Grows wild in the prairies of north-west America. Little iris-like tufts of leaves no more than 3 in./80 mm long are topped by satiny-blue flowers clustered on short stems.

striatum from Chile with its large grey-green iris-like leaves makes another contrast in form among greys. Narrow spires of small creamy-yellow flowers stand above the leaves, followed by almost black seed heads. Sometimes killed by severe frost, but seedlings always survive. (2 ft/600 mm.)

striatum 'Aunt May' (*S. s.* 'Variegatum'). This plant is beautiful, with its bold creamy-yellow stripes on the grey-green background. Has survived several years here under a south wall, very well drained. It's worth the trouble to keep a piece in a well-ventilated cold frame over winter. (18 in./460 mm.)

STACHYS byzantina (*S. lanata*; *S. olympica*), found from the Caucasus to Iran, our old friend 'Lamb's Ears'. I grow two slightly differing forms, both doing well in light soil, and full sun.

– 'Big Ears' ('Byzantinus') is a large-leaved form of *S. byzantina*. Its crowded rosettes of large oval leaves heavily coated in a silky, velvety pile make it useful and handsome as an edging plant or large-scale cover plant. (12 in./300 mm.)

– 'Silver Carpet' is a non-flowering form. Few carpeters are more attractive or hard wearing, with its dense clusters of silky 'Lamb's Ears'. Needs to be dug up occasionally and the best pieces replanted to keep it free of gaps. (3 in./80 mm.)

STROBILANTHES atropurpureus is an uncommon plant from the Himalayas. It thrives in any soil in full sun, and stands drought well considering it makes a large plant

(4 ft/1.2 m) of many branching stems carrying dark green hairy nettle-like leaves. In late summer it becomes a mass of purple-blue hooded flowers when few other plants are offering competition.

SYMPHYTUM ibericum (*S. grandiflorum*) grows wild with *Brunnera macrophylla*. It makes impenetrable weed cover under shrubs. It forms mounds of medium-sized dark green hairy leaves, its shoots surface rooting as they grow. In spring, before the new leaves are fully developed, the fiddleneck clusters of flowers change from burnt-orange buds to creamy-yellow bells. (12 in./300 mm.)

TANACETUM densum subsp. *amani* (*Chrysanthemum naradjani*) from Turkey, has leaves so finely cut they look like curled woolly feathers, clustered into silvery-white rosettes to make one of the prettiest carpeters in full sun. (3 in./80 mm.)

TEUCRIUM fruticans I grow against a south wall in almost pure gravel, but still it shoots up 4 ft/1.2 m of new growth after pruning. Much branched, the stiff white stems are sparsely covered with small pointed leaves, grey above, white beneath, a delicate setting for pale blue lipped flowers.

scorodonia, Wood Sage, is found in dry places in British woods with bluebells and bracken, and throughout Europe and temperate Asia.

– 'Crispum Marginatum' is a delightful variant, making cover in dry shade. Its green crêpey leaves have heavily ruffled edges rimmed with white. The spikes of tiny cream-lipped flowers have quiet charm. (8 in./200 mm.)

THYMUS. There are many different thymes, which for convenience in the garden can be put into three groups:
(A) Very flat carpeters which grow rapidly, making good cover if other plants are not allowed to seed into them. Good in paving crevices, walls, or carefully tended rock gardens.

(B) Those that make deeper piled carpets, standing 3 in./
80 mm or so, more able to hold their own as edging plants.
(C) Little shrublet or bush thymes up to 12 in./300 mm.

× **citriodorus** (*T. pulegioides* × *T. vulgaris*).

– **'Aureus'** makes dense lemon-scented carpets of richly
golden foliage, lovely around a bluish conifer. (B) (4 in./
100 mm.)

– **'Bertram Anderson'** (*T.* 'E. B. Anderson'), a denser, slower
growing carpet with brilliant golden foliage throughout the
year, most brilliant in winter. (A) (2 in./50 mm.)

– **'Golden King'**, very similar in growth but lemon scented
so could have *T. citriodorus* blood. Most attractive in spring
when it makes a neat dome of new golden variegated foliage.
(C) (8 in./200 mm.)

– **'Silver Queen'**, lovely all the year round, strongly variegated grey-green and white, with shades of amethyst in
winter. (C) (8 in./200 mm.)

doerfleri (*T. hirsutus doerfleri*) from the Balkans makes
chunky mats of dark grey woolly wedge-shaped leaves
arranged in short rosettes. Lavender-pink flowers. (A)
(1 in./25 mm.)

'Doone Valley', a splendid plant, introduced by Bill Archer
of Wimbledon. Thrives in the lightest soils making dense
cover. In spring every tip is brick-red gradually developing
irregular gold markings on the small olive-green leaves. It
continues to spread its gold-spangled lemon-scented carpet
throughout the summer, flowering late with large clusters
of soft lavender flowers held above the leaves. (B) (3 in./
80 mm.)

herba-barona, found in Corsica and Sardinia on dry denuded
slopes, making eventually a wiry rigid mound covered with

dark green leaves strongly scented of Carraway. Flowers deep pink. (B) (4 in./100 mm.)

– **Lemon-Scented,** collected by us in Corsica, has the most tantalizing fresh lemon scent. (B) (4 in./100 mm.)

polytrichus subsp. britannicus (*T. drucei*). The wild creeping thyme is found throughout western Europe, including Britain in dry hilly pastures. There are many varieties. Here are a few:

– – **'Albus',** makes dense prostrate mats of bright green starred with little white flowers. (A) ($\frac{1}{2}$ in./13 mm.)

– – **'Coccineus',** dark foliage which is smothered beneath sheets of vivid crimson-purple flowers. (A) ($\frac{1}{2}$ in./13 mm.)

– – **'Coccineus Major'.** Similar but larger everywhere. (A) (2 in./50 mm.)

– – **'Minor'.** Densest of all the flat thymes, the tiny packed rosettes are studded with very wee pink flowers. (A) ($\frac{1}{4}$ in./6 mm.)

pseudolanuginosus of gardens (*T. lanuginosus*) quickly makes carpets of dark grey-green leaves, their top surface glistening with fine woolly hairs, irresistible to touch. (A) ($\frac{1}{2}$ in./13 mm.)

vulgaris. Common Thyme, familiar as a cooking herb, is a typical garigue plant found on poor dry slopes of limestone or clay, from Spain to Italy, and Morocco. It forms a compact wiry bush, up to 12 in./300 mm high, and more across, covered with neat dark green very aromatic leaves. (C)

TRACHYSTEMON orientalis, from the Caucasian mountain woods; it seems to tolerate dry shade fairly well. For large shrubberies it makes useful ground cover, its immense dock-shaped but rough dark green leaves forming impenetrable overlapping mounds. In spring just as the new leaves begin to show, pink stems of blue borage-like starry flowers look deceptively fragile. Good companion for *Pachyphragma* and early daffodils.

Tritonia disticha subsp. rubrolucens (*Crocosmia rosea*). Although a little spindly, perhaps, compared to some of the more recent hybrids, this colour is unique in montbretias – rose pink, on tall delicate stems. In flower for weeks from July to October. There are also many fine named hybrids available.

VALERIANA phu 'Aurea', related to *Centranthus ruber*, I grow on north-facing dry borders or in part shade where, in early spring, its brilliant gold foliage rivals daffodils. The heads of small white flowers on tall slender stems create an interest vertically after the foliage has matured to pale green. (3 ft/1 m.)

VERBASCUM, or Mullein, all like full sunshine and well-drained soil.

chaixii, from central Europe, southern Alps, Pyrenees, Cévennes to Caucasus, found in dry hills, chestnut groves and glades in woods. Here it grows happily in poor gravelly soil in full sun, making a neat rosette of grey-green slightly wrinkled leaves. In late summer it produces slender stems tightly massed with yellow or white flowers with fluffy mauve eyes. A good perennial, it is a useful vertical among rounded grey bushes. ($2\frac{1}{2}$ ft/760 mm.)

olympicum from Bithynia, north-west Turkey. Not a perennial, but by no means dismissible on that account. Sometimes taking two years to make a huge rosette a yard across of beautiful petal-shaped leaves, finely felted silvery-white, it lies on the gravelly soil like a giant dahlia head. When ready it sends up a candelabra of stems, studded with woolly buds which open haphazardly, over a long season, yellow flowers, while the seed head, whipped into curving shapes by the autumn gales, prolongs interest until cut down during the winter tidy-up. (6–8 ft/2.5 m.)

phoeniceum, south-eastern Europe, central Asia, and Russian steppes. The Purple Mullein makes a handsome basal rosette of dark-tinted, glossy veined leaves, sending up spires of large soft purple flowers. There are also pink and white forms, all seeding freely. (2 ft/600 mm.) This plant interbreeds in my garden with *V. olympicum* producing sterile hybrids in shades of pink, lilac and soft tans, all taller than *V. phoeniceum.*

'Vernale'. Forms larger basal clumps of rich green leaves which support a closely branched spire covered with bright yellow flowers, a torch-like feature for weeks in midsummer. (5 ft/1.5 m.)

VERONICA cinerea from Asia Minor makes useful bulb cover or edgings for the dry sunny border. Quick growing mats of narrow ash-grey foliage is smothered in early summer with light blue flowers. (4 in./100 mm.)

prostrata (*V. teucrium prostrata*) from central or southern Europe, on dry hills and grassy places.

– **'Trehane'** is a delight. Tolerates dry soil if not in hot sunlight, so partial shade, where its spreading carpet of brilliant gold foliage can develop all summer while the little spires of tiny Reckitt's Blue flowers make vivid contrast in early summer. (6 in./150 mm.)

VINCA. Periwinkle. Apart from ivies probably the most valued ground cover for dry shade.

difformis, from the west Mediterranean region. Not quite so hardy as the rest, similar in growth to *V. major,* that is, long and straggly, taking time to make dense cover. But this plant merits a sheltered corner where its innocent flowers of milky-blue can be appreciated. There is a darker form called *V. d. dubia.* (15 × 24 in./380 × 600 mm.)

major itself with its long arching shoots and too few flowers is not to my mind worth bothering with.

– 'Reticulata' is better. Less vigorous, its large leaves are quite handsomely netted with golden yellow. (15 × 24 in./380 × 600 mm.)

– 'Variegata' ('Elegantissima') is a lovely plant, not grown and appreciated enough. With *Iris foetidissima* the ground between shrubs in winter can be a joy with lovely trails of boldly variegated cream and green leaves. By pegging them down they will shoot again and fill in the surface more quickly. (15 × 18 in./380 × 450 mm.)

minor. Lesser Periwinkle is the best form to make close mats of ground cover. Its prostrate stems run out from the centre, rooting as they go. If you can put down a layer of peat or crushed bark after planting pieces 18 in./460 mm apart you will relieve yourself of the tedium of weeding between the trailing shoots and in two years you will have total cover. (8 × 24 in./200 × 600 mm.)

– f. **alba** ('Alba'), white flowers, small leaves marbled light and dark green in spring and early summer. (8 × 18 in./200 × 450 mm.)

– 'Alba Variegata' ('Variegata-Alba'). Leaves totally gold, flowers white, best on north- or east-facing aspect. (16 × 18 in./ 150 × 450 mm.)

– 'Argenteovariegata' has prettily-marked leaves in green and white, while the starry flowers are pale blue. (8 × 18 in./ 200 × 450 mm.)

– 'La Grave' ('Bowles' Variety'). Perhaps the best. Simply smothered with large blue flowers in spring.

There are also forms with wine-coloured flowers, both single and double, a double blue, and reputedly a double white, but I have never met anyone who has seen it. (8 × 18 in./ 280 × 450 mm.)

WALDSTEINIA ternata, from eastern Europe, Siberia and Japan is a useful carpeter which will tolerate drought in partial shade, so a north-facing border, or shrubbery edge. It makes spreading mats of dark strawberry leaves, evergreen and glossy, which contrast with the sprays of yellow starry flowers produced around the edges of the clumps. (3 in./ 76 mm.)

YUCCA, from the south-east United States, found on rocky hillsides and sand dunes. Well placed they can make a garden by themselves. Old well-grown specimens may consist of a cluster of multiple trunks each bearing a great rosette of bayonet-like leaves, the whole creating sharp outlines against a velvet-smooth lawn or sun-drenched terrace. When the immense flower spikes tower up to 8 ft/2.5 m, loaded with waxen bells, the effect is breathtaking. The following I grow in full sun in enriched stony gravel.

filamentosa itself has rather flaccid grey-green leaves, not nearly so attractive as:

– concava. This splendid little yucca makes an open rosette of wide concave leaves about 18 in./460 mm long, conspicuously edged with fine curling wisps, and while pointed are not viciously so. Every midsummer it produces a slender narrowly branched stem hung with bronze-flushed ivory bells. This plant does not make trunks. (4 ft/1.2 m.)

gloriosa makes the largest rosettes, eventually forming a trunk as thick as your thigh. Each leaf is a broad, stiff, upturned bayonet, wickedly tipped. Reputedly shy flowerers, mine have flowered repeatedly over the last two or three hot summers. (6–8 ft/1.8–2.4 m.)

recurvifolia is similar in scale, but its older leaves curve downwards away from the new central blades, producing a very exotic and elegant effect. It helps to maintain a smart appearance if you remove the oldest and ragged-looking leaves; this also reveals the developing trunk, and encourages fresh new rosettes to emerge from the base. The flower spike, sometimes 5 ft/1.5 m high, hung with greenish-white waxen bells is glorious.

ZAUSCHNERIA californica (Hummingbird Trumpet Flower) from central and southern California, also the Rockies to Wyoming in dry rocky hills, often in the chaparral. Making underground stems which travel easily through sandy gravelly soils, it sends up firm stems of narrow grey leaves topped in autumn with sprays of narrow scarlet trumpet flowers. Lovely with *Ceratostigma wilmottiana*. (18 in./460 mm.)

Grasses for Dry Sunny Situations

FESTUCA glauca is found in France in dry pastures on limestone, also on calcareous plateaux in southern Sweden with *Potentilla fruticosa* and *Thymus polytrichus* subsp. *britannicus* – all of which look attractive together in the garden. In full sun, on dry soil, this neat compact grass is powder blue, ideal for edgings, in groups for ground cover or as isolated features among low growing thymes. (9 in./ 230 mm.) *F. amethystina* is similar but larger and bluer (over 12 in./300 mm.)

glacialis is endemic in the Pyrenees, and also found on the mountains of central Europe and Spain. It spreads gently little carpets of palest blue powder-puffs only 2 in./50 mm high. Needs to be divided and replanted fairly frequently to look its best.

punctoria is from Greece, and will survive the driest soils. Hard curved leaves like steel bodkins make distinctive clumps that look well among sedums and sempervivums. (6 in./150 mm.)

HELICTOTRICHON sempervirens (*Avena sempervirens*). Western Mediterranean on limestone rocks. A splendid contrast feature plant among softly rounded greys, it makes stiff clumps of radiating stems of steely-blue topped with soft straw-coloured chaffy flowers in midsummer. (3 ft/1 m.)

HORDEUM jubatum (Squirrel Tail Grass) is found in steppes in southern Chile and in overgrazed areas of the prairies of the Great Plains. Not a long-lived perennial, but it seeds mildly, takes up little space, and is always admired when its softly iridescent barley-like heads wave among helianthemums and Blue Rue.

LEYMUS arenarius (*Elymus arenarius*), is a sand-binding grass from the maritime sand dunes of north and north-west Europe. In the right place it is most handsome with its broad-bladed leaves of fine grey-blue topped with tall wheat-like flowers of the same blue shade. It is, however, made to invade, so needs constant watching, if not isolated and mown round. (4 ft/1.2 m.)

PENNISETUM may not be too hardy in very cold districts. Where they can survive they are among the showiest of grasses.

alopecuroides, eastern Australia and eastern Asia, makes a clump of tidy grassy leaves topped with large dark brown bottle brushes. (2½ ft/760 mm.)

macrourum from South Africa needs a very warm site. I have it tucked under a west-facing bank where it sends up hundreds of cats tails, long slim spikes, handsome growing, useful for flower arranging. (4 ft/1.2 m.)

orientale is a grass of great charm. The long fluffy flower heads are like delicate pink and mauve caterpillars on the end of wiry stems. On misty autumn mornings, filled with dewdrops, they droop like fat white lambs' tails. (18 in./ 460 mm.)

STIPA calamagrostis (*S. lasiagrostis*) is a delightful grass that could be more widely enjoyed. It makes a profusion of creamy-buff feathery flowers arching above soft fountains of light green leaves which turn biscuit colour by autumn. (4 ft/1.2 m.)

gigantea grows in Spain with *Genista cinerea*, *Cytisus multiflorus* (*C. albus*), and *Malva alcea*. It makes a superb feature in the dry sunny garden. Above neat arching clumps of narrow green leaves soar 6 ft/2 m stems carrying enormous oat-like heads tinted in gold and bronze. They dry perfectly.

Grasses for Dry Shade

HOLCUS mollis is one of the worst nuisances as a garden weed but *H. m.* 'Albovariegatus' ('Variegatus') can be used successfully in both sun and shade, in poor dry soil. It makes clusters of green and white striped leaves which send out runners with fresh new clusters, easily dislodged if they overstep their allocation. Useful and quick cover, often where nothing else has succeeded. (4 in./100 mm.)

MILIUM effusum is called Wood Millet, a native in British woods as in Europe.

– 'Aureum' is well known as 'Bowles' Golden Grass'. It forms non-running clumps of soft ribbon-like leaves, bright golden yellow in spring, making patches of sunlight in shady places; its many fine stems support a cloud of tiny bead-like golden flowers. (15 in./400 mm.)

11

Plants for Special Purposes

Medium and Large Plants for Hot Sunny Positions

Acanthus spinosus
Achillea, large forms
Agapanthus
Alyssum
Allium, tall forms
Alstroemeria
Anthemis cupaniana
Arctanthemum articum
Artemisia, large forms
Asphodelus
Ballota
Bergenia
Catananche
Centaurea, large forms
Centranthus ruber
Cistus
Commelina
Crambe
Crocosmia
Cynara
Dictamnus
Dierama
Diplarrhena
Echinops

Eryngium
Erysimum
Euphorbia
Ferula
Foeniculum
Fritillaria imperialis
Galtonia
Gaura
Genista aetnensis
   ,, lydia
   ,, hispanica
Geranium
Gladiolus
Glaucium
Gypsophila
Halimiocistus
Halimium
Hebe
Helichrysum
Hieracium
Incarvillea
Iris
Kniphofia
Lathyrus latifolius

Lavandula
Liatris
Libertia
Limonium platyphyllum (L.
    latifolium)
Linaria
Linum
Lotus
Lupinus arboreus
Lychnis coronaria
Marrubium
Nepeta
Nerine
Oenothera
Onopordum
Ornithogalum
Papaver
Penstemon
Perovskia
Phlomis

Phygelius
Potentilla
Ruta
Salvia
Santolina
Sedum, border forms
Senecio
Sisyrinchium striatum
Strobilanthes
Teucrium
Verbascum
Yucca

GRASSES
Helictotrichon
Hordeum jubatum
Leymus
Pennisetum
Stipa

Low Growing Plants for Hot Sunny Positions

Achillea, dwarf forms
Aethionema
Allium, dwarf forms
Alyssoides
Anemone fulgens
    ,,   pavonina
Antennaria
Anthemis marshalliana (A.
    rudolphiana)
Arabis
Armeria
Artemisia, low growing
    forms
Calamintha
Carlina
Centaurea nana 'Rosea'

Cerastium tomentosum
    columnae
Chamamaelum nobilis
    'Flore Pleno'
Chiastophyllum
Crepis incana
Dianthus
Diascia
Eriophyllum
Erodium
Euphorbia myrsinites
Fritillaria, dwarf forms
Genista sagittalis
Geranium, dwarf forms
Gypsophila, dwarf forms
Haplopappus

Hebe
Helianthemum
Helichrysum 'Schwefellicht'
  ('Sulphur Light')
Hermodactylus
Iberis
Iris
Leptinella
Limonium bellidifolium
Lychnis flos-jovis
Lychnis viscaria
Oenothera
Onosma
Origanum
Ornithogalum
Osteospermum jucundum
  (Dimorphotheca
  barbarae)
Paronychia
Penstemon, low forms
Phlox, low forms
Phuopsis
Plantago

Potentilla, dwarf forms
Pterocephalus
Pulsatilla
Raoulia
Rhodanthemum
  hosmariense
  (Chrysanthemum
  hosmariense)
Saponaria
Sedum, dwarf forms
Sempervivum
Silene
Sisyrinchium angustifolium
Stachys
Tanacetum, low forms
Thymus
Veronica
Zauschneria

GRASSES
Festuca
Holcus mollis

Medium and Large Plants for Dry Shade

Acanthus mollis latifolius
Alchemilla mollis
Bergenia
Brunnera
Digitalis
Epimedium
Euphorbia amygdaloides
  „ a. robbiae
Hedera
Helleborus
Hesperis
Hosta
Humulus lupulus 'Aureus'

Hypericum
Iris foetidissima
Lamium galeobdolon
Lonicera
Lunaria
Pachyphragma
Polygonatum
Pulmonaria
Rubus idaeus 'Aureus'
  „ tricolor
Symphytum
Trachystemon
Valeriana phu 'Aurea'

Low Growing Plants for Dry Shade

Ajuga
Alchemilla conjuncta
Anemone blanda
Anemone nemorosa
Anemone sylvestris
Hedera
Lamium maculatum
Liriope

Melissa
Origanum ⎫
   vulgare 'Aureum' ⎬ part shade
Pachysandra ⎭
Rubus pentalobus (R. fockeanus)
Vinca
Waldsteinia

Plants for Flower Arranging

Acanthus
Achillea, large forms
Agapanthus
Alchemilla mollis
Allium
Alstroemeria
Alyssoides
Anaphalis triplinervis
Anemone fulgens
Armeria
Artemisia, larger forms
Asphodelus
Ballota
Bergenia
Carlina
Centaurea
Crocosmia
Cynara
Dianthus
Dictamnus
Dierama
Digitalis
Echinops
Eryngium
Erysimum (Cheiranthus)
Euphorbia

Foeniculum
Fritillaria
Galtonia
Gladiolus
Gypsophila
Hedera
Helleborus
Hosta
Iris
Kniphofia
Lathyrus latifolius
Liatris
Libertia
Limonium
Linaria
Liriope
Lonicera
Lotus (Dorycnium)
Lunaria
Marrubium
Melissa
Nerine
Onopordum
Ornithogalum
Osteospermum
   (Dimorphotheca)

Papaver
Penstemon
Phlomis
Plantago
Pulsatilla
Rubus idaeus 'Aureus'
   ,,   *tricolor*
Ruta
Salvia
Santolina
Sedum

Senecio
Verbascum

GRASSES
Helictotrichon
Hordeum
Leymus (*Elymus*)
Milium
Pennisetum
Stipa

BIBLIOGRAPHY

....

This is a far from complete list of all the books I value on the subject, but a selection of those I refer to constantly, both for pleasure and information.

ANDERSON, E. B., *Rock Gardens*. Michael Joseph.

BEAN, W. J., *Wall Shrubs and Hardy Climbers*. Putnam, 1939.

BLOOM, ALAN, *Perennials for your Garden*. Floraprint, 1972.

FARRER, REGINALD, *The English Rock Garden*. T. C. and E. C. Jack Ltd.

FOURNIER, P., *Les Quatre Flores de la France*. Paul Lechavalier, Paris, 1946.

FISH, MARGERY, *Ground Cover Plants*. David and Charles, 1970.

HILLIER, H. G., *Manual of Trees and Shrubs*. David and Charles, 1974.

JEKYLL, GERTRUDE, *Home and Garden*. Longmans, Green & Co.

LLOYD, CHRISTOPHER, *Foliage Plants*. Collins, 1973.

LLOYD, CHRISTOPHER, *The Well-tempered Garden*. Collins, 1970.

MATTHEW, BRIAN, *Dwarf Bulbs*. Batsford, 1973.

POLUNIN, OLEG, AND HUXLEY, ANTHONY, *Flowers of the Mediterranean*. Chatto, 1965.

ROBINSON, WILLIAM, *The English Flower Garden.* 15th
ed. John Murray, 1934.

ROYAL HORTICULTURAL SOCIETY, *Dictionary of
Gardening.*

THOMAS, GRAHAM S., *Perennial Garden Plants.* Dent,
1975.

THOMAS, GRAHAM S., *Plants for Ground-Cover.* Dent,
1977 (revised edition).

INDEX

....